STONE

Quarrying and Building in England
AD 43~1525

St Mary's Conduit, Lincoln.

STONE
Quarrying and Building in England
AD 43~1525

Edited by
David Parsons

PHILLIMORE
in association with
THE ROYAL ARCHAEOLOGICAL INSTITUTE

1990

Published by
PHILLIMORE & CO. LTD.
Shopwyke Hall, Chichester, Sussex

in association with the
ROYAL ARCHAEOLOGICAL INSTITUTE

ISBN 0 85033 768 2

Printed and bound in Great Britain by
STAPLES PRINTERS ROCHESTER

Contents

List of Illustrations

vii

List of Colour Plates

Between pages 20 and 21

In memory of
Dorothy Pounds

Preface

Most of the papers which make up this volume were read at a conference held in Loughborough in January 1988 and jointly organised by the Royal Archaeological Institute (as part of its regular programme of seminars and meetings) and the Continuing Education Unit of the Department of Adult Education at Leicester University. The intention of the conference was to bring together scholars in different disciplines working on aspects of the history of building stones, particularly those whose research projects involved the collaboration of archaeologists and geologists. Several such projects had been undertaken and the time seemed ripe for an exchange of information, methodologies and experiences. The weekend proved to be as stimulating as expected and the only surprise was the number of such investigations being carried out in England alone. The interdisciplinary nature of the subject was emphasised by the variety of speakers' specialisms: of the fifteen main contributors to this volume six are geologists or environmentalists and nine are archaeologists or historians.

Partly because of the highly specialised nature of most fields of study today and partly because of the tendency to academic comparmentalisation, few people can have all the skills necessary to interpret buildings and to determine their geological background. Even in the recent past archaeologists and art historians have made some ludicrously incorrect identifications of building stones, and geologists are equally capable of making erroneous assumptions about architectural styles or constructional practices. The clear message is that specialists from different fields must work together if we are to make any real progress in identification and interpretation. Several contributions to this volume make it apparent, however, that the possession of geological expertise does not itself guarantee the correct identification of any given block of building stone or its correct attribution to a particular quarry site, and much uncertainty will continue to surround co-operative attempts to determine the source of particular building stones. This volume also reveals the extent to which the derivation of building stone can be obscured by the widespread practice of reclaiming building materials for re-use. Some months after the conference was held, Leicestershire Museums issued a press release describing part of the Shires excavation then taking place in the city of Leicester. The site director remarked that 'the Roman buildings were stripped bare of stone by medieval builders in the 11th and 12th centuries . . . the medieval builder had a well-developed sense of economy'. This is a common experience, and the later re-use of stone continually interferes with our understanding of the patterns of stone supply in earlier periods.

In spite of such drawbacks much has been achieved, especially in the last decade or two. To some extent this volume is a measure of that achievement, but the intention in publishing it is not only to represent the current 'state of the art' but — we hope — to stimulate new work and thought and to lead to a refinement of methodologies and research techniques.

★ ★ ★ ★ ★

It is a pleasure to have the opportunity to thank those who have helped to make this publication possible: Mrs K.B. Penny and her assistants in the Continuing Education Unit at Leicester, who organised the conference; the Department of Adult Education, which has supported me in many practical ways; David Dunning, who keyboarded for computerless contributors; Tim Schadla-Hall and Eric Robinson, who supported and encouraged; the Royal Archaeological Institute, whose Council courageously decided to fund the publication; Noel Osborne and Phillimore, who rescued us from oblivion when our original publication arrangements broke down; and the Geologists' Association, who generously awarded a grant from the Curry Fund to make possible the inclusion of colour illustrations.

David Parsons
Leicester
8 March 1990

Chapter 1

Review and Prospect: The Stone Industry in Roman, Anglo-Saxon and Medieval England

David Parsons

The exploitation of stone for building from Roman times until the end of the Middle Ages can be studied using geological, archaeological, documentary and linguistic information. The picture which emerges is uneven and much affected by the quality and availability of the various forms of evidence at any one time or in a particular area. Not until the late Middle Ages is there sufficient information to allow the identification of a well established and developed industry. In the Anglo-Saxon period in particular there is a paucity of evidence and the status of the quarrying industry is further obscured by the widespread habit of re-using building materials, a practice which was common at all periods. A study of transport networks needs to be added to clarify the sources of supply and the history of the industry's development throughout the period covered.

Introduction

The systematic exploitation of stone for building purposes appears to have begun in Britain during the Roman period. With the collapse of urban and military aspects of Roman civilisation during the 5th century, the need for quarrying became minimal, though there are hints that the techniques of stone production may not have been immediately or totally lost. The conversion of the Anglo-Saxons to Christianity from *c*.AD 600 onward provided the next impetus to erect masonry buildings in imitation of the continuing classical tradition in Rome and Gaul, but the evidence suggests that the many surviving Romano-British buildings were able to satisfy the limited need for stone and that quarrying in the Anglo-Saxon period was the exception rather than the rule. By the time of the Norman Conquest, however, it is clear that the practice of stone quarrying had been re-established, though probably not on a sufficient scale to satisfy the extraordinary demands of the building boom of the late 11th and 12th centuries. At all events, from this period on stone was imported in significant quantities from the north of France, perhaps for the first time since the Roman period. For the rest of the Middle Ages the picture is one of considerable diversity. The quarrying industry became increasingly firmly established, and it became financially worthwhile to transport good quality stone over long distances, especially where water transport was available, as in the case of the French imports. Nevertheless, for the average building project it was normal to obtain the stone from nearby. In some instances there is evidence both for stone being brought in from outside the immediate area and for the exploitation of local resources; the locally dug stone was no doubt used as rubble for wall cores and burnt to make quicklime, a necessary ingredient of mortar. At the same time the tradition of re-using stone from demolished buildings continued apace, and was by no means confined to humble building projects.

It is this continual recycling of material that makes it so difficult to understand the nature of the quarrying industry and its distribution patterns at all periods, except perhaps the Roman. While it may be perfectly possible on petrological grounds to identify the area of origin of a particular block of building stone, as described by John Hudson and Diana Sutherland in Chapter 2, there is no guarantee that quarries in that area were working at the time of the erection of the building concerned or that there was any direct commercial connection between the quarries and the builders at that particular time. Nor is it usually possible on petrological grounds alone to specify precisely the source of any given stone, and documentary and topographical evidence are required to identify the location of most quarry sites.

Stone Supply in Roman Britain

Quarries of the Roman period are particularly hard to recognise, as Tom Blagg demonstrates in Chapter 3. Only where exposures have not been subsequently worked in medieval or modern times is there the slightest chance of making a positive identification. In the case of quarries in accessible locations and yielding good quality stone, such as those in north-east Northamptonshire and the Soke of Peterborough, heavy exploitation in later times makes it inherently unlikely that direct evidence for the use of the sites in the Roman period will ever come to light. In more remote and underpopulated areas Roman quarry faces still survive, though in some instances exposures identified in the past as Roman have since become so weathered as to be unrecognisable, for example the inscribed rock face at Coombe Crag, Cumbria (NGR NY 5909 6500), where the whole of the worked surface seems to have spalled off since the inscriptions were recorded 50 or more years ago (see *RIB* 1946-52, especially the comment on *RIB* 1949). Roman workings are still recognisable elsewhere in the vicinity of Hadrian's Wall, however, particularly in the river valleys just to the east of Carlisle. On the east bank of the River Gelt there are rock faces bearing what seem to be characteristic Roman masons' tooling marks, as though the surface was dressed in advance of the cutting out of the blocks, while the famous 'Written Rock of the Gelt' (at NY 5242 5890, but now practically inaccessible) still bears recognisable traces of its inscriptions (*RIB* 1007-15). More impressive are the inscriptions near Wetheral on the west bank of the River Eden (at NY 4663 5345), where in particular MAXIMUS SCRIPSIT still looks remarkably clear (*RIB* 1004-06). Inscriptions such as these provide first-class evidence for Roman quarrying, but one must be on one's guard against later imitations, even though these often occur in the same locations as genuine inscriptions (see *RIB* under 'Falsa', e.g. no. 2379 at Coombe Crag). The identification of some other sites in the Hadrian's Wall area is less certain, especially where the quarrying appears to have been superficial and – presumably – relatively short-lived. To the east of Haltwhistle Burn,

Northumberland (NY 7140 6615), a number of depressions in the hillside are probably the sites of small quarries, though they are completely grassed over and might equally be the result of natural erosion. However, the presence of small grassy hillocks, which have the characteristic shape of spoil heaps, indicates human activity rather than erosion, though there is no guarantee that this was quarrying for building stone; other extractive processes would leave similar traces. A Roman inscription was recorded here in 1844 (*RIB* 1680).

Apart from examples such as these, the identification of stone sources relies on the petrological examination of building materials discovered by excavation, as Chapter 3 makes clear. On the basis of such determinations it is possible to be confident that stone was quarried in the Roman period in a number of areas, for example Barnack (Cambridgeshire) and Stanion (Northamptonhire). It is often assumed that the stone from sites in this area was distributed through the network of watercourses, both natural and man-made, which are such a feature of the nearby Fenland margin. This is no doubt a correct assumption, and one which in the medieval period is backed up by documentary evidence of various kinds. It is clear, too, that stone from the Wetheral and Gelt quarries must have made the first stage of its journey by water before reaching the Stanegate, which offered ready access to building sites on Hadrian's Wall; if the sites using stone from these quarries were restricted to the western end of the wall, then water transport alone might have been used. Stone from Barnack or Stanion, however, must have travelled overland in the first instance, and the Roman road system may have been as convenient as the waterways for middle- and even long-distance transport. The 'Hills and Holes' area to the south-west of Barnack, widely regarded as a possible source of stone in the Roman period, is only half a mile from the major road known as Ermine Street, and two miles from King Street. The River Welland at its nearest point is one and half miles across country from Barnack, while to reach the River Nene stone would have to travel five miles south on Ermine Street to the crossing point near *Durobrivae*. For journeys farther to the north or the south, the stone would probably continue by road beyond these crossing points. The case for road transport from Stanion is even stronger, since the village lies directly on the presumed line of Gartree Road/Via Devana, by which stone would have had easy access to Leicester in one direction and to Godmanchester and the Essex hinterland in the other. By contrast, both the Welland and the Nene are some four miles from Stanion, and an initial journey by road would be required before the river system could be used. Thus the Roman road network seems to have been of some importance to the exploitation of the quarries at Barnack and Stanion and the link between roads and quarries is further emphasised by sites like Hazelwood (North Yorkshire), where a road actually crosses former quarry workings.

Linguistic evidence

The more extensive quarries of the Roman period, and perhaps some of the smaller ones, must have been noticeable landscape features in the early Anglo-Saxon period, and they – rather than contemporary quarrying activity – may have been the origin of some of the place-name and other Old English linguistic evidence. Stanion is a case in point. The name derives from OE *stan-aern*, and Dr Margaret Gelling has suggested that the second element may be more specific than simply 'house', 'building'. By analogy with comparable name forms (Brewerne, Colerne, Seasalter) Stanion may mean 'stone store' or 'stone workshop'. However, the similar formation 'Potterne' does not necessarily imply current activity on the part of potters. Large quantities of high-quality Iron-Age wares have been discovered in the locality and the OE speakers who coined the place-name may have been referring to this. Similarly, Stanion could be taken to indicate the site of former stoneworking and not the extraction of stone by the Anglo-Saxons themselves. A similar interpretation may be placed on other place-names compounded with *stan*, including perhaps such specific examples as Standhill/Standel (*stan-gedelf*: 'stone quarry'). An interesting case is Stonegrave (North Yorkshire), whose name seems particularly unambiguous and is attested as early as the mid 8th century. A recent re-assessment of the name has suggested, however, that the name arose in the 6th century in the form *staninga-graef* (Morris 1985), which appears to mean 'quarry of the stone people'. These 'stone people' are unlikely to have been identified as such unless they were currently working the material. Since it is hardly credible that Anglo-Saxons would be quarrying at a date before the introduction of Christianity, the implication is that there was a sub-Roman population in Stonegrave still extracting stone, though perhaps only in small quantities and for such purposes as repairing roads or patching stone-built villas or other Romano-British buildings.

Other -grave names do not necessarily indicate diggings (Gelling 1984, 192-94) and even when a case can be made out for this meaning, it should not be taken to imply contemporary quarrying. The same observation must apply to a variety of words which appear in the boundary clauses of Anglo-Saxon charters. Examples from the Cotswolds and elsewhere in the south-west Midlands have been discussed briefly by Dr Della Hooke (1985, 127-28). In addition to *stangedelf*, mentioned above, there are several occurrences of *crundel*, and it has been argued that this term indicates a quarry or chalk pit rather than a natural ravine. Even so, the use of such obvious features to identify the lines of estate boundaries by no means proves that they were being actively used as quarries at the time when the charters were drawn up, as Dr Hooke assumes – perhaps a little too readily. Indeed, one might argue that quarries are likely to pre-date the boundaries which they are used to define, and in the case of charter references as early as the 8th century this would imply a very early start to quarrying activity within the Anglo-Saxon period itself. There is a strong possibility that some, at least, of such quarries were disused at the date of the relevant charters and were last used in the Roman or sub-Roman period. Nevertheless, where a *crundel* is identified by the name of an owner (or his office), this might be taken as indicating a current interest in the site and thus perhaps contemporary exploitation of the quarry. Examples include *leppan crundlas* (Leppa's quarries) at Bibury in Gloucestershire, and *cyninga crundel* (the king's quarry) at Hawkesbury in the same county. The latter is comparable with the *Cnutes delfe* of the mid 11th-century agreement between the abbeys of Ramsey and Peterborough, though this was a watercourse rather than a quarry (Harmer 1952, no.62). I have referred elsewhere to quarries as a possible royal prerogative in the early Middle Ages (Parsons forthcoming, where a number of topics touched upon here are discussed in more detail). Other names in *delf/gedelf* include the Staffordshire examples of Biddulph and Dilhorne, the latter compounded with the suggestive *aern*, mentioned above. Biddulph lies on the coal measures, however, so that the digging may well have had a purpose unconnected with building, but Dilhorne, on the Bunter Sandstone, is a more likely instance of a stone quarry name. Another Staffordshire example is Stony-delph, south of Tamworth. Further instances in West Yorkshire are given by Stephen Moorhouse in Chapter 9 (below, pp. 128-31).

Re-use of stone

The cautious attitude to the linguistic evidence is dictated by the results of archaeological investigations, many of which have suggested that the building industry in Middle Saxon times and later depended heavily on the re-use both of demolition material from earlier structures and of other loose stonework, such as gravestones and memorials. The implication of the widespread recycling tendency is that little or no original quarrying was taking place at the time, for whatever reason. This is not universally true, for in the stone-rich area of Derbyshire Michael Stanley has found no evidence for re-use: fresh stone was ready to hand at most sites of importance (Chapter 11). Elsewhere, however, the evidence tends to point in the other direction. The church at Brixworth, Northamptonshire, is a case in point. The petrological examination of the building stones has revealed that there is only one piece of Barnack stone in the whole fabric, and that can be shown to be intrusive. This is surprising in view of the connexion between Brixworth and the abbey at Peterborough, which later owned quarries at Barnack. Various explanations for this have been put forward (Sutherland & Parsons 1984, 52 & 62), but that interim report failed to discuss the obvious inference that the Barnack quarries may not have been working at the time of the building of Brixworth church. As it is, the primary structure, possibly of 8th-century date, and the secondary fabric of the west tower and attached stair turret, probably 11th-century, both consist very largely of re-used masonry. One of the basic criteria for recognising this is the random distribution in the fabric of burnt blocks of stone, a topic which is explored in detail by Diana Sutherland in Chapter 7. The observation and recording of this evidence is able to establish the fact of re-use, but on its own is insufficient to establish either the date or the location of the building from which the material was robbed. ·

On the question of date, the use of mostly broken bricks in the Brixworth fabric and the recovery of carved and inscribed stones from excavations point unambiguously to the Roman period. This accords well with the evidence, long since recognised, of Anglo-Saxon church fabrics in places close to major Roman sites, where the re-use of building material comes as no surprise. At Escomb, County Durham, many of the stones bear characteristic Roman tooling patterns and the masonry includes a stone inscribed LEG VI, but inverted during re-use. The crypt of the priory church at Hexham, Northumberland, incorporates considerable numbers of carved stones, such as cornices from major Roman buildings, all re-used without any regard to their original architectural context and function, and at least one Roman building inscription. At Wroxeter, Shropshire, many of the Roman stones built into the church fabric are recognisable either by their shape (e.g. column fragments) or by the lewis holes originally intended for the attachment of lifting gear. All of these cases are well known and are described in the standard literature of Anglo-Saxon architecture. Recent work has added to the list of examples. Several churches in York, including the first Norman cathedral of Archbishop Thomas of Bayeux, have been shown to rely heavily on the former Roman buildings for their supply of stone, and there are further examples elsewhere in Yorkshire (Morris 1988).

In most of these instances the stone was ready to hand in the near vicinity, but in the case of Brixworth, petrological analysis suggests that second-hand stone and brick was being brought considerable distances. It is somewhat surprising that this method of obtaining materials should have been preferred to quarrying in the area around the church, where stone of sufficient quality for rubble building is readily available. The discovery in 1987 that the inner ambulatory wall was built directly on the bedrock merely served to emphasise this paradox. Much of the material for the first phase of the building came from the Charnian series of central and north Leicestershire, but with no very significant quantity of stone from any one location. This fact alone would seem to preclude the possibility of any original quarrying by the builders of Brixworth, and the buildings of Roman Leicester suggest themselves as the immediate source for the mixed bag of materials used in the church fabric. In fact, the surviving Jewry Wall consists of a mixed assemblage of stone, some of it non-Charnian, which matches quite closely the composition of the early walling at Brixworth. This prompts one to inquire whether the Jewry Wall and comparable buildings in the Roman city were themselves built initially of recycled material. If that were the case, it would be in keeping with the traditions of Rome itself, and with evidence available from elsewhere in Roman Britain. One of the buildings most frequently referred to by contributors to this volume is the monumental arch at Richborough, whose demolition by the late 3rd century released huge quantities of stone which found its way into a variety of buildings in east Kent, and which was available for further re-use in the Anglo-Saxon and later medieval periods. The importation of stone into Roman Britain for major building projects such as the Richborough Arch may provide an explanation for the use of exotic materials in the early Middle Ages. Examples of such re-use certainly include the Reculver Columns and Cross and perhaps the coloured marble used as paving in Canterbury Cathedral after the Norman Conquest (Chapters 4 and 5).

Despite the development of native quarries and the importation of stone, particularly from northern France, the tradition of re-using old materials continued unabated throughout the Middle Ages, as David Stocker and Paul Everson make clear in Chapter 6. After the Norman Conquest Anglo-Saxon as well as

Roman stonework was available for re-use. Most easily recognisable are the numerous fragments of cross sculpture and architectural details, together with grave covers and other funerary monuments. The stock of this kind of material was constantly being replenished during the medieval period. Apart from the many Lincolnshire examples cited in this volume, instances of Anglo-Saxon or Anglo-Scandinavian sculpture incorporated into later church fabrics can be found in such diverse places as Billingham, Cleveland (in the Saxo-Norman tower), and Winterbourne Steepleton, Dorset (in the possibly late Anglo-Saxon nave). A particularly informative example is the church of St Peter, Northampton, where two loose respond bases from the 12th-century building were cut from blocks of stone previously carved with Anglo-Saxon interlace and cable moulding, which are still preserved on the bottom faces of the two stones. St Peter's is a sophisticated building on a high-status site, and gives the lie to any suggestion that only unimportant local buildings were built of second-hand materials. This is emphasised by the documentary evidence quoted below, all of which refers to buildings of some importance, including royal houses. The re-use of pre-Conquest material can be demonstrated even later in the Middle Ages, for example in the 14th-century west tower at Market Overton, Leicestershire (formerly Rutland), where two cross-shafts of modest size are employed as quoin stones low down in the salient western angles. The interlace panels on the narrow faces of the shafts can be clearly seen in the north and south walls of the tower, and in view of David Stocker's discussion of the symbolic use of old carved stones (Chapter 6) it is tempting to see here a reference to Christ as 'the head of the corner'. This interpretation would be easier to defend, however, if the carving consisted of vine-scroll rather than purely geometrical interlace. Another Midlands example of re-used sculptural material is the west tower of the parish church at Higham Ferrers, Northamptonshire, which was rebuilt in 1631-32 using the original stonework. High up in the west face is a diverse collection of carved fragments including part of a possibly Romanesque Christ in Majesty. All of these stones came presumably from the demolition material of the original medieval tower, though there is no guarantee that they were visible on the surface before the modern rebuilding.

In addition to this material visible in surviving medieval fabrics there is a wealth of documentary evidence for the re-use of building materials. One of the best known cases is St Alban's Abbey, where the late 11th-century fabric includes large quantities of material, mostly brick, from Roman *Verulamium*. The abbey's *Chronicle* relates that this was already available in the builders' yard, having been collected together and stockpiled by two Anglo-Saxon abbots in the 10th century. In the transepts of the present cathedral church there are also baluster shafts, widely accepted as being of Anglo-Saxon origin, so presumably the Norman building also cannibalised its immediate predecessor. In the 13th century an interesting sequence of events took place in Bedford. King John granted the castle there to Falk, count of Bréauté, who set about extending and improving the buildings. In the course of this work he demolished the old-established church of St Paul near the castle and used the stone from it in the construction of the new buildings. Eventually the progress of political and military affairs resulted in some kind of rough justice, for the castle was slighted by Henry III, who granted the demolition materials to the canons of three churches in the area, including St Paul's. Royal property was also the subject of a series of transactions in the early 15th century. In 1399 Richard II had given his manor at Northolt to Westminster Abbey. When a new house was being built for the king at Sutton, the clerk of the royal works bought from the sacrist at Westminster material which had been obtained from the Northolt manor house. The king decided, however, not to occupy the house at Sutton, so it was demolished, and the materials re-used yet again in the construction of a further royal house at Sheen. In this case, not only the stone was re-used, but timber, tiles, and even plaster from the walls and ceilings. The final royally-inspired re-use of medieval building stone was on a grand scale when, after the dissolution of monasteries and collegiate churches in the 1530s and 1540s, the redundant buildings were sold off to the highest bidder, and were converted into stately homes, park walls and even garden ornaments.

The growth of medieval quarrying

Despite the considerable evidence for the large-scale re-use of building stone, the demand for freshly quarried stone gradually grew, and a quarrying industry established itself. This begins to become evident in late Anglo-Saxon times. Some of the sites identified by archaeological means can be dated to this period. The quarry pits recovered by excavation at Raunds, Northamptonshire, are discussed in this volume by Graham Cadman and Michel Audouy (Chapter 12) and the evidence for quarrying and mining in medieval Norwich is presented by Brian Ayers (Chapter 14). Other examples of quarrying within late Saxon towns are recorded in the recent archaeological literature, for instance in Stamford and Peterborough. Many of these would not qualify as quarries in the modern sense of the term, since they are very small-scale affairs, as at Raunds. Such restricted 'diggings', which may have been opened up for a single phase of an individual building, are almost impossible to identify in advance of excavation, especially where they have been backfilled in antiquity. It is therefore possible, indeed likely, that this kind of exploitation was widespread at an early period for which evidence of substantial activity is sparse. David Stocker has privately expressed the view that even the 'Hills and Holes' of Barnack, perfectly evident both from the air and from ground level, may represent an unusually extensive spread of such small diggings rather than an area of systematic quarrying. The area might nevertheless qualify for the description of 'well known quarry' which appears in one of the few pieces of documentary evidence surviving from before the Norman Conquest, the grant in 1061 by Earl Waltheof of property at Barnack to Crowland Abbey. Another document of the period also refers to Barnack. The agreement referred to above (pp. 4-5) between the abbots of Peterborough and Ramsey, conferred on the latter the right to obtain *wercstan* from Barnack and *walstan* from Peterborough itself. The Latin version of the agreement makes it clear that the Old English words refer respectively to dressed freestone and to rough rubble.

The ability to make such a distinction argues for growing sophistication in the stone supply industry by the mid 11th century. It also illuminates the one academic study of the late Anglo-Saxon stone industry so far attempted. A quarter of a century ago Professor E.M. Jope published distribution maps showing that good-quality stone might travel as much as 50 miles from source (Jope 1964). The raw material for his study was carved stonework and dressed stone used as pilaster strips, window surrounds and the like, in other words the *wercstan* of the Peter-borough-Ramsey agreement. The results clearly show a developing network for the distribution of fine stone in late Anglo-Saxon England but they do not indicate the volume of the traffic and thus the level of production at the quarries, and they are not relevant to the question of where *walstan* was produced and how far it travelled. The bulk of the stone industry's production is thus almost totally undocumented. Most of the evidence for Anglo-Saxon quarrying is very late in date, and in spite of the indications of growing sophistication and the establishment of distribution networks the impression remains of a fairly underdeveloped industry at the Norman Conquest. The demands placed on it after 1066 must have been intolerable, since there was a huge acceleration in the rate at which new projects were undertaken, and many of the buildings were on an unpre-cedented scale. By the end of the century substantial progress had been made in replacing cathedrals and major monastic churches (e.g. Winchester; York; St Augustine's, Canterbury) and some castles had stone-built structures (e.g. the White Tower; Durham). In the 12th century many more castles were provided with stone keeps, and houses, both in towns and in rural manors, were added to the list of masonry building projects. It is not surprising, therefore, that the Anglo-Norman builders found it necessary to import stone from northern France. Nearly every author of a regional survey in this volume refers to the evidence for the use of Caen stone in his area, and in Kent there is evidence also for the importation of stone from Marquise and from the Paris basin around Soissons. The story of the building of Battle Abbey shortly after the Conquest neatly points up the situation: local sources of supply were apparently considered inadequate, since arrangements were already in hand to import stone from Caen, when a quarry site was miraculously revealed in the immediate vicinity. This may merely indicate Norman ignorance of the locality, but the intention to import Caen stone does suggest that the conquerors had no great expectation of finding suitable stone this side of the Channel. In spite of the development of the English quarrying industry over the ensuing three centuries, the importation of Caen stone continued until the late 1440s, when the deterioration of the political and military situation made trade with Normandy difficult. This affected the building of Eton College, begun in 1442, and the unavailable Caen stone was replaced by magnesian limestone from quarries at Huddleston and Stapleton in Yorkshire. It is clear from such documents as the York Minster Fabric Rolls that these and other Yorkshire quarries were very active by this date, and several of them supplied stone for buildings in midland and southern England. By no means all the stone for Eton came from as far afield as Yorkshire, but the number of sources used for this one project is instructive. The nearest quarries were at Taynton (Oxfordshire)

and Merstham (Surrey), and stone was also brought from three places in Kent –
Maidstone, Farleigh and Boughton. The later medieval period provides numerous
examples of buildings drawing on a variety of sources, some local and some
farther afield. Exeter Cathedral is a case in point (see Chapter 15). Much of the
stone used in the 14th century came from the city itself or the immediate environs.
For example, the Dean and Chapter bought stone from Barley on the outskirts
of the city until in 1301 they bought a plot of land there from Robert le Hayward
which they presumably intended to quarry themselves. Other sites around the
city also furnished stone, and further supplies came from quarries along the
Devon coast, such as Beer, Branscombe and Salcombe. For specialist purposes,
however, stone came from much further afield. Shortly after the purchase of the
land at Barley the Dean and Chapter paid for the carving of four bosses (presumably for the Lady Chapel vaulting) and for their carriage from the quarries at
Ham Hill in Somerset, while in 1304 they obtained great bosses, bases and capitals
from Portland in Dorset.

The transporting of stone
All of this emphasises the importance of transport, whether by land or by water.
The Ham Hill bosses cost 14s. to carve and 8s. 8d. to transport to Exeter
Cathedral: carriage amounted to almost 40% of the total cost. Much of the other
stone came to Exeter by water, however, and its transport cost relatively less. In
the case of stone imported from northern France, of course, there was no
alternative to using boats, even though crossing the Channel with such a cargo
was a hazardous business. This is graphically illustrated by two of the episodes
from the *Miracles of St Augustine*, recently published in extract with a commentary
(Gem 1987). Both stories are set in the late 11th century, more precisely between
1070 and 1087. In one of them St Augustine was credited with calming a storm
in the English Channel when a boat was sailing from Marquise, near Boulogne,
to Kent with a load of 'great capitals, columns and bases' for the saint's abbey at
Canterbury. The other is a more circumstantial account of an attempted Channel
crossing by a fleet of 15 ships carrying stone from Caen. Fourteen of them,
apparently destined for Westminster Palace, sank in a storm, but the fifteenth,
whose cargo was again intended for St Augustine's, Canterbury, was saved by
the intervention of the saint, and managed ultimately to beach at Bramber in
Sussex before the boat broke in two.

Inland journeys by river or artificial canal were doubtless less hazardous than
sea crossings, but the use of these watercourses was sometimes beset with other
difficulties. In the late 12th century a great deal of unpleasantness was caused by the
monks of Sawtrey, Cambridgeshire (formerly Huntingdonshire), using channels
in the Fens which had been dug by their neighbours at Ramsey Abbey. The Ramsey
monks prevented their brethren from using the channels any further, though they
made an exception of the Whittlesey-Sawtrey canal, which was used for the carriage
of building materials. In contrast to this dispute stands the generosity of Robert
Percy, who granted the archbishop of York free passage on and near the river Wharfe
for stone quarried in Tadcaster for the nave of York Minster, begun in 1291. The

stone must have been taken downstream to the confluence of the Wharfe and the Ouse, and then up the Ouse, perhaps to St Leonard's landing in York, which was certainly used in the mid 15th century for unloading Huddleston stone, brought upstream from Cawood. It would be interesting to know whether the vessels used for this traffic were barges or merely flat pontoons. If the former, they would presumably have had to return in ballast after unloading, so that the further question arises as to what material was available in York to use for this purpose. It is clear that in other contexts it was stone that was used as ballast, which results in the occurrence of exotic materials in unlikely places, a subject which is explored by Paul Buckland and Jon Sadler in Chapter 8.

There is no comparable evidence for water transport in the early Middle Ages, but this seems not to have deterred the builders from bringing stone from a significant distance if it was necessary to do so. The igneous component of the first assemblage at Brixworth church cannot have been obtained nearer at hand than Leicester, which presupposes a journey of at least 28 miles (45km). There is no waterway which could have been used for any part of the journey, and one should perhaps envisage a route along the Fosse Way and Watling Street, a distance of nearly 40 miles (64km). Transport routes of similar length are implied by the distribution patterns mapped by Jope (1964). Even allowing for the fact that his observations apply only to selected types of stonework, the evidence from the Anglo-Saxon period is remarkable, especially in the light of Salzman's calculation for the later period that the cost of transport outweighed the cost of production if the overland journey exceeded 12 miles (19km) (Salzman 1967, 119). This was a powerful factor in the choice of sources of building materials, and it is small wonder that there is so much evidence for the use of local stone. There are good examples in most of the chapters in this volume, and the Northamptonshire researches of Robert Taylor for the Royal Commission on the Historical Monuments of England show that the tendency continues well into the modern period. The example of Exeter Cathedral, discussed above, clearly illustrates the heavy reliance on local sources, notwithstanding the bringing in of special items from Somerset and Dorset. The same pattern emerges from a study of smaller projects, such as the rebuilding of the chancel of Adderbury church (Oxfordshire), consecrated in 1418. Although stone had been bought from the quarries at Taynton, it was necessary to fill in a stone pit in or near the rectory garden after the building was completed. I have suggested elsewhere that the material extracted from this pit may not have been used as walling stone, but for burning to make lime mortar (Parsons forthcoming, 24). This activity may well account for many of the smaller local diggings in limestone or chalk areas which would otherwise be puzzling because of their limited extent and of the quality of the stone that was extracted from them. Nevertheless, this is unlikely to have been the case at Adderbury, for a number of reasons. First, the building accounts contain several entries recording the purchase of quicklime, in several instances from places up to 18 miles (30km) away from the church. This would probably not have been necessary if there had been a lime pit in the immediate vicinity. Second, an earlier entry in the accounts implies that a quarry in Adderbury itself was opened to obtain rough stone, and this is probably identical with the pit being backfilled at the end of the contract. Finally, most of the former rectory garden lies not on limestone or chalk, but on marlstone, which is not normally suitable for lime-burning. Its most likely use would have been as rubble in the foundations and wall core. If this interpretation is correct, then the pattern emerges once again of specialist stone being brought from a distance (ashlars and mouldings from Taynton) while the lower grade stone was provided from local sources.

The later Middle Ages

It is apparent that by the end of the Middle Ages the sources of building stone were many and diverse. Quarrying had become a well developed industry and the transporting of stone over quite long distances had become a more or less routine matter. There is extensive documentary evidence for the production, distribution and use of stone: leases, contracts and fabric rolls give information about these and other aspects of the trade in the last two to three centuries of the medieval period (Salzman 1967, esp. Appendix). Even the names of those engaged in the business at varying levels are known. It is clear, for example, that important master craftsmen such as Henry Yevele were concerned with the buying and selling of stone on their own account as well as with designing and supervising major building projects at cathedrals, castles and royal palaces. The quarries themselves had come into the ownership of private families, who either granted rights in them to those in charge of building projects or simply sold building stone by the load or finished lengths of moulding by the foot. In Yorkshire the quarries on the Hazelwood estate were owned by the Vavasour family, while those at nearby Huddleston belonged to the Langtons. In the south-west the Canon family of Corfe is a well-known example. They specialised in the supply of Purbeck 'marble', a highly fossiliferous limestone, capable of taking a polish, which had been in demand for architectural detail since the end of the 12th century and eventually came to be used for paving. Elsewhere in the country similar limestones were exploited, though not perhaps on the same scale. In the North-East 'marble' from Frosterley in County Durham was frequently used, though it is hardly referred to, if at all, in the documents; and in the East Midlands Alwalton 'marble' has been identified in a few instances. This last, like the other so-called marbles, particularly Purbeck, was used for monuments and other sculptural work; in the late Middle Ages this had become the principal use for such stone. Alabaster, too, was used for screens and reredoses as well as for the ubiquitous funerary monuments, but the carvers working at this craft seem to have been quite separate from the building trades. These two specialist materials are discussed in detail in the appropriate chapters of *English Medieval Industries* (Blair & Ramsey forthcoming).

Research directions

The ability of scholars to produce learned papers on specific topics and areas, such as those published here, and the existence of comprehensive works like Salzman 1967, give the impression that we are generally well informed on matters to do with the extraction of building stone in antiquity and with its distribution. This is a somewhat misleading impression, which is based on the wealth of documentary evidence and the high survival rate of major buildings in the period following the Norman Conquest. Much of the detail is not known, however, particularly in the case of minor buildings for which there is no documentary evidence. For the earlier medieval period and for Roman Britain there is a similar dearth of written source material, and a great deal of further investigation, using archaeological, local historical, geographical and geological techniques, is needed before a convincing and reliable history of the stone supply industry can be written. The need is particularly acute in view of the heavy dependence of the builders in the Anglo-Saxon period on the products of their Roman predecessors. It is clear that a full understanding of the Anglo-Saxon building trade cannot be achieved without more – and more detailed – information about quarrying and stone supply in the Romano-British period. It is not simply a question of identifying further quarry sites, though it is clearly important to do so. What is more important is to define the distribution network as a first step in determining how stone travelled from its original source to its ultimate position in buildings of post-Roman date. Part of this network consisted of cross-Channel shipping bringing stone from abroad. How far this imported stone penetrated beyond the coast may well be obscured by its later re-use in buildings at some distance from the primary sites. Indeed, the original cross-Channel routes may themselves be misunderstood unless evidence from secondary contexts is rigorously excluded. It hardly needs saying that stone was re-used in the Roman as well as in later periods and that this has to be taken into account in considering the primary distribution patterns. Conversely, care must be taken to recognise cases where exotica in apparently secondary contexts in Romano-British buildings are the result of using ballast. These are an indication of trade routes, but not necessarily those of the stone trade.

The initial distribution network of native stone may become clearer from a study of roads and waterways in relation to known quarry sites, but inevitably the greatest amount of information will be gained by working back from stonework discovered by the excavation of Romano-British sites. Here the prime need is for secure petrological determinations based on scientific observation rather than on the subjective impressions that have tended to bedevil the subject in the past. It hardly needs saying that this holds good not only for Roman sites but for the investigation of masonry buildings and artifacts of whatever period.

The fate of the quarries at the end of the Roman period is also a matter of some interest. It has been assumed, perhaps too readily, that production ceased with the collapse of Romanised urban civilisation, but the example of Stonegrave suggests that there may have been a degree of continuity into the early Anglo-Saxon period. There is at present no case to be made out for the uninterrupted continuation of quarrying from the Roman period into the Middle Ages, and the questions that need further attention are: which quarries were re-opened, at what date, and in what circumstances? It appears that quarries were recognisable landscape features when charters were drawn up in the Middle Saxon period, but it is not clear whether any of them were in active use. An intensive study of the boundary clauses in charters and of the place-name evidence might shed some light on these questions.

Whether or not Roman quarries were worked again, it is important to establish to what extent and by what date original stone extraction was developed in the Anglo-Saxon period. The currently available evidence suggests that quarrying was an underdeveloped industry in pre-Conquest England and that there was little or no activity until a relatively late date. This hypothesis needs testing. The pioneering work of Jope needs to be carried further, with more rigorous attention to chronology and geological identifications; in addition, great care must be exercised in distinguishing between primary and secondary distribution. The case of Brixworth implies that a medium-distance trade in stone existed quite independently of any quarrying that may have been going on, and there is also a suspicion that the supply of stone for sculpture was organised quite separately from building stone, at least initially. The processes by which the quarrying of building stone was put on a truly industrial footing after the Norman Conquest are also not fully understood, and complementary investigations of the period before the well documented 14th-16th centuries are much to be desired.

All of these inquiries will be forwarded by the continuation of the kinds of local research described in this volume. It is clear that the discovery of quarry sites will not be confined to rural localities like Raunds. Both the documentary evidence (as at Exeter) and the results of archaeological investigation (as in Norwich) show that quarry sites should be sought in and around medieval towns. Local work on masonry buildings above and below ground will make it possible to argue back from site to source, and thus contribute to an understanding of supply networks. Equally important, however, is the total investigation of one or two major quarry sites known to have been used for considerable periods of time (e.g. Barnack). Such investigations should embrace topographical, archaeological and geological research. Only by studying one site in its entirety will it be possible to demonstrate the chronological development of the exploitation of a particular stone, along with changes in quarrying techniques and the criteria used at different periods for identifying stone good enough to be worth quarrying for building purposes.

Finally, it is worth noting that the study of building stone and its distribution can contribute to other areas of enquiry. An obvious example is that of chronology. Two of the contributors to this volume (Tatton-Brown, Harris) are able to point to the possibility of dating some buildings on the basis of their incorporating certain types of stone. If a particular stone is known to have been quarried or imported into an area only between specified dates, it follows that buildings using such stone in a primary context can be firmly placed in that date bracket. Obviously stone commonly available over a long period of time is not diagnostic, but more exotic types may be useful as indicators of date. Another example, of a more specialised kind, concerns the use of carved stonework to identify high-status ecclesiastical sites in the early Middle Ages. That this criterion should not be uncritically applied is apparent from the example of Bedford Castle, quoted above: on the demolition of the castle, the priories of Caldwell and Newnham are likely to have received stonework from the pre-Conquest foundation of St Paul's, Bedford. Deductions from any surviving pieces of sculpture would apply to St Paul's and not to the two Augustinian houses of later foundation. It is thus important to establish, if possible, the history of fragments of stone-carving incorporated into later masonry. It should not be assumed without question that they were originally intended for the place at which they are found.

BIBLIOGRAPHY

Blair, J., and Ramsay, N. (eds), forthcoming — *English Medieval Industries.* London: Hambledon Press

Gelling, M., 1984 — *Place-Names in the Landscape.* London: Dent, 1984

Gem, R., 1987 — Canterbury and the cushion capital: a commentary on passages from Goscelin's De Miraculis Sancti Augustini, in *Romanesque and Gothic: essays for George Zarnecki* ed. N. Stratford, 83-101. Woodbridge: Boydell & Brewer, 1987

Harmer, F.E., 1952 — *Anglo-Saxon Writs.* Manchester: University Press, 1952 (new ed., Stamford: Watkins, 1989)

Hooke, D., 1985 — *The Anglo-Saxon Landscape: the kingdom of the Hwicce.* Manchester: University Press, 1985

Jope, E.M., 1964 — The Saxon building-stone industry in southern and midland England, *Medieval Archaeol.*, **8** (1964), 91-118

Morris, G.E., 1985 — The significance of the place-name, Stonegrave, *J. Engl. Place-Name Soc.*, **17** (1985), 14-19

Morris, R.K., 1988 — Churches in York and its hinterland: building patterns and stone sources in the 11th and 12th centuries, in *Minsters and Parish churches: the local church in transition 950-1200*, ed. J. Blair, 191-99. University Committee for Archaeology, Monograph **17**, Oxford, 1988

Parsons, D., forthcoming — Building stone and associated materials, in Blair & Ramsay forthcoming, 1-27

RIB — Collingwood, R.G., and Wright, R.P., *The Roman Inscriptions of Britain*, **1**: *Inscriptions on stone.* Oxford: Clarendon Press, 1965

Salzman, L.F., 1967 — *Building in England down to 1540: a documentary history.* Corrected impression, Oxford: Clarendon Press, 1967

Sutherland, D.S., and Parsons, D., 1984 — The petrological contribution to the survey of All Saints' Church, Brixworth, Northamptonshire: an interim study, *J. Br. Archaeol. Assoc.*, **137** (1984), 45-64

Chapter 2

The Geological Description and Identification of Building Stones: Examples from Northamptonshire

J. D. Hudson and Diana S. Sutherland

Building stones should be described as rock types, using terms comprehensible to both geologist and layman, as an essential prerequisite to their assignation to a particular source. Guidelines for the description of some common sedimentary rocks are suggested. Objective description allows the essential facts about a stone to be recorded irrespective of its source. In the absence of documentary evidence, quarries cannot always be specified, but a geological formation usually can; however, some common lithologies recur in more than one formation. Examples are given from the Northampton Sand Ironstone and the Blisworth Limestone of eastern Northamptonshire: both can be confused with better-known stones from other areas.

> And no County in England affording a greater Variety of Quarry-
> stone than this, or exceeding this in the Goodness and Plenty of it,
> upon that account it deserves a more particular Consideration
>
> (Morton 1712, 98).

Introduction

During a survey of the stone types used in the vernacular buildings of North-amptonshire, we have been confronted by the problem of how to describe them. As geologists, it is natural for us to consider stones first of all as rock types (lithologies); there are geological schemes, not always easy for a layman to comprehend, for describing these. Within a given area, a particular lithology normally characterises a geological formation. The fossils contained within a sedimentary rock further serve to determine its geological age. By comparing the lithology of the stones used in buildings with currently available quarries or natural exposures, it is usually possible to assign a stone to a geological formation. By such means we have been able to confirm that in the stone-rich county of Northamptonshire most vernacular buildings prior to the industrial revolution, and most medieval churches, were built of locally available stone. However in the architectural and archaeological literature attention is generally concentrated on the sources of stone that were used over wide areas of the country. These famous stones are usually known by the names of the quarries that yielded them (e.g. Barnack Stone, Ketton Stone), and they are often identified as such with little or no description of their lithology. Some of these stones are indeed highly distinctive and can be recognised unambiguously; also there is often documentary evidence of their source, when used in buildings such as cathedrals, colleges, or great houses. These high-quality stones were also widely used in humbler buildings for special purposes such as quoins or window dressings. But in vernacular buildings we generally lack documentary evidence, and there is a good chance that the quarry that yielded the stone was never recorded and may have entirely vanished. In such cases it is essential to describe the stone before trying to determine where it came from, and we would maintain that it is good practice in all cases, except the most obvious, to do so: An objective description is surely of more use to one's successors than an unsupported guess.

The description of building stones
General
The following section is intended as a guide for those without specialised geological knowledge who are engaged in the study of building materials. Non-specialists are understandably wary of the jargon employed by geologists, but useful observations can, in fact, be made by anybody with the help of a x10 hand lens and a little practice. Of course, certain problems demand specialised petrographic effort (e.g. the Reculver Cross, below, Chapter 4). The aim here is rather to encourage improved day-by-day recording of stone types, using terms with sufficient geological precision but which are comprehensible to a layman.

These notes have been prepared primarily for use within Northamptonshire, but should be readily applicable to the rest of the Jurassic stone-belt. We do not deal with igneous or metamorphic rocks, which would require additional terminology. All the rocks of Northamptonshire are sedimentary and all, apart from the boulder clays, gravels and tufas dating from the last ice age or since, are of Jurassic age (213 to 144 million years ago). The principal types of sedimentary rock are *clays*, *sandstones*, and *limestones*. Clays are not directly of interest in the present context (although they are, of course, used in brick-making), but limestones and sandstones are both important. Within our area *ironstones*, not common rocks worldwide, are also important. The different stone types are discussed in more detail below. The compositional distinction into different stone types is convenient, but it is arbitrary, because all transitions can exist: calcareous (lime-rich) ironstones, ferruginous (iron-rich) sandstones, argillaceous (clay-rich) limestones, etc. (see Table 2.1).

An important property is grain size. Although more elaborate schemes are used geologically, the simple scheme suggested in Table 2.1 should suffice. It is important to note that whereas some rocks are well-sorted (all the grains nearly the same size), others are poorly sorted and contain a range of grain sizes. This is particularly obvious where a rock consists of large fossil shells in a finer-grained matrix.

All sedimentary rocks are more or less *bedded*, that is they consist of layers of differing composition or grain size, corresponding to fluctuations in their conditions of deposition. Sometimes bedding is on a scale of metres, and may not then be apparent in a building block (e.g. Ketton Stone). Since rocks often tend

TABLE 2.1
Characteristics to look for in stone, whether in a quarry or building, using a hand-lens.

GRAIN SIZE
Coarse-grained: Particles easily visible to the naked eye (> about 0.5mm)
Medium-grained: Particles visible with a hand lens
Fine-grained: Particles not visible with a hand lens

	PARTICLES	MATRIX/CEMENT	Examples:
Sandstones	Quartz grains Mica flakes	Quartz Calcite Limonite Hematite	Calcareous sandstone Limonitic, micaceous sandstone

Limestones	Shell fragments
	Ooliths (calcareous)
	Elongate coated
	  grains
	Pellets, etc.
	Recognisable fossils,
	  e.g. oysters, other
	  bivalves, crinoid
	  ossicles, echinoid
	  spines
		Micritic calcite
		Sparry calcite
		Porosity
			Micritic shelly limestone
			Sparry oolitic limestone
			Porous oolitic limestone
			
			Also:
			Micritic limestone with
			  oysters,
			Argillaceous limestone,
			Sandy limestone,
			Ferruginous limestone

Ironstones	Ooliths (chamosite)
	  weathering to
	  limonite
	Fossils,
	  e.g. belemnites,
	  brachiopods,
	  bivalves (often
	  as moulds)
		Fine-grained chamosite,
		Siderite, weathering to
		  limonite
			Limonitic oolite with
			  brachiopods
			
			Also:
			Sandy ironstone,
			Calcareous ironstone

to split along bedding planes, thick bedding is a valuable property in freestones. Most rocks, however, show finer-scale bedding. It may be cross-bedding, formed when layers in the rock were deposited obliquely to the depositional surface (e.g. ripples on the sea-floor), as seen in the stone from Weldon. Millimetre-scale bedding is known as *lamination*. In many sedimentary rocks laminations have been disturbed or destroyed by the burrowing of animals living on the sea-floor, and sometimes the *burrows* can themselves be distinguished (e.g. in the iron-rich sandstone used in Daventry church).

Fossils present in a sedimentary rock are a distinctive feature and often aid identification. If sufficiently well-preserved and distinctive, they can give a precise geological age. In the case of buildings the presence of distinctive fossils such as belemnites, brachiopods, crinoid ossicles, echinoid spines, oysters and other bivalves is always worth recording. (*British Mesozoic Fossils*, published by the British Museum [Natural History], is a convenient source of illustrations.)

Quarries and buildings
The above lithological observations can be made on a stone in a building or in a

quarry. In examining a quarry, the succession of different beds can be observed, and bed thicknesses recorded. Jointing is a particularly relevant additional feature. Joints are natural cracks within the rock usually, though not always, normal to the bedding. They may be regular or irregular, and closely or widely spaced. The combination of bed thickness and joint spacing determines the maximum size of block available.

Conversely, on a building, the size and shape of the blocks used gives a clue to their availability, and often has geological relevance. Average and maximum size of blocks should be recorded, and also their shape and regularity. Frequently, a different stone is used for quoins from that of the walling, and this is usually available in larger blocks or considered more durable. Similarly, special stones are often used (and may be brought long distances) for windows and any features requiring carving. In many medieval churches walls are of random rubble but coursing was used when suitable stone was available, particularly in later medieval buildings (RCHM 1984, xliii).

Sandstones

Sandstones are composed of grains of minerals derived from older rocks, deposited as sand in ancient seas, rivers, or deserts, subsequently hardened by burial beneath later strata and by cementation. Cementation, to a geologist, is the process by which minerals are precipitated from groundwaters after deposition of a sediment, eventually filling the pores and binding the grains together to form a hard rock. The principal mineral grain in most sandstones is *quartz*. It is hard, colourless, and does not fracture easily, hence its durability. The quartz grains may be accompanied by other minerals, of which the most conspicuous is *mica*, occurring as glittering flakes. The principal differences between the Jurassic sandstones of Northamptonshire arise from the minerals present as *cement* or *matrix* between the detrital grains, accounting for most of their striking variations in colour. Quartz, in grains or in cement, is colourless, and so is calcite which is volumetrically the most important cement. Iron minerals are usually strongly coloured, however (see *Ironstones*, below), and a small quantity can colour a rock deeply. In buildings one generally sees the brownish or yellowish colours of the iron oxide, *limonite*, in its numerous varieties. (An exception is the New Red Sandstone of the West Midlands, sometimes seen in western Northamptonshire. It owes its pinkish-red colour to another iron oxide, hematite.) The colour of a sandstone can be much affected by degree of freshness or of weathering. Other points for description, and guides to identification, are grain size, roundness or angularity of grains (the New Red Sandstone often has rounded wind-blown grains, as compared to the sub-angular grains of the water-deposited Jurassic sandstones), bedding or lamination, and contained fossils.

Ironstones

These are composed predominantly of iron-bearing minerals and some of them have been important as iron ores. Their mineralogy is often complex. In addition, because of the susceptibility of iron minerals to weathering, the stones seen in buildings are generally shades of brown, whereas the fresh rock in a quarry may be greenish or grey.

The principal iron minerals are the greenish iron silicate *chamosite* and the grey to colourless iron carbonate *siderite*. Both weather to brown iron oxides. In addition, ironstones are often sandy or calcareous, or both, and may contain fossils. A distinctive form of ironstone that is also an important building stone is composed of *ooliths* of chamosite; the rock is a *chamosite oolite* (colour plate Ia). An oolith is a small spherical or ovoid grain, less than a millimetre across, and in ironstones these are composed of flakes of chamosite arranged around a nucleus which may be a quartz grain or a small shell chip. The ooliths are cemented together by some combination of calcite, siderite, and fine-grained chamosite. On weathering, the ooliths oxidise to brown limonite, but their structure is still discernible with a hand lens. It is in this state that they are seen in buildings. Iron minerals are mobile during weathering processes, and many ironstones contain veins and irregular patches of deep brown limonite that are not parallel to the original bedding.

Ferruginous sandstones

These intermediates between pure sandstones and true ironstones are common in Northamptonshire. Many of them are calcareous also, and their susceptibility to mineralogical change on weathering adds further complexity. The presence of abundant quartz grains is detectable with a hand lens, and so is that of weathered, brown, limonite ooliths that were chamosite originally. Calcareous ooliths (see below) may also be present but are white or pale coloured. Limonite-cemented sandstones are dark brown, but those with a high proportion of calcite cement are paler. Fossils may be present as original calcite, as moulds, or replaced by limonite.

Limestones

Limestones are the most important building stones in Northamptonshire, and include the only building materials exported to other areas to any extent. They therefore merit rather fuller description, particularly because their terminology has caused some confusion.

Limestones are composed mainly of the mineral calcite (calcium carbonate). Most consist of relatively coarse-grained particles that were originally deposited on the sea-floor, like shells on a beach; these form the 'framework' of the rock. Between the particles there may be a fine-grained matrix of lime-mud deposited along with the coarser particles ('*micrite*'), or clear, crystalline calcite cement ('*spar*') precipitated in the original pore-space of the sediment; some porosity may remain. Limestones are described and classified according to the types of coarse particles they contain, and on the presence and relative proportions of *spar cement*, *micrite matrix*, and *porosity*. Freestones are usually somewhat porous; this characteristic assists their property of being easily carved. Walling stones are often spar-cemented; they are durable but less easily carved. Limestones with a high micrite content weather less well.

Ia. Limonite oolite (Northampton Sand Ironstone) from Raunds. The ooliths (0.1 to 0.2mm) were originally composed of the greenish iron silicate, chamosite, weathered to the ochreous-brown hydrated oxide, limonite. Limonite also forms the cement, and veinlets of dark-brown limonite are typical of the effects of 'geological' weathering on this rock type.

Ib. Sparry oolitic limestone (Lincolnshire Limestone) from Barnack 'hills and holes'. The ooliths are poorly sorted, from about 0.2 to 1.5mm.

II. Finedon, St Mary's church. Built of dark limonite-oolite ironstone (Northampton Sand Ironstone), mouldings of oolitic limestone (Lincolnshire Limestone) from the famous quarries at Weldon.

III. Wellingborough tithe barn. Built of the two contrasting stones available locally: limonite oolite from the Northampton Sand Ironstone, and sparry shelly limestone from the Blisworth Limestone.

IV. Barn wall in Mears Ashby, Northamptonshire, showing reddening of Northampton Sand caused by the burning of the adjacent thatched roof.

V. Brixworth church: burnt, reddened limestone among unburnt limestone in the stair turret.

VI. Aerial view from the south-west of open cuts on Parson's Hill, Repton, for
Hollington Formation (Keuper) Sandstone. (Copyright: Leicestershire Museums).

Impurities in limestones affect their properties and appearance. For example, micritic limestones are often also clay-rich (argillaceous); very argillaceous limestones are known as *marls*, which are too soft to be used for building. Sandy limestones, on the other hand, are often good building stones. Small quantities of iron minerals greatly affect the colour of a limestone. The buff colour so typical of many Jurassic limestones seen in buildings is due to the presence of limonite. However, the same rocks in a deep quarry are grey-coloured, gradually oxidising to brown along beds and joints. The grey colour is due to traces of pyrite (iron sulphide), and stones in the half-way stage, with grey cores and buff rims, are known as blue-hearted.

More detailed classification depends on the type of particle present. The commonest particles found are:

fossils and fragments of them – mainly *shells* of molluscs, etc. (illustration 1) and

ooliths – small round or ovoid bodies with a concentric structure of layers of calcite round a nucleus (illustration 2)

(*pellets* – small (<0.2mm) ovoid structureless granules of fine-grained calcite, and *intraclasts* – larger pieces of pre-existing calcareous sediment re-worked on the sea-floor, are generally less dominant.)

Many limestones contain more than one type of particle and these may be concentrated in different laminae. The 'fossils' category is very varied and the type of fossil or fragment can often be specified e.g. oyster shell fragments, crinoid ossicles. Most of the good building stones of the Jurassic stone belt are either *shelly* or *oolitic* or a mixture of the two (illustrations 1-6; colour plate Ib). In some limestones, flat pieces of shell have a thin oolitic coating; we have referred to these particles as 'elongate coated grains'.

Describing a limestone

A description of a limestone should include reference to the main particle types it contains, and to the type of cement or porosity. A useful convention is to place the main particle type next to the word 'limestone', with qualifiers before it: oolitic limestone (e.g. Ketton Stone [illustration 2]), and some varieties of oolite from Barnack (colour plate Ib), which are pure oolites; shelly oolitic limestone (e.g. Weldon Stone [illustration 3], which contains oyster shells). Both Ketton and Weldon freestones appear porous on weathered surfaces: porous oolitic limestone and porous shelly oolitic limestone respectively. In non-porous rock the matrix between the particles will normally be either spar cement or micrite, e.g. sparry shelly oolitic limestone; micritic shelly limestone. (Note that the term 'Rag', sometimes used for coarse shelly limestone is imprecise and not used by geologists.)

A feature which is important when examining buildings, but is not emphasised in purely geological descriptions, is the relative resistance of spar cement and of particles to weathering. In some limestones the shells or ooliths stand proud, in others the spar cement does. In the latter case ooliths may form small holes. We suggest that the term 'prominent' be used to indicate this, e.g. a 'spar-prominent

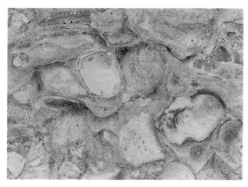

1. Shell-prominent limestone with spar cement (Blisworth Limestone), west of Oundle. Shell fragments here mostly 2 to 4mm.

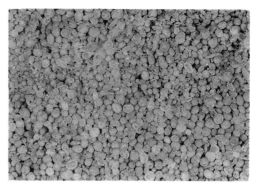

2. Oolitic limestone (Lincolnshire Limestone), Ketton, Rutland. The rock is porous, with minor calcite cement. Ooliths 0.5 to 1mm. Some broken ooliths show their concentric structure. 'Ketton Stone'.

3. Shelly oolitic limestone (Lincolnshire Limestone), Weldon. Ooliths are less than 1mm in diameter. Shell fragments, mostly oysters, about 3 to 5mm across, occur as layers in the rock. Porous, with little cement. 'Weldon Stone'.

4. Carved block of shelly oolitic limestone from Weldon in the tower of Titchmarsh church. The shell layers determine the visible layers of coarser texture.

5. Shelly oolitic limestone with spar cement (Blisworth Limestone), Raunds. The ooliths (0.3 to 1mm) include round ones and elongate coated shell fragments. A band of coarse sparry calcite (centre, left) is a recrystallised fossil shell.

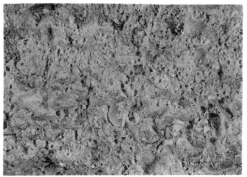

6. Spar-prominent shelly oolitic limestone (Lincolnshire Limestone), Barnack. From the ancient quarry site at Barnack 'hills and holes'. Most ooliths (0.3 to 1mm) are round, but some are elongate. The rock contains alternating layers of ooliths of varying grain-size and of shells (commonly up to 5mm), so it appears banded on weathered surfaces. The so-called 'Barnack Rag'.

shelly oolite' is one in which the spar cement stands proud, as opposed to a 'shell-prominent limestone with spar cement'. (Geologists use the term 'sparite' for spar-cemented limestones, and this is convenient and concise where context makes it obvious to the reader that the rock-type is a limestone. Thus the example above would become a 'shell-prominent sparite'.)

Many limestones are laminated, or bedded on a small scale; this may take the form of flat (originally horizontal) or of cross-lamination. The laminae differ in grain size or in composition; for instance the predominantly oolitic stone from Weldon has cross-lamination picked out by layers of small oyster shells (illustrations 3 & 4). In this example the laminae do not weather differentially to any great extent, but in many cases they do, usually owing to different degrees of cementation, conferring a striped or ribbed effect on the weathered surface (e.g. Barnack 'Rag'; see also illustration 10). These comparatively minor differences are often important practically and aesthetically, and in distinguishing between limestones of generally similar lithology. Later on we discuss examples from Northamptonshire.

We suggest that in a short standard description the main facts of particle type and cementation should be recorded first, with further particulars after the term limestone. The classic Weldon Stone would then be described as:

'Porous shelly oolitic limestone; cross-lamination often visible, defined by oyster-rich layers. Workable as a freestone; available in large blocks.'

Geological formations: stratigraphy

The geological succession in an area of sedimentary rocks consists of distinct layers or strata of differing rock types, which are recognised, mapped and named as *formations*. Their distribution within the region is controlled by the geological structure; in an area of simple structure older formations appear in valleys, younger ones on the hills, and where there is a gentle regional dip, the younger formations appear successively in the dip direction (illustration 7).

Formations are generally named after localities where they are typically developed (Northampton Sand, Lincolnshire Limestone) although they often occur over a wide area. Otherwise, traditional non-geographical names are used (Lias Clay, Cornbrash). Related and contiguous formations are grouped together as Groups (termed Series in older literature) (Table 2.2). Two of these Group names have caused some confusion. The Great Oolite is so named because it is the dominant oolitic limestone near Bath, whence the name originated. The Inferior Oolite lies beneath it; it is not an inferior stone technically or aesthetically. Even more unfortunately, the Middle and Upper Jurassic rocks were formerly labelled on many maps simply as 'Oolites', even though many of the rock types included therein are not oolitic, nor even necessarily limestones. Thus the term 'Jurassic oolite' can be very misleading if it is not made clear whether lithology or stratigraphic position is implied. We advocate avoidance of the term oolite except in a lithological sense.

Each formation is characterised by a particular lithology, or range of lithologies, which can be recognised and described as we have indicated, as well as by

Table 2.2

Stratigraphic succession and building stone sources in and around Northamptonshire

JURASSIC SUCCESSION IN NORTHAMPTONSHIRE	MAIN BUILDING STONE SOURCES
Oxford Clay	
Kellaways Sand and Clay	
Great Oolite Group:	
Cornbrash	
Blisworth Clay	
Blisworth Limestone	Oundle, Raunds, Stanwick, Blisworth, Cosgrove
Upper Estuarine Series (inc. limestone)	Helmdon
Inferior Oolite Group:	
Upper Lincolnshire Limestone	Barnack, Ketton, King's Cliffe, Weldon, Stanion
Lower Lincolnshire Limestone	Collyweston Slate
Grantham Formation	
(Lower Estuarine Series)	Kingsthorpe
Northampton Sand:	
Variable Beds	Mears Ashby, Boughton, Harlestone, Duston, Kingsthorpe 'Pendle', Eydon
Ironstone	Wellingborough, Finedon, Cottingham, Desborough
Lias Group:	
Upper Lias Clay	
Middle Lias inc. Marlstone	Byfield, Hornton
Lower Lias Clay	

particular assemblages of fossils. However the matter is not simple, because a formation rarely consists only of one rock type, and common rock types may also occur within more than one formation. Therefore an accurate lithological description will often, but not always, allow a rock type used as a building stone to be assigned to a particular formation. Quarries may yield different rock types even within the same formation, and conversely some rock types could have come from several possible quarried sources. A sound general principle is that stone for humbler uses such as rubble walling of medieval churches, cottages or field walls is unlikely to have travelled very far, for obvious economic reasons. Local sources should therefore always be suspected and investigated. Freestones, as is also well known, were transported within stone-rich regions as well as outside them to areas, such as East Anglia, lacking local supplies. We do not therefore pretend that accurate description will always lead to accurate identification of source. We now exemplify some of these points by investigating some stone types used in Northamptonshire.

The geological succession in Northamptonshire

The general geology of Northamptonshire is described in Sylvester-Bradley &

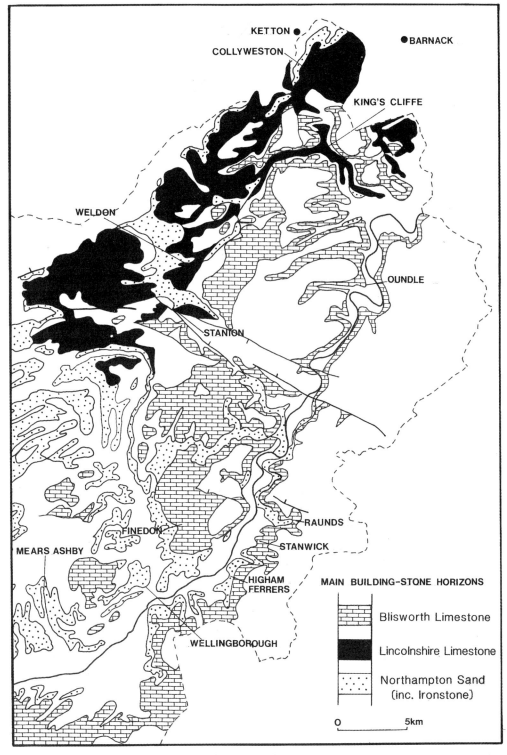

KETTON ●

● BARNACK

COLLYWESTON

KING'S CLIFFE

WELDON

OUNDLE

STANION

RAUNDS

FINEDON

STANWICK

MEARS ASHBY

HIGHAM
FERRERS

MAIN BUILDING-STONE HORIZONS

Blisworth Limestone

Lincolnshire Limestone

Northampton Sand
(inc. Ironstone)

WELLINGBOROUGH

0   5km

7. Simplified geological map of north-east Northamptonshire, showing the distribution of the geological formations yielding the main building stones, with the location of some important quarries and places mentioned in the text.

Ford (1968, 188-290). The county is well supplied with building stones from several of its Jurassic formations (illustration 7, Table 2.2). The gentle easterly dip means that the older formations, for example the Middle Lias Marlstone, outcrop in the west and in valley floors further east, and the youngest, including the Blisworth Limestone, outcrop in the east. The region's best known stone source, the Lincolnshire Limestone, occupies an intermediate position stratigraphically, but dies out southwards, so that it is confined to the region north of Maidwell and Geddington. Its famous freestones, particularly the shelly oolite from Weldon, have long been used within the region and far beyond (Purcell, 1963). Other sources within the county include Stanion and King's Cliffe, and not far outside the county boundary are Ketton and Barnack. All these stones from the Lincolnshire Limestone, as well as others further north in Lincolnshire itself, are well known and well documented both in general works (e.g. Clifton-Taylor 1987, 79-86) and special studies (e.g. Best *et al.* 1978). The other well-known Northamptonshire stones are ironstones and ferruginous sandstones from the Marlstone (found only in the west of the county) and the Northampton Sand. Within the latter, the best and most widely-used stones came from Northampton itself and the surrounding area (Eydon, Duston, Harlestone, Mears Ashby). These quarries yielded tawny to ginger-brown ferruginous sandstones that were durable and capable of being worked as ashlar and, whereas they were never exported to any extent beyond the county, they give a distinctive character to that region.

The building stones of eastern Northamptonshire have been somewhat neglected by comparison with the more famous stones of the county, and moreover have sometimes been mis-identified. They mainly comprise the Northampton Sand Ironstone and varieties of the Blisworth Limestone, and in several places these two contrasting stones are used in combination. We discuss some examples of the description, identification and usage of these stones in more detail.

Northampton Sand Ironstone
The Northampton Sand Formation, where it is best developed around Duston on the western outskirts of Northampton, consists of Ironstone below (locally over 7m thick) and sands, sandstones and calcareous rocks above, known as the Variable Beds, which can be up to 18m thick (Thompson, 1928). Both the Ironstone and the Variable Beds become thinner eastwards, in central Northamptonshire, and between Mears Ashby and Wellingborough the Variable Beds die out. The Ironstone persists in the region of the Nene valley; in the mid 19th century quarrying for iron-ore was revived after a lapse of many centuries, and became a major industry in Northamptonshire in the last 120 years, but the ironstone has a long history of use as a building stone. Ancient quarries have disappeared, having either been built over during town development or obliterated by subsequent iron-ore workings, but the buildings of Wellingborough and Finedon are themselves testimony to the quarrying of ironstone from medieval times to the 20th century.

The parish churches are often the only local survivors of medieval stone buildings. St Mary's at Finedon is a striking example of 14th-century work, built of well-dressed blocks of local dark ironstone and embellished with mouldings of Weldon Stone from the Lincolnshire Limestone (colour plate II). The church of All Hallows, Wellingborough, is less homogeneous, having elements of many periods; ironstone was used extensively, for internal rubble, external facing, for the chamfered blocks of the early Norman doorway and for the octagonal piers and arcades of *c*.1300. The 14th-century porches and buttresses are also of ironstone. It is mostly rich brown in colour, having a dense matrix of dark limonite; with a hand lens one can see the tiny holes where ferruginous ooliths have weathered out, along with a few sand grains. Some of the stone is more ginger in colour, of ochreous limonite, with dark 'knots' of dense iron oxide. The limestone for the later ashlar facing of the south aisle, for several gothic windows and the parapets is Weldon oolite. But the 13th-century tower, up to the third stage, is built of dressed ironstone used in conjunction with Blisworth Limestone in a deliberate pattern of alternating light and dark bands, each of one, two or three courses. This 'polychrome banding' is characteristic of many buildings in eastern Northamptonshire, including the late 13th-century church tower at Irchester, the early 15th-century tithe barn in Wellingborough (colour plate III), and the Bede House at Higham Ferrers. The combined use of these two locally available materials is based on geological circumstance, the Blisworth Limestone forming the upland landscape of eastern Northamptonshire, and the ironstone outcropping on the hillsides some 10m below. Wellingborough is built on ironstone, the nearest Blisworth Limestone occurring on higher ground just over 1 mile (2km) to the west and on all the surrounding uplands (illustration 7). At Whiston church (1534), a similar striped effect is achieved by the use of Northampton Sand sandstone (not Marlstone, *contra* Clifton-Taylor 1987, 91) and Weldon Stone.

Blisworth Limestone
The Great Oolite Group is a major division of the Jurassic of southern Britain, consisting in the Cotswolds and Oxfordshire of several different limestone formations which alternate with clays or marls, and are very variably developed in both vertical succession and geographical extent. They include the famous stones of Bath and Taynton. Blisworth Limestone (Table 2.2) is the name currently employed for the most widely-developed of these limestones in Northamptonshire. Within this region, it was formerly called the Great Oolite Limestone, but this term is insufficiently precise stratigraphically (see above, p. 23). It is also lithologically inappropriate, for much of it is not oolitic.

The Blisworth Limestone has a wide outcrop in the south and east of Northamptonshire (illustration 7), and wherever it occurs it has been used for building; small towns and villages from Brackley in the south to Oundle in the north are at least partly built of it. The limestone is up to 8m thick, the maximum thickness being found at the eastern edge of the outcrop where, dipping gently to the east, it is overlain by the Blisworth Clay and later Jurassic rocks; in the western part of its outcrop the thickness is limited by erosion, the limestone mostly forming a dissected upland plateau and hilltop remnants. It generally consists of individual

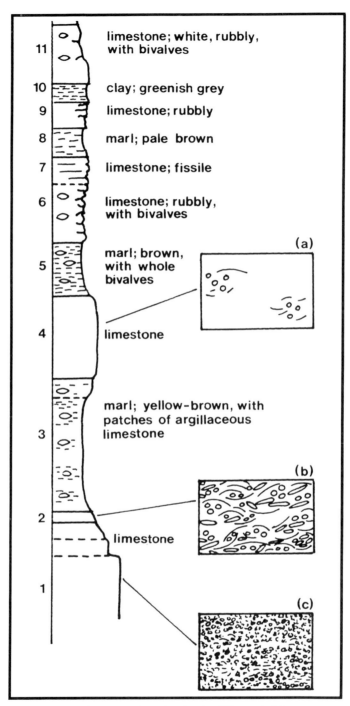

8. Geological measured section in the Blisworth Limestone at Raunds: the Saxon quarry excavated at the Burystead site north of the church (TL 001 733). The diagrammatic sketches indicate the variety of limestone types exposed within this small area (they are a little smaller than actual size): (a) micritic limestone with patches of ooliths and shell fragments; (b) sparry shelly limestone with elongate coated grains and few ooliths; (c) sparry fine-grained oolitic limestone with small shell fragments.

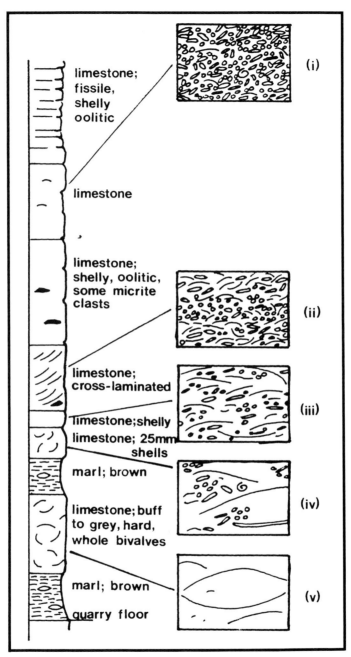

limestone;
fissile,
shelly
oolitic

(i)

limestone

limestone;
shelly, oolitic,
some micrite
clasts

(ii)

limestone;
cross-laminated

(iii)

limestone;shelly

limestone; 25mm
shells

marl; brown

limestone; buff
to grey, hard,
whole bivalves

(iv)

marl; brown

quarry floor

(v)

9. Geological measured section in the Blisworth Limestone at Raunds: section temporarily exposed at Smith's Containers lorry-park extension on the site of medieval and later quarries, 0.7km south-west of Burystead (SP 996 724). The diagrammatic sketches indicate the variety of limestone types exposed within this small area (they are a little smaller than actual size): (i) sparry shelly oolitic limestone with elongate coated grains and some large (15mm) shells; (ii) sparry shelly limestone, with layers of ooliths; (iii) coarse sparry shelly limestone with subordinate ooliths; (iv) coarse shelly limestone with a few ooliths, patchy spar and micrite matrix; (v) fine-grained limestone, partly micritic, partly sparry, with whole bivalves and single shells, including oysters.

beds 1m or less in thickness, alternating between hard limestones and softer, fine-grained limestones or marls. Coarser limestones are often cross-bedded. Details vary from place to place along the outcrop; there were evidently shifting shell banks, areas of lime mud, and patchy deposition of ooliths in the sea that covered Northamptonshire at this time in the Jurassic. Much of the Blisworth Limestone is fine-grained (micritic), often with conspicuous oyster shells, poorly cemented and soft in weathering. The presence of such blocks in a wall generally distinguishes Blisworth Limestone from Lincolnshire Limestone. Other varieties of the stone are generally more durable. Their textures typically include those with abundant shell fragments (many of them oysters), lying flat with the bedding or cross-bedded. Along with the shell fragments are sometimes a few spherical ooliths, or elongate coated grains. The matrix varies from micrite to spar; the better building stones are usually those with spar.

Apart from the rubble stone plentifully available, parts of the Blisworth Limestone occur as thicker beds of good stone. Little is worked for building at the present day, but there were formerly important quarries: Morton (1712, 110) mentions those of 'ancient note' at Cosgrove, 'which have been digg'd under Ground in the form of Caves and Vaults', and they were still active in his own time. There were 19th-century quarries at Blisworth. Within eastern Northamptonshire were quarries at Raunds which Morton listed among those of 'chiefest Note' in his day. There are no quarries there today, but archaeological excavations have revealed evidence of extensive quarrying that goes back to Saxon times (see Cadman & Audouy, below, pp. 192-8). A section through the limestone was temporarily available recently when a factory lorry park was extended, and this together with the section at the Burystead Saxon quarries site is shown in illustrations 8 & 9. The limestone here includes several beds of good building stone. Much of the rock is a sparry, shelly, oolitic limestone, some of it containing small, flat-lying shell fragments, other beds having larger shells. Raunds stone is unusual in the Blisworth Limestone in being conspicuously oolitic, including both round and elongate ooliths (illustration 5). The rock also characteristically shows cross-bedding, with varying grain size and texture in the layers, so that the appearance is streaky and, on a weathered surface, ribbed (illustration 10). This robust, ribbed shelly oolitic sparite is rather similar to Barnack 'Rag' from the Lincolnshire Limestone (compare illustrations 5 and 6). The parish church of St Mary in Raunds, including the Early English tower, was largely built of this local stone, which provided dressed stone and carved mouldings as well as rubble walling.

There were also quarries in the adjacent village of Stanwick; those that remain were overgrown at the time of writing and no section was visible, though the quarries have since been reopened for roadstone. The name 'Stanwick' implies a place where stone was available (Gover et al., 1933, 196). Even in the absence of quarries the buildings themselves are a good indication of the stone that was currently in use. The parish churches of this area, including that of Higham Ferrers, are built of Blisworth Limestone of sufficiently good quality to be used for mouldings and buttresses. At Higham Ferrers the stone is mostly less oolitic than that of Raunds, varying between shell-prominent sparite and spar-prominent limestone with elongate coated grains; it was available in large blocks and employed for mouldings in the elaborate 13th-century west doorway. Whilst the rubble walling is probably very local, the better stone could perhaps have come from Stanwick, less than 2 miles (3km) away. Local ironstone was used in banded courses (in the south aisle, for example), and also carved for the (Perpendicular) clerestory windows. Archbishop Chichele's school (founded 1422), a building of exceptional quality, is not of local stone, but of Weldon oolite. The Bede House (1428) across the churchyard, though, is of Blisworth limestone striped with ironstone; the walling stone is shelly, the string course mostly

10. Building stone of the tower of St Mary's church, Raunds. Sparry shelly oolitic limestone, with cross-laminated structure caused by varying proportions of the components, and brought out by weathering. The rock is local Blisworth Limestone (compare illustrations 5, 8 and 9).

spar-prominent and oolitic. The early 14th-century churchyard cross has a 1.7m long shaft of spar-prominent shelly limestone, cross-bedded, a type probably obtainable in large pieces locally; the replacement carved cross-head is of Weldon oolite.

Further north along the Nene valley, the town of Oundle was described by Leland in 1540 as 'all builded of Stone' (Steane 1974, 158); today, though most of what Leland saw has been rebuilt, there are many delightful historic buildings and the tradition of stone has continued from the 17th to the present century. It has been described as a Lincolnshire Limestone town (Taylor, 1963, 136); though this claim was made by a geologist, it is misleading, if not erroneous. Some of the ashlar buildings are indeed made of oolitic Lincolnshire Limestone brought from Weldon, 7 miles (11km) west of Oundle, including the 17th-century Talbot Inn and much later the school buildings. But Oundle lies on the outcrop of the Blisworth Limestone and, as might be expected, all the rubble-walled cottages and most of the medieval parish church are made of it. However, it is interesting that Blisworth Limestone in Oundle is not confined to rubble walling. Good-quality Blisworth Limestone ashlar was used by the 17th century in Oundle and in the late 16th century for Tresham's Lyveden New Bield, 3 miles (5km) to the west.

Oundle-type Blisworth Limestone is very shelly, the shell fragments being flat-lying and close-packed in a spar cement, generally without ooliths (see illustration 1). The remains of old quarries close to Oundle are now built over or infilled. A few kilometres to the west are hills and holes (now the golf course) and there are signs of old workings on the banks of the river to the south of Barnwell mill. For evidence of medieval working we can only look at the church. Whilst the Blisworth Limestone here is used mainly as rubblestone, the 14th-century tower is of fairly large blocks (150 x 300mm) of well-dressed local shelly sparite. Most of the decorative mouldings, and the 15th-century two-storey porch, are of imported Lincolnshire Limestone (including Weldon, Ketton, and Barnack-like oolites). But good-quality Blisworth Limestone was also used with these stones, for example in some buttresses. It can also be recognised in other churches of the area, including Fotheringhay.

It is clear from our investigations, and from the evidence of quarrying at Raunds described by Cadman & Audouy (below, Chapter 12) that the Blisworth Limestone was a more important medieval stone source in the Nene Valley area than has generally been realised, and comprises several recognisably different lithologies. Some of these are distinctive, others confusingly similar to better-known sources, especially Barnack. Much enjoyable geological, archaeological and architectural detective work will be needed to solve the remaining problems.

ACKNOWLEDGEMENTS

We acknowledge with thanks the co-operation of the Northampton Archaeology Unit in the work on the various medieval quarries in Raunds, and the assistance of Smiths Containers Ltd. in allowing us access to the geological section on their premises; our thanks also to Mr Jack Stock, resident of Raunds, for much help and information. Sue Button prepared the map in the Geology Department at the University of Leicester.

BIBLIOGRAPHY

Best, J.A., Parker, S., and Prickett, C. M., 1978 — *Using the Environment*, no.6 (a): *Quarries – Weldon & Ketton*. Northampton: Nene College, 1978

British Museum (Natural History), 1983 — *British Mesozoic fossils*. 6th ed. London: British Museum (Natural History), 1983

Clifton-Taylor, A., 1987 — *The Pattern of English Building*. 4th ed., London: Faber & Faber, 1987

Gover, J.E.B., Mawer, A., and Stenton, F. M., 1933 — *The place-names of Northamptonshire*. Cambridge: University Press, 1933

Morton, J., 1712 — *The natural history of Northamptonshire*. London: Printed for R. Knaplock and R. Wilkin, 1712

Purcell, D., 1967 — *Cambridge Stone*. London: Faber & Faber, 1967

Royal Commission on Historical Monuments, England, 1984 — *An inventory of the historical monuments in the county of Northampton* **6**: *Architectural Monuments in North Northamptonshire*. London: HMSO, 1984

Steane, J.M., 1974 — *The Northamptonshire Landscape*. London: Hodder & Stoughton, 1974

Sylvester-Bradley, P.C., and Ford, T. D., 1968 — *Geology of the East Midlands*. Leicester: University Press, 1968

Taylor, J.H., 1963 — *Geology of the country around Kettering, Corby and Oundle*. Mem. Geol. Surv. Gr. Br., Sheet 171, London: HMSO, 1963

Thompson, B., 1928 — *The Northampton Sand of Northamptonshire*. (Reprinted articles from J. Northamptonshire Nat. Hist. Soc.), London: Dulau, 1928

Chapter 3

Building Stone in Roman Britain

T. F. C. Blagg

Roman building in Britain involved new enterprises in discovering sources of stone, few of which had previously been exploited. The earliest stone buildings were supplied by a variety of means, including from across the Channel. When stone was in more regular use, regional variations indicate that accessibility of local supplies was the main factor. Quantification of the material required for some individual buildings gives insight into the logistics of supply, and the relative scale of the projects. Direct evidence of Roman quarrying, often lost through later workings, survives best in the military north. Purbeck marble and the relatively rare but spectacular uses of imported Mediterranean marbles are discussed.

Introduction

For Britain, building in stone in the Roman manner involved not just the introduction of new techniques of construction but also a requirement for quarrying and supply for which there were few precedents in native British industry. Stone was certainly quarried in the Iron Age for querns, from sources specifically sought out for the purpose (Peacock 1987). The use of stone for building, however, seems to have depended essentially on what was conveniently to hand.

In some hill-fort defences, stone available as an incidental product of digging the defensive ditches was put to systematic use in facing the rampart. Later repairs sometimes led to fresh stone being dug within or immediately outside the fort. Maiden Castle (Dorset) is a rare instance where a rock extraneous to the site was employed: the fort is on chalk, but the later rampart and east entrance works were faced in the Lower Purbeck limestone which outcrops 2 miles (3km) to the south (Wheeler 1943, 34). Where stone was used for building houses, mainly in the upland regions, it seems essentially to have been what was available on the ground surface or in stream beds.

Other mineral resources in Britain, such as iron, lead and tin, were known prior to the conquest, and were an economic incentive for it, described by Tacitus (*Agricola*, 12) as the reward of victory. The searching out and exploitation of building stone, largely an unknown quantity previously, was a demonstration of victory. By its use, the built landscape of Britain was transformed, a process described ironically by Tacitus (*Agricola*, 21) in the context of Britain's urban development, as enslavement by an alien culture, eagerly adopted by native Britons who thought it was civilisation.

Early building in stone

It is appropriate, then, to begin with an examination of some of the earliest stone buildings in Roman Britain, and the sources of the materials, to get some insight into the pioneering stages of the systematic quarrying and supply of Britain's building stones which, apart from the pagan Saxon hiatus, have formed its architectural heritage for nearly two millennia. It should be borne in mind that such pioneering was a relatively new experience for the Romans. In much of their empire, the stone sources had long been known to and quarried by the native population: Greeks, Carthaginians, Numidians, Iberians and others. In Italy, the opening up of travertine limestone and Carrara marble quarries in the 1st century BC are special, but perhaps significant, precedents for the early imperial organisation of quarries in North Africa, Egypt and Turkey. It was only with Julius Caesar's conquest of Gaul (58-51 BC), however, that the Romans came into contact with a large region, rich in building stone, but with no vernacular tradition of using it for any architecture of distinction (Dworakowska 1983, 10-17). Although Caesar conquered Gaul a century before the emperor Claudius conquered Britain in AD 43, it was not until Claudius's time that, in the parts of Gaul outside Provence, a real start was made to building in stone. The whole business of looking for stone suitable for the various uses which had been developed in the context of Mediterranean architecture was thus a relatively new experience for those involved in the conquest of Britain. Consequently, it is no surprise that the earliest Roman buildings in Britain constructed of stone do not demonstrate a systematic application of resources, but rather a variety of improvisations. Some of them were to be of great future importance.

To build in Britain in the Roman manner, stone of the variety of types suitable to the following purposes was required: (1) wall facing, of which the main types were ashlar, and a coursed rubble of small regular-sized blocks; (2) Roman concrete, as it is convenient to call the use of an aggregate of rubble laid in a matrix of lime mortar; (3) decorative stonework, including architectural ornament, sculpture, inscriptions and marble inlay; (4) roofs, floors and drains. The initial demand came from two sources: officially inspired prestige building; and the social requirements of the army.

The most important of the prestige buildings was the Temple of Claudius at *Camulodunum* (Colchester, Essex), which was probably begun after AD 54 and may still have been under construction in AD 61 at the time of Boudicca's rebellion (Drury 1984, 24). The substructure of this temple was a massive vaulted podium of mortar-laid septaria blocks. Hull has remarked that many of them were water-worn and obviously came from a beach (Hull 1958, 167). For the superstructure, the problem would have been the local absence of suitable stone for decorative carving, principally for the columns. The solution for the temple, when it was reconstructed after the Boudiccan destruction, was to build the columns of segmental tiles and cover them in fluted stucco (Drury 1984, 27 & 42). That must have been for reasons of economy or practicality, because suitable stone had been available in *Camulodunum* previously, if to a limited extent, for the commemorative tombstones of the centurion M. Favonius Facilis and the cavalryman Longinus. The former's has been identified as being of Bath oolite (Phillips 1975, 102).

If that identification is correct, it is a rather surprisingly distant source, when one considers the sources of limestone exploited for the palace buildings in Fishbourne (West Sussex: see below), the early use of Marquise stone (Worssam & Tatton-Brown, below, pp. 56-58), or the later use of limestone of the Lincolnshire series for monumental building in London (below, p. 40). If Bath was the source, the explanation may be connected with the early knowledge acquired of that region, where there was an important road junction near the river crossing of the Avon (Cunliffe & Davenport 1985, 9-10). For the earliest masonry buildings at Bath, the temple of Sulis Minerva and the adjoining baths, there was of course no problem of stone supply. The ornamental detail suggests that stonemasons from northern Gaul were employed (Blagg 1979, 106), and it may be thought likely that quarrymen also were brought over from Gaul to open up the quarries. The Neronian/early Flavian date for the Period I buildings allows the possibility that work on them had begun before the Colchester tombstones were carved; these appear to have been erected before AD 61, assuming that it was in Boudicca's rebellion that they were damaged and overthrown (Phillips 1975, 102). The funeral altar of the procurator Classicianus at London, erected a few years later, has also been identified as of Bath stone (Williams 1971b, 95).

The stone identified in the buildings at Fishbourne came from a remarkable range of sources (illustration 11). In the Neronian proto-palace, the Corinthian capitals are different from those at Bath, and have been considered to be probably the work of south Gaulish craftsmen. They were carved from a foraminiferal Lower Eocene limestone, identified as probably from the Mediterranean region (Cunliffe 1971, 1 & 14-15), though Mr Worssam wonders whether it might not be Calcaire Grossier from around Soissons (personal communication, and cf. below, p. 56). It is possible that these capitals were imported ready-worked. The column drums, however, were of a glauconitic sandstone comparable generally with specimens from quarries in Wiltshire and Dorset, but in particular with the off-shore reef of Church Rocks, near West Wittering (West Sussex). By contrast, the columns of the Flavian palace of *c.*AD 75 were identified as being of three types of stone: a possibly Mediterranean or French Lower Eocene limestone; Inferior Oolite, similar to that found at Temple Guiting in Gloucestershire; and, the majority, probably Caen stone; in view of the work on Marquise stone (Worssam & Tatton-Brown, below, p. 53), that might be an alternative, and re-examination of samples is desirable. The stylobates were of limestone from the Isle of Wight, the coursed rubble walls of the north and east wings were of limestone comparable with that from Pulborough (West Sussex), those of the west wing were of fossiliferous limestone from Selsey Bill, to the south-east of Fishbourne, and the gutters in from of them were of glauconitic sandstone from the Weald (Cunliffe 1971, 1-2), a source which was probably known as the result of the quarrying of the greensand for quernstones in the Iron Age (Peacock 1987).

The marble employed in both these Fishbourne buildings for *opus sectile* floors (see further below, pp. 47-48), as also the quality of the mosaic floors and wall-paintings, demonstrates that the owner, whether or not he was the client king Ti. Claudius Cogidubnus, was evidently one who could call upon very widespread

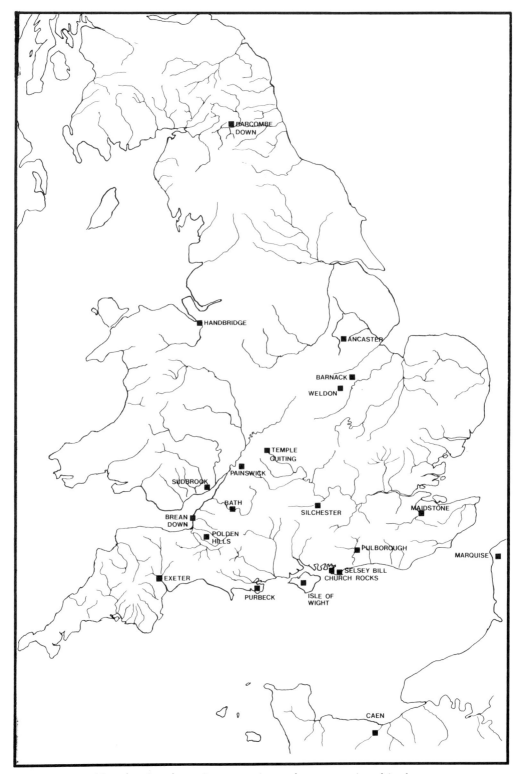

BARCOMBE
DOWN

HANDBRIDGE

ANCASTER

BARNACK
WELDON

TEMPLE
GUITING

PAINSWICK

SUDBROOK

BATH

BREAN
DOWN

POLDEN
HILLS

SILCHESTER

MAIDSTONE

PULBOROUGH

MARQUISE

EXETER

SELSEY BILL
CHURCH ROCKS

PURBECK

ISLE OF
WIGHT

CAEN

11. Map showing the main quarry sites and areas mentioned in the text.

resources, not only within the presumed area of the kingdom of the Regini, but extending to Mediterranean craftsmen and materials. It is perhaps that which best explains the extraordinary variety of stones employed. Fishbourne's location on the south coast, with a harbour, was no doubt particularly convenient for importing material from the continent, as well as from the Isle of Wight. It seems unlikely that stone in blocks large enough to make whole columns and capitals came as ballast; though some, but surely not all, of the large quantity of walling stone required may have come that way (cf. Buckland & Sadler, below, Ch. 8). The origins of some of the material might, however, be better explained by the owner's network of social relationships, if only we knew what they were, than by geographical factors.

The legionary baths at Exeter (Devon) contrast with contemporary Fishbourne in exploiting a variety of local resources, several of which are also discussed by Professor Pounds (below, pp. 233-35) in relation to Exeter Cathedral. The main building stone was trap, the red basalt local to the site. A calcareous sandstone which outcrops in East Devon was used for such architectural details as column bases. Mudstone and white Lias limestone were used for floor tiles, the latter also for roof tiles, as also Devonian slate. The only material likely to have come from more than 20 miles (32km) away was the Purbeck 'marble' used for small decorative mouldings (Scrivener 1979).

In these early buildings, we see a number of expedients being adopted for the supply of stone, including the import of it from outside Britain; the transport to one site of stone from a variety of different sources; and the beginnings of local exploration and exploitation. All the buildings discussed so far were in some sense official, either built under the patronage of high-ranking Romans, or connected with military establishments.

Logistics of stone supply

The situation of local urban communities who wished to build in the Roman manner was rather different. If they were fortunate enough to live in an area of good building stone, there was not much problem of supply, and what was required was the technology. Cirencester (Gloucestershire), which had magnificent columns in its forum basilica, became a centre for stone carving at an early date, probably acquiring the technical information from Bath. One wonders whether what are generically described as the Bath stone quarries were under some sort of imperial control. Bath stone was used extensively in wall-building at the legionary fortress at Caerleon (Gwent), as well as for columns and other architectural features. It was not available to the town of Caerwent (Gwent) in such quantity, even though Caerwent is a few miles nearer the source. The architectural decoration there was executed in the yellow Triassic sandstone which outcrops on the coast at Sudbrook, 3 miles (4.5km) away, a stone which was also used, in conjunction with Bath stone, at Caerleon (Brewer 1986, xv).

Elsewhere, it was probably the difficulty of organising the supply of stone which led to the construction in timber of the first forum basilica at Silchester (Hampshire), identified in Professor Fulford's recent excavations (Fulford 1985, 47-49). It was not rebuilt in stone until AD 125-150, and Bath stone was then used for the columns and their Corinthian capitals. At Canterbury (Kent) Gaul provided a closer source of limestone for the decoration of public buildings than any in Britain, and that used in the early 2nd-century temple and probably in other buildings appears to have come from Marquise in the Boulonnàis (below, p. 58).

With the development of towns both in their public and in their domestic architecture, and likewise with the development of villa estates, we are dealing with the acclimatisation of Roman architectural ideas among a largely native population. That was a matter not just of cultural assimilation but also of economic resources, in terms of the accessibility of appropriate building materials. John Williams's studies of the distribution of those materials in the south-east and the south-west of Britain review the evidence (Williams 1971 a & b).

Taking south-eastern Britain, much of the area is not in close reach of good freestone. The main materials of vernacular building were flint, greensand and ragstone, brick and timber. Fine architectural details are unusual in this region, compared with both the towns and the villas of the south-west, even in relatively costly buildings. The villa at Bignor (West Sussex) is one of the few in south-east Britain to have had stone columns, and then not before the late 3rd century, two centuries after the first house was built (Frere 1982). The mouldings and proportions of these columns are very close in detail to those of columns from three other rather distant sites; the temple at Nettleton Shrub (Wiltshire), just north of Bath; a building at Caerleon; and a villa just outside Leicester (Blagg 1981, 176). I have previously interpreted this as evidence for an itinerant stonemason, but it is possible that it was the completed columns, rather than the mason, which travelled. Unfortunately, none of the columns has been identified petrologically, an essential test of the hypothesis, though they all appear to be of oolitic limestone. The masonry of the Bignor house in that period was of Lower Greensand blocks, that of the earlier structure having been of mortared flint (Frere 1982, 139).

The evidence that survives for the walls of Bignor, as for many other Romano-British buildings, particularly villas, rarely consists of more than a few courses above the footings. It cannot be assumed that the whole superstructure of such buildings was of masonry, rather than of timber framing infilled with lath and plaster, or daub. On many sites, the small quantities of debris seem insufficient to suggest a stone superstructure. The evidence from villas in the south-west, indicating their dependence on very local materials, even when finer stone was available only a few miles away, suggests that for many owners, stone was laborious and expensive to acquire. The ashlar masonry and grand columnar façades of English Palladian country houses were derived from an aspect of Roman architecture which had not been a regular feature of the Romano-British countryside, however spacious and relatively luxurious some of the finer 4th-century villas may have been.

Unfortunately, we do not have any building accounts for Roman Britain, not even the record of what any one building originally cost. Calculations can, however, be made about the quantities of material required, which gives us some insight into the scale of effort and investment involved.

Probably the most significant single requirement for building stone was that of the defensive walls of towns and military forts. In the case of most towns, masonry defences were not constructed before the 3rd century. George Boon (1974, 100-02) has calculated the amount of material required for the walls of Silchester, which are 2,430m long and 16.45m² in average cross-section. The calculations are expressed in terms of a theoretical waggon-load of 500kg. Most of the material for the core of the wall was flint in lime mortar. Boon's calculations indicated over 20,000m³ of flint, from the local Upper Cretaceous chalk, i.e. 105,000 waggon-loads, and half that quantity of chalk and sand for the mortar. The bonding courses were of a variety of stones, including several Middle and Upper Jurassic limestones, probably from the Bath area, but mainly of glauconitic sandstone from the Upper Greensand, for which until recently the nearest likely source was thought to be around Farnham, Surrey (Sellwood 1984), but which has now been discovered a few kilometres from Silchester (M.G. Fulford, personal communication). These stones comprised nearly 9,500m³, or 45,000 waggon-loads, and by any standards that must have been a very expensive undertaking for the local community in terms of labour and transport, even if the stone came mainly from municipal land (a matter for conjecture).

For the walls of London, built about AD 200, Kentish ragstone was extensively used. The ragstone found in the wreck of a ship with marine barnacles on its hull at Blackfriars, London, was interpreted specifically as cargo, not ballast, and the source was the Hythe Beds of the Lower Greensand; it was probably brought down the Medway from the area of Maidstone (Kent) and then up the Thames (Marsden 1967, 39-41). In contrast with Silchester, however, London, as the provincial capital, might well have had its walls built at imperial expense.

That, of course, was the case with military fortifications, for instance the Saxon Shore fort at Richborough (Kent). As at Silchester, the aggregate for the concrete core was mainly of local flint. The wall facings were predominantly of Kentish ragstone, with levelling courses of tile. Several vertical divisions have been noted in the masonry, in particular one on the north wall, where the division is marked by the presence to the west of it of periodic courses of alternating chalk and ferruginous sandstone blocks (the latter probably from the Folkestone Beds of the Lower Greensand), laid for decorative contrast with the ragstone (Johnson 1981, 28 & pl.IV). The division indicates a break between one season's building and the next, and also a change in the stone supplied for the respective seasons' work. The chalk and flint were conveniently to be had within a radius of less than 6 miles (10km), from Thanet or the Deal area. The ragstone and other stones required a minimum sea journey of 50 miles (80km) from the Medway or the south coast.

The most convenient source of material, however, was from the demolition of the late 1st-century monumental arch on the site of Richborough itself. This had also probably been an imperial building project, the only building in Britain known to have been covered externally in marble veneer, which was imported from the Carrara quarries in Italy. From Strong's estimate (1968, 60) of the size of the monument, which would have stood over 25m high, I have calculated that nearly 400 tonnes of marble would have been required to face the building, between one and four shiploads (Blagg 1984, 73). The quantity of greensand, oolitic limestone, flint and other materials for the bulk of the monument's superstructure, however, was about 20,500 tonnes (41,000 waggon-loads, using Boon's Silchester figures). In addition, a similar quantity of material was required for the massive mortared flint foundations, which were over 9m deep. The demolition of the arch would have provided materials for the new fort walls (in which re-used stone is visible) at a great saving in the time and labour of quarrying and transport.

Returning to London, a much smaller monumental arch raises a different aspect of stone supply. It was also demolished to provide building material, in that case for the late Roman defensive wall along the Thames, which incorporated in its lower courses the decorated blocks of Lincolnshire Limestone from the level of the archway and above (Blagg 1980). This ornamented part of the arch was 7.57m wide, 3.37m high and 1.15m from front to back, and decorated on all four sides. It is not known whether this stood free, or surmounted an entrance gate through a wall. The fact that the whole of it could have fitted within the main passageway of the Richborough Arch emphasises the difference in scale.

The quantity of freestone required for the Arch's ornamental carving was relatively small: the volume calculated from the reconstructed dimensions is 23.6m³, about 59 tonnes weight, which would be a small boat-load, or 118 waggon-loads. This demonstrates a point already implicit in earlier discussion in this paper, that even for a fairly small project such as this, the accessibility of the sources of stone, and the sites where it was to be used, to transport by water was obviously a key factor in the economics of stone supply. The stone used for the London Arch was identified as Lincolnshire Limestone, from two sources: Barnack and Weldon were suggested (Dimes, in Hill *et al.* 1980, 198-200). Carriage overland would thus have involved a distance of at least 90 miles (145km) by road to London, possibly further: the palaeontological evidence from the specimens analysed was not conclusive in identifying the source of stone, and it could not be ruled out that Ancaster, for example, was one of them. Had precise identification of the sources been possible, firmer conclusions could have been drawn about the alternative routes of supply and the logistics of transport and handling. The difficulty illustrates the wider problem in discussing Roman sources of building stone in Britain, the recognition of Roman quarries.

Quarries

One result of the Roman success in prospecting for and winning the wide variety of building stones which have been identified was that their discoveries remained as a visible legacy to later generations, whose workings seem to have removed most traces of those of the Romans, particularly in southern and central England. For example, at the small Roman town of Ancaster (Lincolnshire), the outcrop of the Jurassic ridge where the Roman road Ermine Street descends northwards to cross the valley of a small river was the probable source of the stone used for building, sculpture and sarcophagi. Here, the extent of the modern quarry has cut the rock face back far beyond the likely site of Roman workings in the valley side.

As the discussion of the London Arch has already illustrated, it is notoriously difficult to pinpoint the exact sources of oolitic limestones transported for use elsewhere, since they can vary appreciably within a small area, and the particular variety employed in the Roman period may all now have been worked out. This may also be so, even when the likely sources of stone used are relatively close. Williams's study (1971b) of Roman building materials in the south-west showed a great variety in the use both of oolitic and of lias limestones, it being quite common for different qualities of stone to be found in one bulding, or in different periods of construction at one site (Williams 1971b, 99-105). In some cases, e.g. the Gloucestershire villas at Barnsley Park, Chedworth, Frocester, Spoonley Wood and Wadfield, old quarries can still be seen nearby, but it should not necessarily be assumed that they were actually exploited in the Roman period, in the absence of positive evidence. Carriage of stone for a few miles from an existing quarry may have been preferable to opening a new one closer to hand.

If, for example, the Lower Freestone of the Inferior Oolite used in Gloucester was quarried at Painswick (Williams 1971b, 100), it may well have been more convenient for the 2nd-century villa at Hucclecote, just to the east of the city, to have been supplied from Painswick through Gloucester, than from Birdlip. That potential quarry is nearer, and on the Roman road from Cirencester to Gloucester, but at the top of a very steep hill which would have made haulage difficult. Neither at Painswick nor at Birdlip has Roman quarrying been proved.

By contrast, the 4th-century temple on Brean Down (Somerset) had walls built from carboniferous limestone which was evidently quarried on site. A test trench excavated in the quarry pit immediately north-east of the temple produced potsherds of 4th-century type from the quarry floor (ApSimon 1965, 253). Carboniferous limestone is intractable to cut, however, and Bath stone and yellow Triassic Breccia were used for the dressings in the first period of construction. In the second period, quoins were made from blue Lias limestone from the Polden Hills, 15 miles (25km) to the south-east, and some dolomitic conglomerate, available from the Mendips 2-3 miles (3-5km) to the east, was employed in the walls, in preference, it may be thought, to further quarrying on site (ApSimon 1965, 253-55; Williams 1971b, 103).

As these examples show, most of what can be said about Roman quarrying is more a matter of deduction from the petrological identifications of the stones employed in building, and the location of geologically appropriate areas in relation to the Roman pattern of settlement, than of direct evidence from the quarry sites themselves. Sadly, it is not possible for a book to be written about Roman quarrying in Britain comparable with Bedon's (1984) on Gaul, though Williams (1968, 20-21), after considering the organisation of quarrying, has listed the quarries of known or probable Roman date in Britain.

The areas from which the most direct information is available are those associated with military fortifications in the north. At Handbridge, directly opposite Chester on the south bank of the Dee, the quarry for the red sandstone used in the legionary fortress is identified by a relief carving of Minerva on the rock face, and by the quantities of quarry waste and pottery dating to about AD 100 found in archaeological excavations there (Thompson 1965, 52–53). Cheshire sandstone, presumably from this quarry, was also transported for use in the fort of Caernarfon (Gwynedd), accessible down river and along the north Welsh coast and also, more remarkably, to inland fort sites over 45 miles (70km) away at Caer Gai (Gwynedd) and Caersws (Powys) (Brewer 1986, xvi).

The most informative area of Roman quarry workings, however, is that of Hadrian's Wall, particularly its central sector, little populated since Roman times, where consequently several Roman quarries have remained subsequently unworked. Thanks to the Roman army's epigraphic habit, several of these quarries in Cumbria and Northumbria were identified from the inscriptions found by 17th-century and later antiquarians (*RIB* 998–1015, 1442, 1680, 1946–54), and some are still visible (illustration 12).

12. Quarry inscription of Flavius Carantinus (*RIB* 1442) from Fallowfield Fell, Northumberland (scale = 0.2m).

Something of the variety of the Roman army's exploitation of local stone resources may be seen near Milecastle 42 at Cawfields, near Haltwhistle Burn (Northumberland). At this point, the Wall follows the crests of the ridges of dolerite which are such a spectacular feature of the local landscape. This very hard stone was extracted in the course of digging the ditch in front of the wall, and in levelling for its foundations and for fort buildings. It was only serviceable as aggregate in the mortared core of the wall. What was also needed was limestone

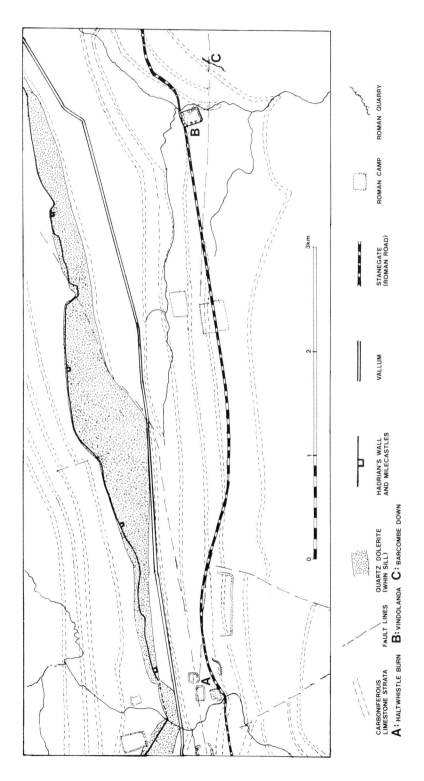

CARBONIFEROUS
LIMESTONE STRATA

QUARTZ DOLERITE
(WHIN SILL)

ROMAN CAMP

ROMAN QUARRY

FAULT LINES

HADRIAN'S WALL
AND MILECASTLES

VALLUM

STANEGATE
(ROMAN ROAD)

A: HALTWHISTLE BURN   **B**: VINDOLANDA   **C**: BARCOMBE DOWN

0   1   2   3km

13.   Hadrian's Wall east of Haltwhistle Burn, Northumberland: solid geology and Roman sites.

for the mortar, and a stone which could be dressed, for the wall facing and for columns and other architectural detail in the fort buildings.

Outcrops of carboniferous limestone overlie the dolerite about half a mile (1km) to the south of Milecastle 42, near the Haltwhistle Burn fort on the Stanegate, the east–west road which formed the initial line of Roman occupation (illustration 13). A quarry is still to be seen there, worked in the 19th century but also in the Roman period: an inscription of the Sixth Legion was recorded there in 1844 (*RIB* 1680). The presence of these limestone deposits was an important factor in the original design of Hadrian's Wall. West of the River Irthing the Wall was initially planned to be of turf because of the local unavailability of limestone for the mortar, and it was only later rebuilt in stone.

The limestone is not suitable for dressing, and gritstone was employed both for wall facing and for sculpture. In the central sector, this overlies the limestone beds further south. The quarry at Barcombe Down above the fort at *Vindolanda* (illustration 14), 4 miles (6km) further east from Haltwhistle Burn along the Stanegate, provided the yellow gritstone used in the fort and probably for the facing of the Wall to the north. It is of interest that among recently discovered writing tablets from *Vindolanda* is part of a letter referring to the transport of stone by waggon on a fairly large scale (Bowman & Thomas, 1987, 129).

14. Barcombe Down, Northumberland, from the west, showing the quarry face in the hillside above *Vindolanda* fort, top right.

In the Barcombe Down quarry face, as evidence of the Roman working, there remain three wedge holes in vertical line, so placed as to run parallel with a natural fissure in the rock (illustration 15), and a large phallus incised further along the face. At Limestone Corner (Northumberland) wedge holes may be seen in the blocks of dolerite which it proved too difficult to dislodge from the Wall ditch. The technique of splitting blocks of stone from their bed by driving in a line of wedges is well-attested in other parts of the Empire (Ward-Perkins 1972; Bedon 1984; Dworakowska 1983). I have not seen evidence in Britain for another Roman method of quarrying, the cutting of separation-trenches with a pick to remove blocks of stone in steps going down the face. I have discussed briefly elsewhere the small amount of evidence for the tools used in Romano-British quarrying (Blagg 1976, 154-55). It will be clear that, so far, Britain has added little to what is known of Roman quarrying methods.

15. Barcombe Down, Northumberland: wedge holes in the Roman quarry face (scale = 0.2m).

It is likely that much of the preliminary dressing of the stone took place at the quarry, partly to reduce the weight of stone to be transported. One site which has produced evidence of this, though the nature of the stone makes it rather a special case, is Norden on the Isle of Purbeck, Dorset (Sunter & Woodward 1987). In the Roman period, Purbeck 'marble' was used for mortars, inscription tablets and decorative mouldings and veneers, and the industry has been the subject of studies by Dunning (1948) and Beavis (1970). It should be noted that it was not the only hard fossiliferous limestone so used in Britain, and it is probable that, among earlier references in particular, the name 'Purbeck' has been loosely applied to such similar metamorphosed limestones as Sussex and Alwalton 'marbles', which lack Purbeck's distinguishing fossil gastropod, *Paludina carinifera* (otherwise *Viviparus carinifenis*; Beavis 1970, 183-85).

At Purbeck, the exact site of the Roman quarry is not known, but it was probably somewhere near the centre of the outcrop, which runs east–west across the middle of the Isle (illustration 16). Norden, situated 1 mile (2km) to the north at the gap in the Purbeck Hills next to Corfe Castle, was well-placed for associated industrial workings, including that of Kimmeridge Shale bracelets and other

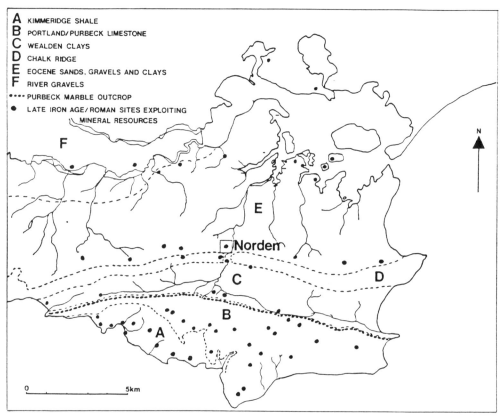

16. Isle of Purbeck, Dorset: 'marble' outcrop and Roman sites (after Sunter & Woodward 1987).

ornaments. Roughed-out mortars and fragments of sawn veneers found in the excavations indicate that Purbeck 'marble' was being worked on the site from the 2nd to the late 3rd or 4th centuries. This has led to a revision of Dunning's suggestion that the industry declined after the mid 2nd century (Beavis 1970, 204; Sunter & Woodward 1987, 43). Mudstone and chalk inlays were also being made at Norden.

The special techniques required for Purbeck 'marble', particularly the sawing of veneers and the abrasion to give the stone the polish which is its characteristic feature, might suggest that it would have been more economical to work it near the quarry rather than on the site where it was to be used. While the Norden excavations show that this was being done to some extent, there is also evidence for working on site, notably from Fishbourne, where in the builders' working yard associated with the proto-palace there were found unfinished mouldings and slabs of a variety of marbles and other hard stones, including large quantities of

Purbeck 'marble' (Cunliffe 1971, 16-17; Beavis 1970, 193-94). Fishbourne is one of the earliest sites at which the stone was employed, and the evidence from Norden might suggest a rather different organisation of the industry later in the Roman period.

Imported marble

Purbeck 'marble' and geologically similar British stones could only partially satisfy the early Imperial taste for decorating floors and internal walls with geometric inlays. Britain's remoteness from the resources of white and coloured marbles available around the Mediterranean was, however, an inhibiting factor. Freestanding and relief sculptures in marble, for example those found in the Walbrook Mithraeum, London, are rare in Britain, and most if not all were probably imported in a finished state (Toynbee 1986, 55). For working the marble imported for architectural decoration, however, specially trained craftsmen would have been required.

The workshop at Fishbourne has already been mentioned. As well as Purbeck 'marble', Pouillenay Rose breccia from the Côte d'Or and some Carrara marble was used in the proto-palace, and a much wider range in the Palace which succeeded it c.AD 75, with material from Greece and Turkey as well as from Italy and southern France (Cunliffe 1971, 16-17). A marble workshop has also been claimed at Colchester (Taylor & Collingwood 1921, 221). The foreign marbles found in the precinct of the Temple of Claudius at Colchester came from Italy, Greece, Turkey, Egypt and North Africa (Hull 1958, 173, 188-89; Pritchard 1986, 187-88). Drury, however, has argued (1984, 34-35) that they were not associated with the 1st-century temple, but with the basilican building which replaced it in the early 4th century. If he is right, that would appear to have been a special case. Otherwise, apart from in London, the period when marble was being imported into Britain seems to be restricted to the late 1st and early 2nd century. Clarke, in a paper on the villa at Woodchester (Gloucestershire), observed that the few villa sites where marble wall and floor veneers have been found are, where datable, all early (e.g. Angmering, Sussex, and Rivenhall, Essex), suggesting a relatively short-lived demand (Clarke 1982, 209-11).

There is the question of how this demand was met. London must have been one of the main importing centres, as is indicated by the much greater diversity of ornamental stone found there. Pritchard's recent study (1986, 171-75) identifies 21 different types of marble and other exotic rocks, originating from France, Italy, Greece, Turkey and Egypt, and found on 44 different sites all over the city. The variety suggests that London may to some extent have been the source of supply for other British sites, but differences in the pattern of distribution indicate other possibilities. Pritchard noted (1986, 187) that the *campan vert* limestone from the Pyrenees, the fifth most common (6.78%) of London imports and found also at Silchester and Woodchester, is absent from the eastern towns of Colchester and Canterbury. Considering the unique scale of the monumental Arch at Richborough, and the site's geographical position, direct order and shipment from Italy seems most likely. At Canterbury, the precinct of what was probably a temple produced over 600 fragments altogether (Blagg forthcoming). Carrara marble accounts for 63% of the total (56% by weight). Possibly there was material left over from building the Richborough Arch about thirty years before. Certainly, the relative proportions of white (including veined and bluish-white) marble, compared with Purbeck/Sussex 'marble' at Canterbury, the two main categories (76% and 15%) contrast with equivalent figures for London (24% and 34% respectively). Even among the comparatively small quantity (3%) of imported coloured marbles at Canterbury, there are rocks which have not been recorded at London.

It should be remembered that the quantities of some are extremely small: six of London's imported marbles are each represented by one fragment only. Their arrival may have been quite fortuitous, in contrast with Carrara, Proconnesian and *campan vert*, present in quantities sufficient to indicate deliberate ordering and shipment. The use of those was restricted. The Richborough Arch is the only building in Britain known to have been veneered externally in marble. No Roman building in Britain had whole columns of imported marble, as Becket's shrine did in Canterbury Cathedral (Tatton-Brown, below, p. 75). Compared with the amount of native British stone in transit, imported marble was of minor economic significance. That is not to deny, indeed it emphasises, the striking effect which would have been achieved in buildings where marble was used.

Conclusions

So far as Britain's resources of building stone are concerned, the Romans came with a virtually blank geological map, and they sought out and found a great many of the stones which have been found useful for building in Britain ever since. That is a remarkable achievement. One point for investigation seems to be whether old Roman quarries were sufficiently visible to be an obvious point of return for late Saxon and early Norman builders. Roman buildings were themselves quarries of stone to be re-used; they had been so in the Roman period already (e.g. the Richborough and London arches), and the fact that such re-use was recurrent was noted by several contributors to the conference (notably Parsons and Stocker: see above, pp. 5-8, and below, Ch.6). The difficulty in proving a Roman date for quarry workings means that most of our knowledge of the sources of stone depends on petrological identifications. Further studies of the kind represented by the contributions of Senior, Worssam and Tatton-Brown to this volume need to be made of the use of particular types of stone in the Roman period. In considering questions of stone supply, those interested in the world of classical antiquity in general, and Roman Britain in particular, lack the sort of documentation, especially building accounts, available to social and architectural historians of the medieval and later periods. Within limits, however, the materials required for a particular building may be quantifiable, and that can give some insight into the logistics of supply involved for the community or patron concerned.

For ordinary building stone, local availability was the main consideration, particularly in private building. It was rarely carried from further away than 20 miles (30km), often much less. Stone for particular types of work, especially for decoration, might need to be brought from considerably further, and an element of prestige enters the calculations. The same applies to some of the largest undertakings, particularly defensive walls, where the purpose of the construction could not always be served adequately by what was locally available.

BIBLIOGRAPHY

ApSimon, A.M., 1965 — The Roman temple on Brean Down, Somerset, *Proc. Univ. Bristol Spelaeol. Soc.*, **10**.3 (1965), 195-258

Beavis, J., 1970 — Some aspects of the use of Purbeck Marble in Roman Britain, *Proc. Dorset Nat. Hist. Archaeol. Soc.*, **91** (1970) 181-204

Bedon, R., 1984 — *Les carrières et les carriers de la Gaule Romaine.* Paris: Picard, 1984

Blagg. T.F.C., 1976 — Tools and techniques of the Roman stonemason in Britain, *Britannia*, **7** (1976), 152-72

Blagg, T.F.C., 1979 — The date of the temple of Sulis Minerva at Bath, *Britannia*, **10** (1979), 101-07

Blagg, T.F.C., 1980 — The sculptured stone, Hill *et al.* 1980, 125-93

Blagg, T.F.C., 1981 — Architecture and patronage in the western provinces of the Roman Empire in the third century, *The Roman West in the third century*, ed. A. King and M. Henig, 167-88. Br. Archaeol. Rep. international series, **109**, Oxford, 1981

Blagg. T.F.C., 1984 — Roman architectural ornament in Kent, *Archaeol. Cantiana*, **100** (1984), 65-80

Blagg, T.F.C., forthcoming — Architectural stonework, *The Archaeology of Canterbury*, **6**

Boon, G.C., 1974 — *Silchester, the Roman town of Calleva.* Newton Abbot: David and Charles, 1974

Bowman, A.K., and Thomas, J. D., 1987 — New texts from Vindolanda, *Britannia*, **18** (1987), 125-42

Brewer, R.J., 1986 — *Corpus Signorum Imperii Romani, Great Britain* **1**. 5: *Wales.* Oxford: University Press, 1986

Clarke, G., 1982 — The Roman villa at Woodchester, *Britannia*, **13** (1982), 197-228

Cunliffe, B., 1971 — *Excavations at Fishbourne, 1961-1969*, **2**: *The Finds.* Res. Rep. Soc. Antiq. **27**, Leeds, 1971

Cunliffe, B., and Davenport, P., 1985 — *The Temple of Sulis Minerva at Bath.* University Committee for Archaeology monograph **7**, Oxford, 1985

Drury, P.J., 1984 — The temple of Claudius at Colchester reconsidered, *Britannia*, **15** (1984), 7-50

Dunning, G.C., 1949 — The Purbeck Marble industry in the Roman period, *Archaeol. News Letter*, **1**.11 (March 1949), 15, reprinted **6**.12 (1960), 290-91

Dworakowska, A., 1983 — *Quarries in Roman provinces.* Wrocław: Polish Academy of Sciences, 1983

Frere, S.S., 1982 — The Bignor villa, *Britannia*, **13** (1982), 135-95

Fulford, M.G., 1985 — Excavations on the sites of the amphitheatre and forum-basilica at Silchester, Hampshire: an interim report, *Antiq. J.*, **65** (1985), 39-81

Hill, C., Millett, M., and Blagg, T., 1980 — *The Roman riverside wall and monumental arch in London.* London & Middlesex Archaeol. Soc. Spec. Pap. **3**, London, 1980

Hull, M.R., 1958 — Roman Colchester. Res. Rep. Soc. Antiq., **20**, Oxford, 1958

Johnson, S., 1981 — The construction of the Saxon shore fort at Richborough, *Collectanea Historica: Essays in memory of Stuart Rigold*, ed. A. Detsicas, 23-31. Maidstone: Kent Archaeol. Soc., 1981

Marsden, P.R.V., 1967   *A ship of the Roman period from Blackfriars in the City of London.*
                             London: Guildhall Museum, 1967

Peacock, D.P.S., 1987   Iron age and Roman quern production at Lodsworth, West Sussex.
                             Antiq. J., **67** (1987), 61-85

Phillips, E.J., 1975   The gravestone of M. Favonius Facilis at Colchester, *Britannia*, **6**
                             (1975), 102-05

Pritchard, F.A., 1986   Ornamental stonework from Roman London, *Britannia*, **17** (1986),
                             169-89

RIB   R.G. Collingwood and R.P. Wright, *The Roman Inscriptions of Bri-
                             tain*, Oxford: Clarendon Press, 1965

Scrivener, R.G., 1979   Geological report on building materials, *The Legionary Bath-house
                             and Basilica and Forum at Exeter*, P.T. Bidwell, 135. Exeter: City
                             Council and University of Exeter, 1979

Sellwood, B.W., 1984   The rock-types represented in the town wall of Silchester, *Silchester:
                             Excavations on the Defences 1974-80*, M.G. Fulford, 224-30. Britannia
                             monograph **5**, London, 1984

Sunter, N., and   *Romano-British industries in Purbeck*. Dorset Nat. Hist. Archaeol. Soc.
    Woodward, P., 1987   monograph **6**, Dorchester, 1987

Taylor, M.V., and   Roman Britain in 1921 and 1922, *J. Roman Stud.*, **11** (1921), 200-44
    Collingwood, R. G.,
    1921

Thompson, F.H., 1965   *Roman Cheshire*. Chester: Cheshire Community Council, 1965

Toynbee, J.M.C., 1986   *The Roman art treasures from the temple of Mithras*. London & Middlesex
                            Archaeol. Soc. Spec. Pap. **7**, London, 1986

Ward-Perkins, J.B., 1972   Quarrying in antiquity; technology, tradition and social change,
                            Proc. Brit. Acad., **57** (1972), 3-24

Wheeler, R.E.M., 1943   *Maiden Castle, Dorset*. Res. Rep. Soc. Antiq. **12**, Oxford, 1943

Williams, J.H., 1968   Stone building materials in Roman Britain. Unpublished M.A.
                            thesis, University of Manchester, 1968

Williams, J.H., 1971a   Roman building materials in south-east England, *Britannia*, **2** (1971),
                            166-95

Williams, J.H., 1971b   Roman building materials in the south-west, *Trans. Bristol & Glouces-
                            tershire Archaeol. Soc.*, **90** (1971), 95-119

Chapter 4

The Stone of the Reculver Columns and the Reculver Cross

B. C. Worssam and T. W. T. Tatton-Brown

Two Anglo-Saxon columns from Reculver church are of Marquise oolite from the Boulonnais, while the Anglo-Saxon Reculver cross survives as six finely carved fragments of foraminiferal limestone with Ditrupa, *from the Calcaire Grossier (Middle Eocene) of the Paris Basin. Both types of stone occur elsewhere in east Kent in Roman and Anglo-Saxon contexts. Calcaire Grossier was also used for an Anglo-Saxon cross head at Pagham, West Sussex. The geology of the Oolithe de Marquise and the Calcaire Grossier is examined.*

Location

Reculver is situated on the south shore of the Thames estuary. It was originally a Roman fort near the north end of the then navigable Wantsum, a tidal channel between the Isle of Thanet and the Kentish mainland (illustration 17). The tides from each end of the channel would have met at Sarre (Steers 1964).

A monastery was established in the abandoned Roman fort between 669 and 679, when Theodore of Tarsus was Archbishop of Canterbury. Though its sacking by Danes, who wintered on Thanet in 850-51, is not recorded, the monastery did not survive into the late Anglo-Saxon period. But its church found use as a parish church, belonging to the Archbishop of Canterbury from the mid 10th century onwards.

Owing to coast erosion, it was decided in 1809 to dismantle the church and to build a new one at Hillborough, a mile or so inland. The twin west towers of the church had proved so valuable a navigation aid that Trinity House ensured their preservation, and they form a seamark to this day. The ruined church, together with the remains of the Roman fort, is in the care of English Heritage. Excavations by Peers (1927) showed the nave to have been of 7th- to 8th-century date, whilst the west end was remodelled and the towers, of Transitional style, were added in the late 12th to early 13th century; the chancel was extended a short distance eastwards in the 13th century.

The Reculver Columns
History

At the time of dismantling of Reculver church, an arcade of three round arches of Roman brick, supported on two massive cylindrical stone columns, stood between the nave and chancel. In 1859 the columns were re-erected in the Water

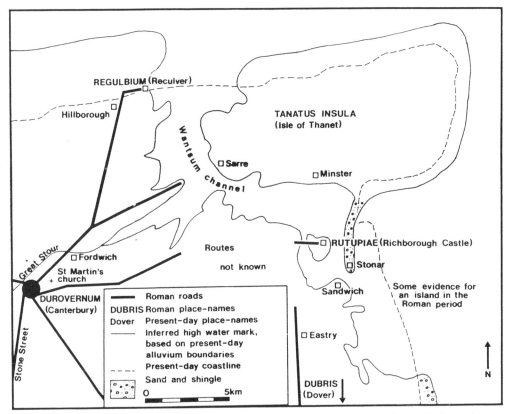

17. Conjectural east Kent coastline in Roman and early Anglo-Saxon times. Estimated amounts of coastal recession (Holmes 1981) are an average 1.8m per year for the Tertiary strata at and westward of Reculver, and 0.6m for the chalk cliffs of the Isle of Thanet.

Tower garden of Canterbury Cathedral (illustration 18), and in 1932 they were brought for shelter into the cathedral crypt. The columns have unusual plain capitals and decorated moulded bases. Measurements by Peers (1927) give them a height of some 4.5m, with shafts, each consisting of nine drums, tapering from 0.68m diameter at the bottom to 0.58m at the top.

The columns are generally regarded as dating from the original (c.670) construction of the church at Reculver. Blagg (1981) gave reasons for considering that their form and decoration derive from late Roman and early Byzantine ecclesiastical architecture.

The stone of the columns

The type of stone used for the Reculver Columns aroused interest in the Victorian period. Sir George Gilbert Scott noted among the stones used in Anglo-Saxon work at St Mary-in-Castro, Dover, which he was engaged in restoring, 'a very peculiar kind of coarse oolite' (Scott 1863), of the same type as the stone of the Reculver Columns, and as the oolite noted by Hussey (1858) in the quoins of St Mildred's church, Canterbury, and at Richborough Castle, a Roman fort. Dowker (1878; 1900) confirmed the use of the coarse oolite for the Reculver Columns and its presence at Richborough. Although none of these authors could say where the stone had come from, Stebbing (1928) was able to write of Richborough that the castle had for long been noteworthy 'for its massive blocks of Hythe Greensand and still larger blocks of the oolite of Marquis [sic] near Boulogne'. These various observations seem to have been lost sight of in recent years.

The columns consist of a distinctive pale grey oolitic limestone of 'millet-seed' type, consisting of closely-packed well-rounded grains (which may be pseudo-ooliths) of 0.2 to 0.5mm diameter. Two varieties of the stone form different drums of the columns. One is characterised by scattered very coarse subrounded grains or oncoliths (i.e. botryoidal aggregates of ooliths enclosed in a thin outer coating), of 2mm diameter; in places it includes casts of bivalves up to 50mm across, infilled with crystalline calcite; and tends to show signs of cavernous weathering, suggestive of burrowing activity during deposition. The other variety, probably from a somewhat higher-energy environment of deposition, is a more even-grained oolite, without oncoliths.

The stone has a Jurassic appearance but is unlike any English Jurassic building stone; apart from its texture, it is not white enough for Portland stone, and it lacks the yellowish tinge of Cotswold and Lincolnshire oolites, most of which are fragmental-shelly biosparites. However, its resemblance to the grey oolitic lime-

18. The Reculver Columns, as re-erected in the Water Tower garden of Canterbury Cathedral in 1859. Reproduced from *Archaeologia Cantiana*, **3** (1860), by permission of the Kent Archaeological Society.

stone of Marquise (see Appendix), now shown to have been used in early Norman work at Canterbury (Gem 1987; Tatton-Brown, below, pp. 73-74), is close enough for it to be regarded as from that formation.

The Reculver Cross

History

A finely carved and painted stone cross in the shape of a tall column, standing 'yn the enteryng of the quyer' of Reculver church, was described in some detail by the historian John Leland, writing in about 1540. No such monument existed at the time of dismantling the church, nor was it mentioned in late 18th-century descriptions of the church, and it is assumed to have been broken up by 16th- or 17th-century Puritans. Peers (1927) found five carved pieces of a cross shaft in the church at Hillborough. The present church is a late Victorian (1876) replacement of that built in 1809 (Newman 1983), and the cross shaft fragments were reposing on its window-sills in the 1930s (Jessup 1936). Peers (1927) excavated two small cross fragments 'in the old church'; one was part of a cross head. Jessup (1936) published a photograph of a sixth large fragment, in the possession of Canon Livett. It had been found on a garden rockery in Canterbury. In 1949 the five pieces from Hillborough (numbered I to V) and Canon Livett's piece (L) were taken into the care of Canterbury Cathedral. Peers's two fragments had meanwhile been lost; only his photographs of them (Peers 1927, 253, figs. 8 & 9) remain.

The extant stones are sectors of cylindrical drums. Most of the drums would have had a diameter of about 0.45m, but stone IV came from a drum no more than 0.38m in diameter. The fragments have flat, sawn-off top and bottom surfaces that truncate their sculptures, and none is taller than 0.38m. The sculptures depict groups of classically garbed figures; some correspond well with figures that were described by Leland. All the stones except L bear traces of paint. As an example, stone III is sketched in outline in illustration 19. It shows a draped figure leaning over a block, against which is displayed an outstretched hand, in what may be part of a Baptism of Christ or a Raising of Lazarus (Beckwith 1969), a Sacrifice of Isaac (Tweddle 1983; 1986), or a Crucifixion scene (Kozodoy 1986).

An extensive literature has grown around these pieces of stone. Dr Kozodoy (1986) expressed a firm view that the cross – except for stone L – is of 7th-century date, describing it as more closely related in style to the Byzantine and Byzantine-Italian art of the 6th and 7th centuries than to that of any other culture. Stone L she dated to around AD 800. Other authors have assigned the cross to the 7th century (Peers 1927; Clapham 1930; 1951; Jessup 1936; Brown 1937; Beckwith 1969; Newman 1983), to the late 7th or early 8th (Jope 1965, n.46), to the 8th or early 9th (Stone 1965; Taylor 1969; Tweddle 1983; 1986), or to the 10th century (Saxl & Wittkower 1948; Talbot Rice 1952). Kendrick originally (1938) assigned the cross to the 7th century, but later (1949) accepted a 10th-century date.

The stone of the cross

Peers (1927) submitted his cross-head fragment to Dr L.R. Cox of the British Museum (Natural History), who described the stone on the basis of its fossils, notably the foraminifer *Alveolina*, as definitely Eocene, non-British, and probably from the Calcaire Grossier of the Paris neighbourhood. Kozodoy (1986, 69), while admitting that a continental source for the stone of the cross head had been given general credence, pointed out that there was no proof that Peers's stones came from the same monument as the extant pieces, and accepted an opinion of the late Dr F.W. Anderson that the cross was of Barnack stone. This suited her idea of the cross being entirely Anglo-Saxon in workmanship. Stone L differs somewhat in dimensions and, in her view, in style from the others, and she accepted other advice that it was of ' "clunch", a Kentish Rag'.

All extant fragments of the cross are actually of a whitish grey, finely granular limestone, with particle size 0.1 to 0.2mm, and including a little fine-grained quartz (grains 0.1mm or less). It is not oolitic, which precludes it from being Barnack stone. The rock contains hollow moulds of shell fragments and of some near-complete fossil shells, but most immediately noticeable are the more or less numerous small white-ringed perforations that are the cross-sections of tubes of Serpulid worms. The tubes are of 0.8 to 1.2mm internal diameter, and the walls 0.2 to 0.3mm thick, consisting of an inner compact layer and an outer layer of radially arranged crystalline calcite. They are 20 to 40mm or so in length, smooth surfaced, gently curved and slightly tapering. These features place them in the genus *Ditrupa* (see Wrigley 1951). Where most numerous, the tubes are spaced at two or three to the square centimetre. In stones II, III, IV and L they are numerous, and in V they are sparse, while none have been discerned in stone I. This variability is only what might be expected in different beds from one quarry. Stone L has a darker colour than the others, but no more than would be consistent with it having acquired, while on its rockery, a thin algal coating that has darkened on drying out. Another effect of weathering is that worm tubes are conspicuous on the carved face of this stone, whereas on the carved surfaces of the others they are largely concealed by a thin plaster-like coating. The contrast with stone L suggests incidentally that the other stones have never been subjected to any prolonged period of weathering in the open.

Ditrupa has a Tertiary to Recent date-range. It indicates a marine environment of deposition for the rock, as do the other macrofossils. These include echinoid fragments; a mould of an ornamented spired gastropod on the base of stone IV; moulds of two ribbed bivalve shells impressed one on top of the other on the front of stone III (illustration 19); and an impression of part of a large, gently convex bivalve with pronounced growth lines on the back of stone II. Dr Noel Morris, of the British

O   50   100mm

19. Outline drawing of stone III of the Reculver Cross.

Museum (Natural History), reporting on a latex cast made from the last-mentioned, remarked that in itself this fossil is not diagnostic of geological age, for similar forms are found from the Carboniferous onwards; however, in view of its association with *Ditrupa*, he considered its features consistent with its being *Crassatella ponderosa* (Gmelin), from the Calcaire Grossier (personal communication, Jan. 1988).

Cox (in Peers 1927) made no mention of Serpulid worm tubes, but these do not occur in all the existing cross fragments, while his observation that shells occurred as 'casts' is consistent with their mode of preservation in the extant fragments. His evidence, therefore, leads to a strong presumption that the cross head was of the same type of stone as the rest of the cross.

A Tertiary age, and an attribution of the Reculver Cross rock to the Calcaire Grossier, receive indirect support from the finding by Mr D. Curry (personal communication) that an Anglo-Saxon cross-head fragment at Pagham in West Sussex (Tweddle 1980) is a mid-Lutetian limestone of Calcaire Grossier facies. On his evidence, *Ditrupa* points to an origin between Creil and Laon for the stone. The Pagham fragment may be a re-used stone from Roman Chichester, or, more certainly, from the nearby Fishbourne palace. A recent visit to the Fishbourne site museum established that some columns of Eocene foraminiferal limestone there (Sanderson in Cunliffe 1971) are of *Ditrupa* limestone with *Orbitolites*.

The distribution of stone of Reculver Column and Reculver Cross types in east Kent

Introduction

This study started with the involvement of one of us (BCW) in the identification of stone types for the south-east England volume of the British Academy's *Corpus of Anglo-Saxon Stone Sculpture*. The Reculver columns and cross were examined as part of that project, and the co-operation of both authors started when the two types of stone used for those monuments began to be recognised elsewhere, not only in Anglo-Saxon, but in Roman and (so far as the oolite is concerned: Tatton-Brown, below, pp. 73-74) in early Norman contexts. There follows a list of Roman and Anglo-Saxon sites where we have found Marquise stone, or *Ditrupa* limestone, or both.

Roman occurrences

Richborough Castle: This name is given to a late 3rd-century Saxon Shore fort (*Rutupiae*), the walls of which survive largely intact. Centrally situated in the fort is the Great Foundation, which is all that remains of an enormous marble-faced four-way triumphal arch, decked with bronze statues, which was erected around AD 85 to mark the completion of the Roman conquest of Britain. The excavation report mentions that blocks of masonry from the arch, some of greensand, others of 'white oolite', are still to be found lying on the site or built into the walls of the fort (Strong 1968). As noted on a previous page, 19th-century authors had remarked on the resemblance between the Richborough oolite and that used in Anglo-Saxon buildings in east Kent. It takes one back to the Heroic Age of geology to learn from Hussey (1858) that 'the late Dr Buckland, on a slight examination of a piece which he broke off this last mentioned specimen [a block of oolite in Richborough castle] said he believed it came from the neighbourhood of Weymouth'.

About twenty large irregular blocks of oolite, of 0.6m in diameter or so, lie around the Great Foundation. Their lithology supports their identification by Stebbing (1928) as Marquise stone. One block includes 2-mm oncoliths and casts of large bivalves in crystalline calcite, as in the Reculver columns; another, of oncolithic limestone with rhynchonellids, has been reduced to a soft and flaky condition by frost action. In the site museum a carved slab with a low-relief draped figure of a goddess, probably Hygeia (Health) or Abuntia (Abundance) – 'good provincial work of the 1st century AD' – is of millet-seed oolite, possibly also Marquise stone. As well as those of oolite, there are some large blocks of a dark green glauconitic sandstone or sandy limestone, no doubt from the upper part of the Hythe Beds (Aptian, Lower Greensand Group) of the Hythe or Sandgate vicinity (cf. Smart *et al.* 1966, 52, 77).

What have not previously been noticed are the half dozen or so blocks of *Ditrupa* limestone, almost identical in appearance with that of the Reculver Cross. One block measures about 1m x 0.5m across and is 0.2m thick. *Ditrupa* limestone is also to be seen *in situ*, as large blocks used for constructing a stone-lined drain, aligned north–south, just to the west of the Foundation. The drain (Bushe-Fox 1949, 54, 58, pl. XIIIa; Cunliffe 1968, 237-42, fig. 29) was made to facilitate the construction of the triumphal arch, and on completion of the arch, about AD 90, was filled with stone debris.

Numerous small fragments of *Ditrupa* limestone occur in a gravel perimeter track on the Foundation site – the excavation report mentions the finding of debris from a Roman masons' yard. By permission of English Heritage, a few fragments were recovered for examination. They give final confirmation that the stone of the Reculver cross originated in northern France. Freshly-broken surfaces show that the rock is crowded with foraminifera, mostly poorly preserved. One fragment broke up to reveal a mould of a gastropod, identified by Dr Noel Morris as a turritellid, cf. *Turritella carinifera* Deshayes non Lamarck, = *T. oppenheimi* Newton 1912, ? = *T. imbricataria* Lamarck, a Lutetian species illustrated by Pomerol (1973, fig. 3.16) (N. Morris, personal communication, Feb. 1988). The *Ditrupa* tubes show all the features of the London Clay species *D. plana* (J. Sowerby), which according to Wrigley (1951, 191) has no clear distinction from the Calcaire Grossier fossil *D. strangulata* (Desh.).

Mr Curry has kindly examined two of the fragments and reports that they are of a material closely similar to that of the Pagham cross; as well as *Ditrupa* he noted *Orbitolites* and, in one fragment, *Alveolina*. Crushing of a small amount of each revealed foraminifera including *Reussella*, *Hanzawaia* and miliolids, as well as marine ostracods of three species, including the mid/late Eocene *Schizocythere tessellata* (D. Curry, personal communication, Feb. 1988).

We are, finally, indebted to Dr A. Blondeau of the Département de Géologie Sédimentaire of the Université Pierre et Marie Curie, Paris, for his comments on two further fragments of limestone from Richborough Castle. Under a binocular microscope he recognised abundant *Ditrupa strangulata*, numerous miliolids, five *Orbitolites complanatus*, two elongate *Alveolina* of *A. boscii* type, and a bryozoan. He adds:

> Le 'grain' de la pierre est constitué par des microorganismes (Foraminifères, Ostracodes, Algues en débris). Les grains de quartz détritiques sont petits et très rares.
>
> Je peux affirmer qu'il s'agit de 'calcaire grossier', lutétien moyen, niveau a *Ditrupa* pour les géologues, ou banc de St-Leu-d'Esserent pour les carriers de la région de la vallée de l'Oise près de Creil.
>
> J'ai comparé vos échantillons avec ceux de différentes régions: il faut exclure Paris, l'Ouest de Paris et le Vexin, ou les *Ditrupa* sont rares et la pierre très mauvaise à ce niveau (sandy limestone). J'ai retenu la vallée de l'Oise (St-Leu-d'Esserent, Noyon), du Therain (St.-Vaast-les-Mello), mais *surtout* la vallée de l'Ourcq (Echampeu, Marolles, La Ferté-Milon) et dans le Soissonnais (Vierzy, St.-Gobain, Soissons), plus à l'Est (Laon). Les échantillons du Soissonais (Vierzy) et de l'Ourcq (Echampeu) sont très riches en *Ditrupa* et possèdent le même 'grain' (personal communication, Mar. 1988).

Dover: In Dover Museum is a Roman statue of a goddess, presumed to be Venus, found in 1877 in excavations for the foundations of the Carlton Club, in the Market Place, Dover (Payne 1889). It is carved from a single block of greyish-white oolite consisting of closely-packed, well-rounded, 0.3-to 0.5-mm diameter grains with scattered 1- to 2-mm diameter oncoliths, and shows some signs of cavernous weathering – all typical Marquise oolite features. In its present state the statue is 1.2m high, but its legs are broken off just above the ankles and the original block must have been at least 1.5m long by 0.6m wide.

Canterbury: In the care of the Canterbury Archaeological Trust, from the excavation of a site in Castle Street, Canterbury, are fragments of Corinthian capitals described as of a well-known Romano-British type, introduced from north-east Gaul in the last third of the 1st century AD (Blagg 1985). One fragment is of a fine-grained, yellowish, millet-seed variety of Marquise stone. Some column fragments are of coarser, oncolithic limestone.

Middle Anglo-Saxon occurrences

Some instances of the use of oolite and *Ditrupa* limestone can be dated to the Middle Anglo-Saxon period (*c.*AD 600-800). Where building stone and the smaller items of sculptural stone are concerned, re-use of stone from Roman sites seems likely; whether the major sculptural works are of re-used Roman stone is perhaps an open question.

Reculver church: As already mentioned, the Reculver Columns are generally ascribed to the 7th century, while some would regard the cross also as of that date.

Dowker (1878) and Peers (1927) found what they both took to be the foundation of the cross centrally in the nave of Reculver church, just in front of where the arcade had stood. Measuring 7ft by 3ft 3ins (2.1 x 1.0m), the foundation was described by Dowker as built of fragments of stone, 'some of which is coarse oolite'. The difference in stone type from the rest of the cross, as well as its dimensions, fairly certainly preclude this foundation from being part of the cross itself. Taylor (1969) thought it likely to have been the base of an altar.

Blocks of Marquise stone form the base of each jamb of the central doorway in the late 12th-century west front of Reculver church. One block is beginning to crumble under the influence of weathering, but the others have a sharpness of arris that indicates a weathering resistance surpassing that of the local Thanet Beds sandstone, the Reigate stone and the Purbeck 'marble' of the doorway, much of which, in this exposed coastal situation, has crumbled away almost completely. A few blocks of *Ditrupa* limestone occur, together with Caen stone, in a pilaster buttress about 2m south of the doorway, and in the plinth course of a 13th-century buttress on the south side of the chancel.

Canterbury, church of St Pancras: This ruined church, on the St Augustine's Abbey site, is of 7th-century date, with walling largely of Roman brick and flint. On a low dividing wall between nave and presbytery is the lower part of a column, of classical appearance, described by Blagg (1981) as 'almost certainly the earliest piece of Saxon architectural decoration in England', carved, he concluded, in a Roman tradition transmitted through the ecclesiastical architecture of the late Roman and Byzantine Mediterranean. It consists of a smooth, cylindrical shaft of 0.4m diameter, which stands on a moulded base and that in turn on a relatively tall plinth. The base and plinth together appear to have been carved from one block. The shaft is of yellowish-weathered limestone with *Ditrupa*, the base and plinth of similar limestone with some perforations but no obvious *Ditrupa* tubes.

Canterbury, St Martin's church: East of the city, St Martin's church is where St Augustine started his mission in AD 597. The west end of the chancel may be of 6th-century or even of late Roman date, and the nave 7th-century, built within a half century or so after 597 (Tatton-Brown 1980). Calcaire Grossier limestone is conspicuous in the fabric of the nave (illustration 20). Squared blocks form the lower parts of the south-east quoin, of an adjacent setback buttress, and of a half-round buttress halfway along the south nave wall. A few pieces occur in reconstructed walling at the south-west corner of the nave, where two angle buttresses have been removed. The north-west corner of the nave also originally had two angle buttresses, of which the west-facing one remains, extending nearly to roof level and built largely of squared blocks of Calcaire Grossier. The north-east corner of the nave is concealed by a 19th-century vestry wall. The widely spaced blocks near the foot of the western part of the south nave wall are probably part of the original structure. Some 80% of the Calcaire Grossier stones in this wall contain *Ditrupa*. A solitary piece of Marquise oolite has been seen, on the half-round buttress.

Only a few adventitious pieces of Marquise oolite and of Calcaire Grossier occur in the south wall of the chancel. This underlines the structural contrast with the nave that is shown by the style of brickwork (Tatton-Brown 1980). Part of an Anglo-Saxon inscription is to be seen on one of the oolite blocks, in the western jamb of a now blocked-up round-headed doorway. The stone, of a

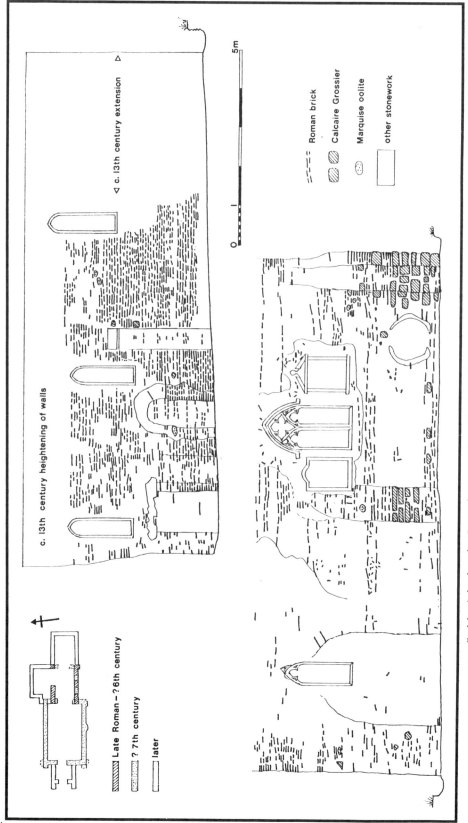

c. 13th century heightening of walls

▽ c. 13th century extension

5m

Roman brick

Calcaire Grossier

Marquise oolite

other stonework

Late Roman – ?6th century

? 7th century

later

20. St Martin's church, Canterbury: south wall of the chancel (above) and of the nave (below).

yellowish colour, has closely packed grains of around 0.5mm in diameter, and appears to be of an even-grained facies of Marquise stone.

Sandwich: Two small grave-markers with runic inscriptions are in the Canterbury Royal Museum. They are of fine-grained soft limestone with *Alveolina*, and thus Calcaire Grossier. They are dated to early in the Middle Anglo-Saxon period, and their simplicity of design has been cited as evidence against so accomplished a carving as the Reculver Cross being equally early (Tweddle 1983).

Anglo-Saxon occurrences of late or uncertain date
Canterbury, Augustine's Abbey: The abbey was founded in *c*.598 but complete rebuilding of its church started in the later 1070s. Excavations in 1915 to 1916 revealed a nearly complete Composite capital and parts of two others built into the Norman foundations (Peers & Clapham 1927; Peers 1929). According to Tweddle (1986), nothing closely comparable is known from Anglo-Saxon England. Taylor and Taylor (1966) remarked that the capitals are most closely paralleled on the continent in the crypts of the abbey of St-Germain at Auxerre, fairly reliably dated to 841-865.

The capitals are at present kept in store at Dover Castle by English Heritage. The near-complete one is 0.32m in height and 0.46m square across the top. All are of fine-grained greyish-yellow limestone and one includes numerous *Ditrupa*. All three can, therefore, be assigned to the Calcaire Grossier. The detail of their carving has survived in remarkably fresh condition.

The massive foundations of the Saxon Abbot Wulfric's octagon (mid 11th-century) under the east end of the Norman nave contain at least one piece of *Ditrupa* limestone and some Marquise stone fragments. One of the latter is a sector of a column drum of 0.5m diameter, which Dr Richard Gem suggests may have come from the arcade between nave and chancel in the original church of SS Peter and Paul (personal communication, Feb. 1988). The two eastern columns and bases in the Norman crypt, which are also of Marquise stone, are probably re-used, and may have come from the same source.

Canterbury, St Mildred's church: The south-west (illustration 21) and south-east quoins of the late Anglo-Saxon nave of this church are built of large blocks, some of Marquise oolite, others of a dark greenish-grey Hythe Beds sandstone. Hussey (1858) noted that the lowest and largest stone in the south-west quoin showed on one side what appeared to be a slot for a lewis, stopped with cement, and also that each quoin contained one stone taken from a large arch. His 'lowest and largest' stone is a pale grey limestone with white oncoliths, scattered casts of shells, and traces of large burrows. Some smaller stones, of yellowish oolite, show distinct cross-bedding.

Canterbury, St Dunstan's church: The quoins of this church are similar to those of St Mildred's church, and the north-west quoin of the nave includes two oolite blocks (the rest are Lower Greensand). St Dunstan's church was first documented in 1085, and as Lanfranc (1070-79) did not encourage the cult of St Dunstan, it is

21. St Mildred's church, Canterbury, viewed from the south-west in the 1850s; it looks little different today. Reproduced from *Archaeologia Cantiana*, **1** (1858), by permission of the Kent Archaeological Society. The light-coloured blocks of the lower part of the south-west quoin are of Marquise stone, the darker ones, above, of Hythe Beds sandstone.

very likely that this church dates from before the Conquest. Like St Mildred's church, it is probably early 11th-century.

Dover, St Mary-in-Castro: This late Anglo-Saxon church, which probably dates from the late 10th or early 11th century (Clapham 1930), though a 9th-century date is possible (Brooks 1984, 35), is the largest surviving Anglo-Saxon building in Kent. Scott's (1863) comment on the use of a coarse oolite in the Saxon work has been mentioned. The church is built largely of Roman brick and rough flint, with quoins of ragstone and some 'megalithic' blocks of Marquise stone, probably re-used from Roman buildings.

Other reported occurrences

Dowker (1878; 1900) reported the use of a coarse oolite similar to that of Richborough and the Reculver Columns in the Anglo-Saxon 'basilica' at Lyminge, Kent, while Hussey (1858), as well as describing oolite at St Mildred's, Canterbury, and Richborough, also mentioned its occurrence in Roman villas at Hartlip, Kent, and Bignor, West Sussex.

We have not been able to confirm the presence of oolite at Lyminge, for little is now to be seen of the earliest Anglo-Saxon building there, to which Dowker was referring; large ragstone blocks were used in late Anglo-Saxon work, and are to be seen in the churchyard. Hussey, unlike Dowker, was not referring specifically to coarse oolite. We have not investigated Hartlip, but at Bignor there are a number of small columns of an even-grained, sparry oolite, probably Bath stone (Combe Down Oolite). The use of Marquise stone would hardly be expected in so late a villa (4th-century).

Concluding discussion

A rapid survey of Roman and Anglo-Saxon sites shows that in the Roman period two types of building stone were imported into east Kent: Marquise oolite from near Boulogne; and a foraminiferal limestone with *Ditrupa* from the Calcaire Grossier of the Paris basin. The former is the more common of the two. They were used together with dark green calcareous sandstone of the Hythe Beds from near Hythe for the great marble-faced triumphal arch at Richborough. The oolite and Hythe Beds sandstone were used for some major buildings in Canterbury and, to judge from the Marquise stone blocks of St Mary-in-Castro, in Dover. Marquise stone was used for sculptures at Dover and Richborough.

All three types came in large blocks, the Marquise stone blocks being the largest. The Calcaire Grossier limestone shows uniformly good weathering resistance. The Marquise stone also weathers well, though some blocks show a tendency to cavernous weathering, and a small proportion have flaked and crumbled.

There is a contrast with Roman London, where those major sculptural and architectural works from that period on display in the Museum of London (if not of Italian marble) are of Lincolnshire Limestone, including Barnack stone, or of Bath stone. There is also a contrast with Roman Chichester, where, although Calcaire Grossier was used for columns at Fishbourne Palace (together with Caen and various local types of stone), there was no import of Marquise stone, so far as is known.

Both Marquise oolite and the Calcaire Grossier were used, or re-used, in churches of the Anglo-Saxon period in Kent. The oolite attracted the attention of 19th-century archaeologists; they realised that it had been introduced by the Romans, though they were unable to locate its source. Its origin at Marquise, where the outcrop is quite restricted in area (see Appendix), is now beyond doubt. Shipment from there (Tatton-Brown, below, p. 73) would have presented little problem.

Dr Blondeau has suggested likely sources of the Richborough *Ditrupa* limestone in the Paris Basin (illustration 22). Its route for shipment is conjectural. Richborough is the only site at present known for Roman use of Calcaire Grossier in east Kent, though the quantities involved may have been large. Blagg (1985) has calculated that the Richborough monument, at 86ft (26.2m) high, would have had a volume, allowing for arches, of 8,201m^3. He estimated the volume of its marble facing alone as 145.6m^3.

The Reculver Cross is unlikely, on historical grounds, to have been made after 850, when the Vikings first wintered on neighbouring Thanet. Now that the cross is seen to be of the same type of stone as that used for the 7th-century column in St Pancras's church, and in construction of the probably 7th-century nave of St Martin's church, does this help to place its date so early in the Anglo-Saxon period? Or does it add to the enigma of what Kendrick (1938, 118) called 'the most baffling and incomprehensible carving in the country'?

APPENDIX
The Geology of the Oolithe de Marquise and the Calcaire Grossier

Oolithe de Marquise

The Boulonnais forms the eastern end of the Wessex Basin of Mesozoic deposition, and of the succeeding, Tertiary, Wealden Anticline. Devonian and Carboniferous rocks of the Palaeozoic basement, known only in boreholes in the Weald, there come to the surface. Their eroded, planed surface is penetrated by sandy fissure-deposits of late Triassic or early Jurassic (Liassic) date, above which come Jurassic

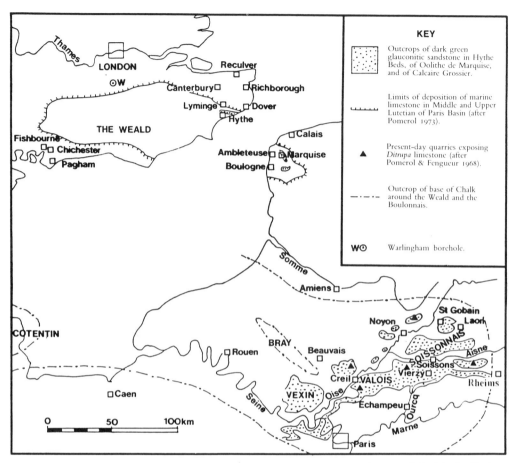

22. Location map, showing outcrops of dark green glauconitic sandstone of the Hythe Beds, of the Oolithe de Marquise and of the Calcaire Grossier.

strata only recently assigned to ammonite ones (Magniez *et al.* 1984). The pre-Callovian sequence comprises, in ascending order, five formations: the Sables d'Hydrequent, up to 4m thick, and assigned to the Bajocian; the Marnes d'Hydrequent, 1.5 to 3.5m thick, fossiliferous interbedded marls and limestones of Upper Bajocian age; the Calcaire de Rinxent, some 9m of fossiliferous limestones with Lower Bathonian (Zigzag zone) ammonites; the Oolithe de Marquise, 7 to 8m, with the brachiopod *Burmirhynchia hopkinsi*, attributed to the Middle Bathonian; and the Calcaires des Pichottes. These last-mentioned beds (Magniez *et al.* 1984, 606) rest with a sharp, bored junction on the Oolithe de Marquise. They comprise a lower marly unit, the Marnes des Calhaudes, 1.5m thick, with upper Bathonian rhynchonellids; and an upper 2 to 2.4m of fossiliferous limestones with end-Bathonian (Discus zone) ammonites in their lower part and early Callovian ammonites in their upper part. Pruvost and Pringle (1924) pointed out that the lower unit corresponds to the Forest Marble, the upper to the Cornbrash of south-east England.

The Oolithe de Marquise has a main outcrop only 10km or so in extent along the strike, centred on Marquise village, and a smaller outcrop 5km to the south, near Belle. The beds dip gently south-west. On a brief visit in February 1988, much evidence was seen in the stonework of older buildings in Marquise village of the use of an oolitic or pseudo-oolitic limestone containing scattered 2-mm oncoliths and sparse shell debris, quite similar to that found in east Kent.

Although there are numerous small quarries on the outskirts of the village, most if not all are filled in or built over. However, a little to the north the disused Queue du Gibet quarry, on the east side of N1 road west of Leulinghen-Bernes, still clearly exposes a section as described by Bonte *et al.* (1958), showing the upper part of the Calcaire de Rinxent and the basal 4m of the Oolithe de Marquise.

The Oolithe de Marquise in the quarry consists of whitish to beige pseudo-oolitic limestones with millet-seed texture. Bed 12 (Bonte *et al.* 1958, 12), 0.9m thick, is notable for large pellets or intraclasts, some exceeding 10mm in diameter. Its appearance under a hand lens (illustration 23) closely matches that of some of the fragments lying loose on the Richborough Monument site. Professor D.T. Donovan, on the same visit, collected the following fossils from the Oolithe de Marquise of the quarry: *Plagiostoma subcardiiformis* Greppin; *?Wattonithyris sp. indet.*, and an indet. rhynchonellid, and the following from the Calcaire de Rinxent: *?Ancliffia pumila* (J. de C. Sowerby), *Modiolus imbricatus* (J. Sowerby); *Epithyris sp. indet.*, and *Kallirhynchia 'concinna'* (J. Sowerby) (close to figs. 7 & 8 of T. Davidson, *The Fossil Brachiopoda: Oolitic*, 1852, pl. 17). He reports that all are typical Bathonian forms, though one or two have longer ranges (personal communication, Mar. 1988).

A hardground marks the top of the Calcaire de Rinxent, the limestones of which, in the 2m or so exposed, are distinctly finer in grain than those of the Oolithe de Marquise, as well as being, in some beds, slightly silty.

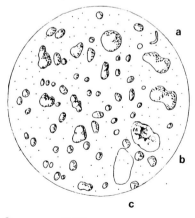

23. Marquise oolite, bed 12 of the Queue du Gibet quarry near Marquise, as seen under a hand lens. A matrix of fine-grained (*c.*0.2mm diameter) ooliths or pseudo-ooliths, cemented by clear crystalline calcite, together represented by stippling, includes well-rounded grains, probably pseudo-ooliths, of 0.5 to 0.7mm diameter; scattered oncoliths of up to 2mm diameter; and one small shell fragment (a). Two of the larger grains have broken cleanly across: one (b) is composed of 0.5mm ooliths in close contact, cemented by crystalline calcite; the other (c) has a structureless, micritic appearance.

0   5mm

The ruins of a small limekiln in a corner of the quarry suggest that the stone there was worked primarily for lime-burning. On a valley side some 500m to the north are two small openings that could be entrances to adits, raising a possibility that the large blocks of stone formerly extracted for masonry and sculptural purposes were won by mining.

The Bathonian succession in the Boulonnais, totalling less than 30m, is inevitably condensed with that in the central Weald, where boreholes show the thickness (Sellwood *et al.* 1986, fig. 10) increasing steadily westwards to more than 100m. It would be surprising, however, if lithostratigraphical continuity between these two parts of the same basin of deposition were limited to the Forest Marble and the Cornbrash. In particular, the lithological resemblance between Oolithe de Marquise limestones and the millet-seed oolites that occur in the lower part of the White Limestone, which underlies the Forest Marble in the Warlingham, Surrey, borehole (Worssam & Ivimey-Cooke 1971), is close enough to suggest some equivalence between the two formations. Warlingham lies about half-way between the Boulonnais and the Oxfordshire outcrop of the White Limestone (illustration 22).

Calcaire Grossier

The Paris basin during the early Tertiary period was subject to alternate marine transgressions and regressions (Curry 1967). An extensive transgression in the mid-Eocene Lutetian stage resulted in marine sands and limestones being deposited eastwards beyond Paris almost as far as Rheims (illustration 22) and extending locally beyond earlier Tertiary beds on to the Chalk.

The resulting Calcaire Grossier formation (Pomerol 1973; Blondeau *et al.* 1980) attains a total thickness of up to 40m or so northwest of the River Oise and of 20m in the vicinity of Paris. In the lower part of the formation are glauconitic sands, the 'glauconie grossière'. These are overlain by richly fossiliferous foraminiferal limestone beds that provide high-quality building stone. They include the Banc de St-Leu, 6 to 8m thick, and, at a higher level, the Banc Royal, up to 12m thick north-west of the Oise but decreasing to 1 to 1.5m under Paris. These terms are based on the usage of quarrymen, who employ them, and others such as 'banc franc' in an informal, lithological sense. The uppermost 5m or so of the formation consists of thinly-bedded, more variable limestones, with a restricted fauna including cerithiids

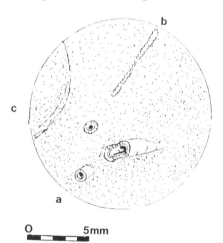

24. *Ditrupa* limestone of the Calcaire Grossier: a loose fragment from the site of the Great Foundation, Richborough Castle, Kent, seen under a hand lens. Within a fine-grained matrix (stippled) are tubes of *Ditrupa* (a), a cross-section of the large discoidal foraminifer *Orbitolites* (b), and part of a bivalve cast.

and miliolids that are adapted to variations in salinity and which indicate the onset of marine regression.

The *Ditrupa* limestone found in east Kent is identified by Dr Blondeau as from the Banc de St-Leu. The degree of diagenesis that this rock has undergone leads to foraminifera in the groundmass being difficult to make out except on freshly broken surfaces, though scattered *Orbitolites* in cross-section (illustration 24) can be discerned, as white streaks with a finely cellular structure. By contrast, Banc Royal specimens from the St-Maximin quarries near Creil, in the Natural History Museum collection, show extremely well preserved foraminifera, clearly distinguishable under the hand lens.

The Calcaire Grossier at outcrop (illustration 22, based on Pomerol 1973) dips gently southwards, to form an escarpment extending eastwards from the north of Paris almost as far as Rheims, with outliers capping plateaux north of the Oise and the Aisne. The dip carries the formation beneath the city of Paris, where the limestone was formerly mined. Resulting instances of subsidence of the ground surface brought about a ban on such working early in the 19th century. Some of the old galleries form the Paris 'catacombs'.

ACKNOWLEDGEMENTS

For access to Roman and Anglo-Saxon items in their care we are indebted to Mr Paul Bennett of the Canterbury Archaeological Trust, to Mr Brian le Mar, Clerk of Works to Canterbury Cathedral, to Mr Nicholas Moore of English Heritage, to Mr David Rudkin, Director of the Fishbourne Roman Palace and Museum, and to Mrs Lesley Webster of the Department of Medieval and Later Antiquities, British Museum. Illustration 20 is based on scale drawings of the stonework of St Martin's church, Canterbury, by Mr John Bowen and Mr Laurie Sartin. To Dr Noel Morris and Professor D.T. Donovan, who have kindly provided identifications of fossils, and to Dr Eric Robinson and Mr R.W. Sanderson we are indebted for much helpful discussion. Professor Rosemary Cramp has commented helpfully on the manuscript. Our particular thanks are due to Mr Dennis Curry for identifying the Calcaire Grossier and for his advice on Tertiary palaeontology and stratigraphy, and to Dr A. Blondeau, both for confirming the Calcaire Grossier identification and for indicating likely sources of the stone in the Paris Basin.

BIBLIOGRAPHY

Beckwith, J., 1969   Reculver, Ruthwell and Bewcastle, *Kolloquium über früh-mittelalterliche Skulptur*, ed. V. Milojcic, 17-20. Mainz: von Zabern, 1969

Blagg, T.F.C., 1981   Some Roman architectural traditions in the early Saxon churches of Kent, *Collectanea Historica: essays in memory of Stuart Rigold*, ed. A.P. Detsicas, 51-53. Maidstone: Kent Archaeological Society, 1981

Blagg, T.F.C., 1985   Roman architectural ornament in Kent, *Archaeol. Cantiana*, **100** (1984), 65-80

Blondeau, A., Cavelier, C., Labourguigne, J., Megnien, C., and Megnien, F., 1980   Eocène Moyen, *Synthèse géologique du Bassin de Paris* 1, ed. C. Megnien, 367-77. Mémoire du Bureau des Récherches Géologiques et Minières, 101, Orleans 1980

Bonte, A., Collin, J. J., Godfriaux, I., and Leroux, B., 1958   Le Bathonien de la région de Marquise et Wealdien du Boulonnais, *Bulletin de la service de la Carte geologique de la France*, 56. 255 (1958), 9-28

Brooks, N.P., 1984   *The early history of the Church of Canterbury*. Leicester: University Press, 1984

Brown, G.B., 1937   *The arts in early England*, 6 (2): *Anglo-Saxon sculpture*. London: John Murray, 1937

Bushe-Fox, J.P., 1949   *4th Report on the excavations of the Roman fort at Richborough, Kent*. Res. Rep. Soc. Antiq., 16. Oxford: University Press, 1949

Clapham, A.W., 1930   *English Romanesque architecture before the Conquest*. Oxford: Clarendon Press, 1930

Cunliffe, B.W., 1968   The development of Richborough, *5th Report on the excavations of the Roman fort at Richborough, Kent*, ed. B.W. Cunliffe, 231-250. Res. Rep. Soc. Antiq., 22, Oxford: University Press 1968

Cunliffe, B.W., 1971   *Excavations at Fishbourne 1961-1969*, 2: *The Finds*. Res. Rep. Soc. Antiq., 27, London: Society of Antiquaries, 1971

Curry, D., 1967   Problems of correlation in the Anglo-Paris-Belgian Basin, *Proc. Geol. Assoc.*, 77 (1966), 437-67

Dowker, G., 1878   Reculver church, *Archaeol. Cantiana*, 12 (1878), 248-68

Dowker, G., 1900   On the Cross and Platform at Richborough, *Archaeol. Cantiana*, 24 (1900), 201-19

Gem, R., 1987   Canterbury and the cushion capital: a commentary on passages from Goscelin's De Miraculis Sancti Augustini, *Romanesque and Gothic: essays for George Zarnecki*, ed. N. Stratford, 83-101. Woodbridge: Boydell and Brewer, 1987

Holmes, S.C.A., 1981   *Geology of the country around Faversham*. Mem. Geol. Surv. Gr. Br., Sheet 273. London: HMSO, 1981

Hussey, R., 1858   St Mildred's, Canterbury, *Archaeol. Cantiana*, 1 (1858), 143-46

Jessup, R.F., 1936   Reculver, *Antiquity*, 10 (1936), 179-94

Jope, E.M., 1965   The Saxon building-stone industry in southern and midland England, *Medieval Archaeol.*, 8 (1965), 91-118

Kendrick, T.D., 1938   *Anglo-Saxon art to AD 900*. London: Methuen, 1938

Kendrick, T.D., 1949   *Late Saxon and Viking art*. London: Methuen, 1949

Kozodoy, R., 1986   The Reculver cross, *Archaeologia*, 108 (1986), 67-94

Magniez, J.M., Marchand, D., Theirry, J., and Vadet, A., 1984   Nouvelles observations (stratigraphie, biostratigraphie, paléogéographie et paléobiogéographie) sur les sédiments affleurants du Jurassique moyen et supérieur du Bas-Boulonnais (France), *Comptes Rendus Acad. Sci. Paris*, 298, ser. 2 (1984), 605-08 (note no.14)

Newman, J., 1983   *North-east and east Kent*, 3rd ed. Buildings of England, Harmondsworth: Penguin, 1983

Payne, G., 1889   On a Roman statue and other remains in the Dover Museum, *Archaeol. Cantiana*, 18 (1889), 202-05

Peers, C.R., 1927   Reculver: its Saxon church and cross, *Archaeologia*, 77 (1927), 241-56

Peers, C.R., 1929   The earliest Christian churches in England, *Antiquity*, 3 (1929), 65-74

Peers, C.R. and Clapham, A.W., 1927
St Augustine's Abbey church, Canterbury, before the Norman Conquest, *Archaeologia*, **77** (1927), 201-18

Pomerol, C., 1973
Ère Cénozöque. Paris: Doin, 1973

Pomerol, C., and Feugueur, L., 1968
Guides géologiques régionaux: Bassin de Paris et Ile de France. Paris: Masson et Cie, 1968

Pruvost, P., and Pringle, J., 1924
A synopsis of the geology of the Boulonnais, including a correlation of the Mesozoic rocks with those of England, *Proc. Geol. Assoc.*, **35** (1924), 29-56

Saxl, F., and Wittkower, R., 1948
British art and the Mediterranean, London: Oxford University Press, 1948.

Scott, G.G., 1863
The church on the Castle Hill, Dover, *Archaeol. Cantiana*, **5** (1863), 1-18

Sellwood, B.W., Scott, J., and Lunn, G., 1986
Mesozoic basin evolution in southern England, *Proc. Geol. Assoc.*, **97** (1986), 259-89

Smart, J.G.O., Bisson, G., and Worssam, B. C., 1966
Geology of the country around Canterbury and and Folkestone. Mem. Geol. Surv. Gr. Br., Sheets 289 & 305-06. London: HMSO, 1966

Stebbing, W.P.D., 1928
Richborough Castle, *Archaeol. Cantiana*, 40 (1928), 181-84

Steers, J.A., 1964
The coastline of England and Wales, 2nd ed. Cambridge: University Press, 1964

Stone, L., 1955
Sculpture in Britain: the Middle Ages. Pelican history of art, Harmondsworth: Penguin, 1955

Strong, D.E., 1968
The Monument, *5th Report on the excavations of the Roman fort at Richborough, Kent*, ed. B.W. Cunliffe, 40-74. Res. Rep. Soc. Antiq. **23**, Oxford: University Press, 1968

Talbot Rice, D., 1952
English art 871-1100. Oxford History of 1952 English Art, **2**, Oxford: Clarendon Press, 1952

Tatton-Brown, T., 1980
St Martin's church in the 6th and 7th centuries, *The parish of St Martin and St Paul: historical essays in memory of James Hobbs*, ed. M. Sparks, 12-18. Canterbury: Friends of St Martin's Church, 1980

Taylor, H.M., 1969
Reculver reconsidered, *Archaeol. J.*, **125** (1969), 291-96

Taylor, J., and Taylor, H.M., 1966
Architectural sculpture in pre-Norman England, *J. Br. Archaeol. Assoc.*, ser. 3, **29** (1966), 3-51

Tweddle, D., 1980
The fragment of pre-Conquest sculpture, in D.J. Freke, Excavations in the parish church of St Thomas the Martyr, Pagham, 1976, *Sussex Archaeol. Collect.*, **118** (1980), 245-56

Tweddle, D., 1983
Anglo-Saxon sculpture in south-east England before 950, *Studies in Medieval sculpture*, ed. F.H. Thompson, 18-40. Occ. Paper (ser. 2), **3**, London: Society of Antiquaries, 1983

Tweddle, D., 1986
The pre-Conquest sculpture of south-east England, 3 vols. Unpublished PhD thesis, University of London, 1986

Worssam, B.C., and Ivimey-Cooke, H.C., 1971
The stratigraphy of the Geological Survey borehole at Warlingham, Surrey, *Bull. Geol. Surv. Gr. Br.*, **36** (1971), 1-111

Wrigley, A., 1951
Some Eocene Serpulids, *Proc. Geol. Assoc.*, **62** (1951), 177-202

Chapter 5

Building Stone in Canterbury *c.*1070-1525

T. W. T. Tatton-Brown

No good building stone is available in east Kent, so during a series of major building campaigns in Canterbury in the later Middle Ages, stone had to be imported by sea from many different quarries in France and England. Because of changing political and economic conditions, and because supplies dwindled in certain quarries, many different types of stone were used in different building campaigns; only Caen stone from Normandy was supplied almost continually for over 400 years. After the Reformation, red brick came into its own, and was often used together with re-worked stone from dissolved religious houses.

Introduction

Virtually no building stone suitable for high quality dressed ashlar masonry is available in east Kent and apart from the use of flint, chalk, local sandstone and tufa for rubble infill or for walling, all the finer masonry buildings in Canterbury use imported stone brought in by sea. With the arrival of Lanfranc as Archbishop in 1070 a massive new building campaign got under way and from then until the early 16th century a great deal of exceptionally well documented building work took place in the city. The ordinary houses of the city were always made of timber, but apart from the cathedral many other masonry buildings were erected and many of these buildings survive, quite a few of which are now ruins. The largest complex of masonry buildings of the period 1070-1525 consists of Christ Church Priory and the Archbishop's Palace (immediately north of the cathedral), but there is also a large area of ruined masonry at St Augustine's Abbey and there are the remains of many churches and hospitals as well as the early Norman castle keep, the Westgate and the city walls and towers.

With their wealth of documentation, the buildings of Canterbury can often be closely dated, and one of the most interesting things to emerge is that many of the imported building materials are only used at one particular time. This allows some other, undated, buildings in the surrounding area to be given a closer date range than was hitherto thought possible. So, for example, Shoulden church, near Deal, has small-block Quarr stone used in the south-west quoin of the nave. No original windows or architectural features survive in this heavily restored church, so on the face of it we can only suggest a 'medieval' date for the building. The use of Quarr in the quoins, however, allows us, on the evidence given below, to suggest a late 11th- or early 12th-century date for the nave.

In discussing the various stones used in Canterbury between 1070 and 1525, I will deal with them in four main chronological phases: Early Norman; Later Twelfth Century; Thirteenth Century, and Late Medieval (14th/15th centuries); and in each section I will deal in turn with each of the main types of stone that are used. For a further discussion on the buildings themselves, see the four volumes of the Archaeology of Canterbury and my paper on the buildings of St Augustine's Abbey (Tatton-Brown forthcoming).

Early Norman (c.1070–1120)

With the arrival of Lanfranc in Canterbury in 1070 a whole series of building campaigns was set in motion. The cathedral itself (1070–77) was followed soon after by the main claustral buildings of Christ Church Priory and the Archbishop's Palace to the north and north-west (Willis 1845). From c.1077 St Augustine's Abbey was completely rebuilt, and in the mid 1080s the very large new hospital of St John the Baptist was erected outside the Northgate of the city, opposite the new priory of St Gregory. Ruined 11th-century buildings of the former still survive, though the priory has been completely demolished. From 1096 onwards the cathedral was almost doubled in length, with the building of Archbishop Anselm's great presbytery and choir, and at the same time a very large new stone keep was being erected at the castle at the south end of the city. Many new parish churches were being built at this time (there were 22 by the mid 12th century) as well as other ecclesiastical establishments like St Sepulchre's Nunnery and St Lawrence's Priory (founded 1137) outside the walls on the south east. For all this building work three main types of material were used:

(a) re-used Roman material;
(b) local materials (flint, tufa, etc.);
(c) newly imported cut stone (Caen, Quarr and Marquise).

The Roman material that was used was mostly fragments of brick and tile, but occasional lumps of *opus signinum* are also found, as well as some re-used building stone. Most of this material is used for rubble infill in walls and it can best be seen today at St Peter's church or in the ruins of Canterbury Castle keep and St Augustine's Abbey.

The commonest material to be used is, of course, flint, which can still be found today in fields on the Upper Chalk to the south and east of the city. These, as well as some large water-rounded flints, were used unknapped in courses in many large Norman walls in the city. The flint, which is bedded in a yellow pebbly mortar, is quite often laid herringbone fashion, and the courses of flints, unlike in the later medieval period when chalk block was used inside, go right through the wall and use very large flints. This can best be seen in the walls of the castle keep, where flint and a greeny-brown hard calcerous sandstone (which perhaps comes from the top of the Thanet Beds near Reculver, ten miles north-east of Canterbury) are the commonest materials. The castle walls and parts of the crypt at St Augustine's also contain a clay-ironstone which must come from further away, probably the Hastings Beds of the High Weald. The other local material much used in the early Norman period is tufa. Being relatively light in weight, this was mostly used for vaulting; it can be well seen in the Norman period spiral staircases in the cathedral and in the vaults of the great dormitory and reredorter at Christ Church Priory. In the great dormitory (built c.1080) the vaults are also made (to a lesser extent) with re-used Roman brick, and large blocks of tufa can also be seen used in the upper walls of the buildings. The tufa is a spring-head deposit and must come from the lower reaches of the dry valleys of the chalk dip-slope south-east of Canterbury, where they are watered by intermittent streams or 'nailbournes'. It was clearly available in thick deposits (hence the large blocks of tufa found in both Roman and Norman buildings in Canterbury) until it was worked out, perhaps in the 13th century.

The most important result of the Norman Conquest in terms of the new building work in the city was the importing of three new building materials for good quality ashlar work. These three new stones, Caen from Normandy, Quarr from the Isle of Wight and Marquise from near Boulogne, were all brought in by sea, and the importing of two of these materials (Caen and Marquise) is actually documented in the almost contemporary account by Goscelin of the Miracles of St Augustine (Gem 1987). One of these miracles mentions the bringing of Caen stone 'for bases, for columns, for capitals and for imposts' for the building of St Augustine's Abbey, in a ship which was saved from shipwreck by St Augustine himself. Another miracle refers to the bringing of 'great capitals, columns and bases' which had already been cut out; they came by sea from Marquise, described as a vill in the Boulogne province of Flanders 'abundant in stone'.

The use of Caen stone in south-east England after the Norman Conquest is, of course, very well known. In the early Norman period it was mainly brought in as small blocks (only from the 1180s did the size of blocks increase) but it was also used for bases, columns (some being monoliths), capitals and imposts, as mentioned in Miracles. Very large quantities must have been imported through the port of Fordwich in the period from c.1070 to c.1120, as it is found in every building of that period. In the great buildings, like the cathedral, it covers all the walls inside and out, while at the castle keep, St John's Hospital, and other lesser buildings it is used only for quoins, doorways, windows, stair-towers, etc. The rest of the walling is (as described above) in flint and sandstone rubblework. Mixed in with the Caen, and in much smaller quantities, is Quarr stone from near Ryde in the Isle of Wight (Anderson & Quirk 1964). This stone is also found in small quantities as ordinary blockwork (it can be seen as this at St Augustine's Abbey and on the outside of the cathedral choir) but as it is much harder than Caen stone it was used particularly for string courses and, at the castle keep, for the moulded plinth blocks. It is also used in some capitals, bases, etc., as with Caen, and is easy to recognise, as it is full of broken comminuted gastropod shells, weathering to a greyer colour than the Caen. No documentary evidence survives for the use of Quarr in Canterbury, but a charter of William II grants Walkelin, Bishop of Winchester

> half a hide of land in the Isle of Wight for the building of his church [Winchester Cathedral], just as my father [William the Conqueror] at his death [1087] had granted it to him for the good of his soul. Reserving my rents, I have given him licence to dig for stone not only there but also throughout my land on the island, in open country, and in woodland, that is if the woodland is so small that the horns of a stag can be seen going through it (Galbraith 1920).

All of the Norman cathedral at Winchester was built of Quarr stone, as well as many other Norman buildings in the Hampshire basin area, and no doubt other charters once existed allowing Archbishops Lanfranc and Anselm and the Abbots Scotland and Guido, of St Augustine's, to acquire Quarr stone for use in their buildings in east Kent. Quarr can be seen not only at the cathedral and St Augustine's Abbey, but also in quite a few of the churches belonging to these two establishments, as well as at St Martin's Priory, Dover. It can still be seen, for example, at St Michael's parish church at Harbledown, just outside the city on the west. It can be seen best, however, at Brook parish church near Ashford. Here all the main quoins of the late 11th-century church (and the chancel arch) are in Quarr stone and it is only when one gets to the western tower (built last but in direct sequence) that Caen stone takes over. At Canterbury Castle keep, Quarr stone is only found in the lowest stage (particularly in the plinth) and all the quoins and windows higher up are of Caen, suggesting that after about 1120 Quarr was no longer being imported into east Kent, perhaps because the best beds in the Isle of Wight were already being worked out (Tatton-Brown 1980). None of the mid and later 12th-century work in Canterbury contains any Quarr stone.

The third imported stone brought into Canterbury in the early Norman period is an oolitic limestone from the Marquise area of the Boulonnais that is halfway between Calais and Boulogne (see illustration 22, above, p. 64). This stone, which is known as the *Oolithe de Marquise*, comes from the Bathonian stage of the Middle Jurassic. It characteristically contains some very large ooliths as well as other areas of less oolitic material though much of the matrix is of fine to medium grained (0.2-0.5mm) ooliths. The stone was perhaps mostly laid down in 'a shallow, sometimes agitated sea' that at times had 'much quieter water' (Ager & Wallace 1966, 400). The stone quarries probably had easy access to the sea down the estuary of the river Slack, which leads from Marquise westwards to the sea at Ambleteuse (about 7km) (Ager & Wallace 1966, 414). Earlier this was an estuary which was apparently called the Amfleat. It is mentioned under this name in Bede's *Ecclesiastical History* (I, 33) as the place where the first abbot of St Augustine's, Canterbury, was drowned in AD 602. It is possible that the great storms of the 13th century which devastated Romney Marsh and the east Kent marshes also caused the Marquise estuary to become blocked with sand and shingle. This, in turn, would have destroyed the easy access the quarries had to the sea, and hence the ease with which stone could have been brought to Kent. Unlike Quarr and Caen stone, which were never used in Canterbury before the early Norman period, Marquise was used in Canterbury and east Kent in the Roman and Anglo-Saxon periods (see Worssam & Tatton-Brown, above, pp. 53, 56-62). In the early Norman period Marquise can best be seen as the large flat capitals and bases in the undercroft of the great dormitory at Christ Church Priory (built c.1080). It is also clearly seen in many plinth blocks, bases and capitals throughout the abbey church at St Augustine's, as well as in the column shafts at the east end of the crypt. It can also be found in the early Norman columns, capitals and bases at the west end of the crypt (Gundulf's crypt) at Rochester Cathedral, and this ties in well with the statements in Goscelin's *Miracles of*

St Augustine that 'great capitals, columns and bases' were cut at Marquise for St Augustine's Abbey. After the early Norman period, Marquise stone does not appear to have been used again in the city, though re-used Marquise oolite is found in the plinth only of the Trinity Chapel and corona at the east end of the cathedral.

Later twelfth century (*c.*1120-1200)

By the middle of the 12th century the very large-scale building programme which had started eighty years earlier was nearing completion. At this time much work was being carried out under Prior Wibert (1152-67) and this work is characterised by its use of highly decorative elements. It can best be seen at the 'Aula Nova' (with its famous Norman staircase) and Green Court gate as well as at the Treasury on the north side of the cathedral, with beneath it the monumental porch and gateway leading into the east side of the monastery from the monks' cemetery. In the mid-12th century the cathedral was also receiving its finishing touches by the building of towers and turrets. Some of the latter survive and are characterised by elaborate decoration on the outside.

For all of this mid-12th-century work the commonest stone used is Caen (no Quarr or Marquise has yet been found in this period, except the re-used material mentioned above), but with the Caen stone comes the use, for the first time, of 'marble' shafting, using Purbeck and onyx marble. Probably the earliest use in Kent of decorative monolithic shafts is at Rochester, where Tournai and onyx marble are used on the east side of the cloister on the chapter house and dormitory façade of the mid 12th century. Onyx marble was also used on the west front of Rochester Cathedral. Tournai was not apparently used at this time at Canterbury (the only use of Tournai marble in Canterbury is in the early 14th-century tomb of Archbishop Meopham). In Prior Wibert's time (*c.*1155-65), however, Purbeck 'marble' and onyx marble were imported, and for the great rebuilding of the choir in *c.*1175-84 Purbeck was brought in large quantities for internal shafting, string courses, etc. The rock comes from the Lower Cretaceous Durlston formation of the upper part of the Purbeck Group of the Isle of Purbeck in Dorset. It is composed of near-complete shells of the small gastropod *viviparus cariniferous* in a green or red matrix. Purbeck 'marble' was, of course, commonly used all over south-east England in the late 12th and 13th century (Leach 1978), but its use at Canterbury in the mid 12th century is exceptionally early. Purbeck 'marble' of this date can best be seen in the surviving east walk of the infirmary cloister at Christ Church Priory where it is used for abacus blocks, capitals and bases. It is also used in roughly alternate piers for pairs of 'barley sugar' columns (and a quadruple column at the north-east corner of the infirmary cloister). Purbeck 'marble' was also used for the Norman staircase of the 'Aula Nova' but its most interesting use was for the double-width voussoirs of an arcade. The surviving blocks showing this are all scattered around and not *in situ*, but it seems most likely that this was for Prior Wibert's cloister arcades in the great cloister. These arcades, which are depicted in the contemporary 'waterworks' plan of *c.*1160 (Willis 1868), were replaced in the early 15th century by the surviving arcades and vaults (see below) and it is likely that the earlier arcades were taken down at this time and re-used as rubble – hence the loose fragments.

The other exotic marble introduced in Prior Wibert's time is onyx marble. This was used for the alternative, wider diameter shafts in the infirmary cloister east arcade as well as probably in the south arcade which was demolished in *c.*1220 when the undercroft of the Prior's chapel was being constructed. Onyx marble is used as the central shafts in the windows of this undercroft, and it must be re-used from the earlier arcades. Onyx marble can also be found in the late 13th-century arcade on the west side of the chapter house. Here it has been recut to form shafts that are quatrefoil in cross section, but it is very likely that the onyx marble here also comes from mid 12th-century arcade columns. Onyx marble in a mid 12th-century (original) context can also be found in the one surviving shaft outside the north door of western crypt where it leads up to the Martyrdom, as well as in the thick and tall double pairs of shafts at the back of the monumental gateway below the Treasury. Where this stone comes from is not yet known, but it seems possible that its ultimate source is in North Africa or the Middle East. Whether it was cut and first used in the Roman period is still an open question, but if this was the case it must have been for a Roman building in the Mediterranean area and not in Roman Britain.

After the great fire in the choir in 1174, the eastern arm of the cathedral was rebuilt to the very highest standard, under the direction of William of Sens and William the Englishman from 1175 to 1184 (Willis 1845). This work, as already mentioned, made much use of Purbeck 'marble' for internal shafting. The great foliated capitals in the choir, which are some of the finest sculptures of their kind in England, appear to use a very high quality form of Caen stone, though the material and source has not yet been closely considered. Under these capitals is a series of very large columns, the drums of which are made of a white pelletal limestone (also probably from Caen). When one moves eastwards to the Trinity Chapel, the columns become double and there the eight double shafts alternate the use of three different materials in the column-drums. These materials are the white pelletal limestone (Caen), Purbeck 'marble' and a pink marble. This pink marble, whose source is also unknown (it may come from Tournai in Belgium or from the Mediterranean area), is only used in the central part of the Trinity Chapel, i.e. in close proximity to the shrine of St Thomas Becket. Pink marble is also found in diamond lozenges in the floor and in strips at the eastern and western ends of the shrine podium (also in the floor), as well as for capitals, shaft rings, and spurred bases in the ambulatory on either side of the Trinity Chapel (Tatton-Brown 1981, fig. 1). A few surviving fragments of the shrine itself (now kept in the cathedral library) are also of pink marble. The pink marble of the column-drums must have been brought to Canterbury by the early 1180s and it is noticeable that the eastern columns in the Trinity Chapel only have pink marble for the bottom drums; the tops are finished in Purbeck 'marble'. Clearly the pink marble had run out. The other decorated marbles used in the Trinity Chapel are all in the *opus alexandrinum* floor west of the shrine. This floor, which uses marble inlays, was put in perhaps in the early 13th century (before 1220) rather than in the late 1880s (Toke 1930). All the rest of the floor in the Trinity Chapel is paved with a mixture of Purbeck and Bethersden 'marbles'. The latter, from the Lower Cretaceous Weald Clay formation, is composed of closely packed shells of the large gastropod *Viviparus fluviorum*. Although a detailed survey of the floors has not yet been made, it is possible to see in the polished surfaces the many different colours and textures that exist in these two freshwater limestones. The fossilised shells both of gastropods and bivalves (probably *Unio*) are to be seen, and as the latter is not uncommon in Bethersden marble it is probable that the floors are largely made of this material, with Purbeck being used for the columns, capitals, bases, etc., but only sparingly in the floor. The Bethersden marble beds were never thicker than about 0.3m and could therefore only be used as a flooring material (and locally in the Weald as a rough building material). In the infill areas below the flying buttresses of William of Sens' choir at Canterbury Cathedral (1175-80) large blocks of tufa are used for lightness. In the neighbouring Trinity Chapel almost the whole of the solid inner wall of the triforium is also made of large blocks of tufa.

Thirteenth century (*c*.1200-1320)

The most important building project at the very beginning of the 13th century in Canterbury was the construction of the vast great hall and solar range of the Archbishop's Palace (internal dimensions of the hall *c*.168ft x 64ft). The main imported materials used here are Caen stone and Purbeck 'marble' (the very tall five-fold shafts of the piers, as well as the capitals and bases, and the central mullion and transom are of Purbeck), but another new material made its first appearance at this time, Reigate or Merstham stone. This stone, a fine-grained pale grey very finely glauconitic sandstone, was used initially for small blockwork and it can be seen in the surviving ruins of the porch and on the outside of the neighbouring window. Only the top of this window is in Caen stone. It is possible that after the loss of Normandy by King John and after the long Interdict in the latter part of John's reign, Caen became much more difficult of access and so the Archbishop's masons had to look westwards to the underground quarries in the Upper Greensand around Reigate and Merstham.

Later in the 13th century various new building complexes were being erected (the biggest being the Dominican and Franciscan friaries) and both Christ Church Priory and St Augustine's Abbey were undertaking major rebuilding campaigns. Again Caen was the commonest imported material, though as we have seen Reigate was also used. Flint continued to be used for ordinary walling, and for the first time knapped flint was used for facework, with chalk on the inside faces and for the core. In the early 14th century some exceptionally fine knapped flint work is found. For example, beautifully finished tabular flint can be seen on the face of the east side of the 'Table Hall' at Christ Church Priory. One new local material, perhaps best described as 'iron-cemented gravelstone', made its first appearance in the rubble-work of 13th-century walling. This comes in large lumps and it can be seen in the mid 13th-century walls of the refectories at both St Augustine's Abbey and the Dominican friary. It is also found in the wall foundations of the kitchen at the former place, as well as in the end walls of the 13th-century prior's chapel at Christ Church Priory. A small amount is also found in a slightly later 13th-century wall at the Archbishop's great hall. Just outside Canterbury, iron-cemented gravelstone is best seen in the walls of Sturry parish church (particularly in the 13th-century vestry on the north-east side of the church) and in the nearby Chislet and Westbere parish churches (particularly in the heightened tower of the former and in the eastward extension to the chancel at Westbere of c.1300). This material apparently comes from river terraces of the Stour, north of Canterbury. A similar hard-cemented gravel was exposed on Rough Common (at 70m above OD) a few miles outside the city on the north-west, when a new housing estate was being built a few years ago. Why this material was apparently only used in the Canterbury area in the 13th century is still not known. Perhaps a supply first came to light at that time and was then used until worked out. A very similar material is used in a group of churches around Heathrow on the west side of London, which sit on the Taplow terrace just beyond the edge of the London clay outcrop, and here Dr Eric Robinson has suggested that the material is perhaps formed as an iron pan in the river gravels near the base of the local water table (Robinson 1988).

One other very different material which has only very occasionally been found in Canterbury at this period is blue roofing slate, which probably comes from the Delabole area of north Devon (see Pounds, below, pp. 231-32). It is commonly found in buildings of this period all along the southern coast as far east as Dover (Jope & Dunning 1954) but in Canterbury the main roofing material throughout the later medieval period was, of course, Kent pegged tiles. On the great buildings, like the cathedral, lead was apparently always used.

In the 13th century also occurred the first use of Kentish ragstone, particularly for weatherings and quoins on buttresses (for example, at the great hall of the archbishop's palace), but it was not until the 14th century that ragstone was really used in a large way in Canterbury.

Late medieval period (c.1320-1525)

During the early and middle years of the 14th century some building work was undertaken in the city, but it was not until the 1370s that a whole series of large new building campaigns was carried out in Canterbury. On the one hand a large scale rebuilding of the Roman city walls, starting with the Westgate, was required because of real threats of invasion from France. At the same time, however, the very bold step was taken to demolish the short cathedral nave between the Norman west towers and the western transepts and to rebuild it in the totally new Perpendicular style. The artistic and military genius behind this work was the royal master mason, Henry Yevele (Harvey 1944 & 1985), who was financially supported at the beginning by Archbishop Simon of Sudbury, until his untimely murder in the Peasants' Revolt of 1381. After a pause in the work at the cathedral from 1382 to 1391, it was carried on and completed by Prior Thomas Chillenden (1391-1411) who was described by Leland as 'the greatest Builder of a Prior that ever was in Christes Church'. Chillenden went on to rebuild the great cloister, the chapter house and many other priory buildings, some of which had been damaged in the earthquake of 1382. Work then carried on steadily at the cathedral in the 15th century with the rebuilding first of the south-west tower and porch, then of the south-west transept and, after a pause in the mid 15th century, the north-west transept (the Martyrdom). The culmination of all this work was the rebuilding of the huge central tower ('Bell Harry' tower) at the very end of the century, under another architectural genius, John Wastell, the royal master mason, who was again backed financially by the Archbishop, at this time John Morton, Chancellor of England.

Various chronicles and detailed records of some of this work survive, and the purchasing and transporting of stone is quite often recorded. Caen was, of course, still used in large quantities, as well as Reigate or Merstham stone, but we also have records of Beer stone and a stone called 'northern stone' being brought in as well as Kentish ragstone. A Christ Church chronicle has, under the year 1414, a record of *petra de Beyr et Carne* (i.e. Beer and Caen) worth £80 at the priory (Woodruff 1911, 83). This was the year the rebuilding of the great cloister was finished. On the south side of this cloister, in the wall that is also the north wall of the cathedral, many large blocks of Reigate stone can be seen. Their size varies between 12 and 28 inches (300-700mm) long, by 12 to 18 inches (300-450mm) high. Large blocks of Merstham stone can also be seen in the lower nave aisle walls on both sides. The areas of webbing in the vaults above are of a chalky material; this is presumably where the Beer stone was used. The lierne vaults of the Black Prince's chantry chapels in the crypt (1363), also use chalk (perhaps Beer stone) and Reigate stone. Why local chalk could not be used is unknown. Perhaps the harder Beer stone from the Middle Chalk on the east Devon border was considered a much better vault material, and this could easily (but more expensively) be brought along the south coast by sea. Outside Canterbury to the east, on the (Old) Dover Road, is a large chalk quarry, which was used presumably for lime, from at least the 12th century. This quarry is in the Upper Chalk and would have produced flint and chalk block.

Detailed fabric accounts of building work in the 15th century at the early years of the rebuilding of the south-west tower of the cathedral (rebuilt 1424-34) do survive and have been published (Woodruff 1933), and a summary is given below of the accounts dealing with the acquisition of building materials for the tower:

1424

227 tons of stone bought (at Sandwich) for	£78	17s.	4d.
Cost of carriage of this stone from Sandwich to Fordwich	£15	10s.	0d.
Cost of carriage of this stone from Fordwich to Canterbury	£7	6s.	8d.

1425

71 tons of stone 'bought from northern men at Monkton' (at 6s. per ton)	£21	6s.	8d.
128 tons of stone carried by water from Sandwich to Fordwich (at 12d. per ton)	£6	18s.	0d.
Winding and cranage at Fordwich, of stone brought by the Lord Prior's barge			23d.
Paid to Richard Bonvyarer of Dover for 22 tones of Caen stone (at 6s. 2d. per ton)	£9	17s.	4d.

Carriage of aforesaid 103 tons of stone from Fordwich to Canterbury (at 10d. per ton)	£4 15s.	10d.
Paid for 82 tons of Northern stone (at 6s. per ton)	£24 12s.	0d.
28 cartloads of flints bought by Edward Duraunt (Works Supervisor)	21s.	4d.
60 cartloads of sand at ¾d. for the load	7s.	6d.
Paid to Edward Duraunt for 214cwt of burnt lime bought at 53s. 3d. per hundred)	114s.	0d.
A thousand of iron bought for the same work	46s.	8d.

1427

178 tons of Caen stone (at 6s. per ton)	£53 8s.	0d.
Paid to William Edmund for 258 tons of Caen stone (at 6s. 4d. per ton)	£81 14s.	0d.
For carrying the above 436 tons and 22 tons left over from the preceding year, from Fordwich to Canterbury at 10d. per ton	£14 1s.	8d.
For 80 tons of Merstham stone bought from Peter Ryder at Battersea (at 4s. per ton)	£16 0s.	0d.
Paid to William Stephens for water carriage of the same to Greystone (at 16s. per ton)	£5 6s.	8d.
And for carting the same from Greystone to Canterbury (at 16d. per ton)	£4 0s.	0d.
201 quarters of quicklime bought price per hundred	53s.	4d.
In loading sand	8s.	4d.
John Morys, warden of the masons, expenses for going to Merstham to order the stone	20s.	5½d.

These accounts show that the Caen stone was brought into Sandwich and then purchased as required for between 6s. and 6s. 4d. a ton from the intermediaries (William Edmund and Richard Bonvyarer of Dover). The priory then had it shipped up the Wantsum and Stour to Fordwich (for one shilling a ton, unless they could use the prior's barge). Here it would be off-loaded onto carts and taken to Canterbury for 10d. a ton. The Merstham stone was cheaper to buy (at Battersea, only 4s. per ton compared to 6s. a ton for northern stone or Caen) but more expensive to transport (2s. 8d. per ton for the sea journey to Greystone, which is perhaps near Faversham, and then overland to Canterbury).

The south-west tower of the cathedral, where all these materials were used, has been very heavily restored on its outside, but it is fairly certain that the Merstham stone was only used internally, with the Caen stone on the outside. The 'northern stone' was perhaps for the now replaced pinnacles. In the south-west transept at the cathedral, which was rebuilt at about the same time, Caen stone can be seen in profusion in the internal and external faces of the main walls, but going up the spiral stair in the south-west corner of the transept quite a number of Merstham stone blocks can also be seen. For all this rebuilding work at the cathedral virtually no Kentish ragstone is used. The main exception is in some of the quoins on the buttresses on the south side of the nave.

Elsewhere, however, particularly in the city walls and at the Poor Priests' Hospital, the rebuilding work of the late 14th and early 15th centuries sees a great deal of Kentish ragstone ashlar being used. The finest example of all is in the

Westgate, which has fine quality ragstone used from top to bottom. This gate was both a defensive structure and a status symbol for the city, so the expensive ragstone was used throughout (again with financial help from Archbishop Simon of Sudbury). Elsewhere on the city walls only the battered plinths of the towers and the parapets used ragstone ashlar. The rest of the facework was in knapped flint. As yet, it is not clear which source of Kentish ragstone was used most. Quite large quantities of ragstone appear to have been brought in from the Lower Greensand beds in the Hythe to Folkestone area in the later Middle Ages and this is one likely source for the ragstone used in the city walls, and at the Westgate. However, the best later quarries for ragstone were in the area around Maidstone, and the stone from here was shipped out down the River Medway. When St George's Gate was rebuilt from *c*.1483, the city accounts tell us that ashlar stone for the work was brought by water from Maidstone to Whitstable. Until more detailed accounts are found, the site of the actual quarries for the medieval ragstone for Canterbury has to be left open. One note about repairs to the large window in the east (internal) side of the Westgate in 1491-92 mentions the use of nine cartloads of 'le Foldstone'. This is presumably Folkestone stone. When Sandgate castle was being constructed in 1539-40 (Rutton 1893, 234) Hythe stone was obtained nearby from a quarry that was partly submerged at high tide. No doubt this quarry also supplied stone by sea to other places at an earlier date.

In the 15th century we see for the first time the use in Canterbury of brick for building. The earliest brickwork was perhaps only used for fireplaces and to infill timber-frames, and the bricks are smaller and lighter in colour (buff to reddy-yellow) to those used later. Red brick was perhaps first used in the 1470s and it can be seen internally in the north gable of the north-west transept at the cathedral. Most important of all, however, was the building of the whole upper stage of 'Bell Harry' tower with red brick between 1493 and 1497. Again the outside face was in Caen stone, but all the rest is in good quality red brick in English bond. Other works at Christ Church Priory in the last years before the Dissolution also used red brick. A stair tower at the prior's new lodging (now the Deanery) of *c*.1500 is in brick, whilst the Christ Church Gate (built in *c*.1500-17) and its neighbouring porter's lodge on the north-west are also of brick. Once again, however, all the external facework on the main gateway is in Caen stone with a ragstone plinth.

The Burgate, rebuilt from *c*.1525, is perhaps the earliest major building in the city with external red brickwork (though the quoins were still in Caen stone). The Roper chantry chapel at St Dunstan's church and the Roper gateway, which are of similar date, are also of red brick. The latter is particularly fine, with moulded brick and no Caen stone being used.

One other building technique is quite commonly used from the late 15th century, and that is chequer work, using alternate squares of flint and ashlar in the facework. It can also be seen, for example, on the upper walls of the north-west transept at Canterbury Cathedral or on the Atwood chantry chapel of *c*.1512 on the south-east side of St Mildred's church.

Coda

With the dissolution of the monasteries and the Reformation in the mid 16th century virtually all major building work ceased. Where new work was carried out, for example, at the King's Lodging at St Augustine's in 1543, or at the Archbishop's Palace in the 1560s, red brick was the standard material. Much use was also made of materials from the dissolved religious houses, and places like the ruins of St Augustine's Abbey became builders' yards (virtually quarries) where stone of all sorts was sold off by the load.

Only at the end of the 18th century, and particularly during the 19th century, did much new building stone come into the city. Ragstone came from the Maidstone area, and once again Caen stone was imported in the early to mid 19th century for restoration. Unfortunately this Caen stone was often much softer than the medieval Caen, and it has weathered very badly in the century or so since its use. Some Portland stone was also brought in, and from c.1908 to 1920 Doulting stone was used at the cathedral for restoration. Another very unsuitable Jurassic stone, Bath Box Ground, was used from c.1949 to 1968. Since then, all restoration carried out at the cathedral has used Lepine stone from near Poitiers in France.

ACKNOWLEDGEMENTS

My interest in the building stone of Canterbury goes back over fourteen years and it was the late Stuart Rigold who first pointed out to me the more unusual stones (like Quarr). Recently my debt to Bernard Worssam has been very great and I am very grateful to him for reading and supplying many helpful comments to the first draft of this paper.

BIBLIOGRAPHY

The Archaeology of Canterbury

1 P. Bennett, S.S. Frere and S. Stow, *Excavations at Canterbury Castle*, 1982

2 S.S. Frere, S. Stow and P. Bennett, *Excavations on Roman and Medieval Defences of Canterbury*, 1982

3 P. Bennett, S. Campbell and S.S. Frere, *Excavations in the Cathedral Precincts*, **1**: *The 'Aula Nova', Almonry Chapel and Lanfranc's dormitory*, forthcoming

4 J. Driver, J. Rady and M. Sparks, *Excavations in the Cathedral Precincts*, **2**: *'Meister Omers', Linacre Gardens and St Gabriel's Chapel*, 1990

(all published in Maidstone by Kent Archaeological Society for the Canterbury Archaeological Trust)

Anderson, F.W, and Quirk, R. N., 1964 — Appendix note on the Quarr stone, in Jope, E.M., The Saxon building stone industry in southern and midland England, *Medieval Archaeol.*, **8** (1964), 115-17

Ager, D.V., and Wallace, P., 1966 — The environmental history of the Boulonnais France, *Proc. Geol. Assoc.*, **77** (1966), 385-435

Galbraith, V.H., 1920 — Royal charters to Winchester, *Eng. Hist. Rev.*, **35** (1920), 382-400

Gem, R.D.H., 1987 — Canterbury and the Cushion Capital: a commentary on passages from Goscelin's De Miraculis Sancti Augustini, *Romanesque and Gothic: essays for George Zarnecki*, ed. N. Stratford, 83-101. Woodbridge: Boydell and Brewer, 1987

Harvey, J.H., 1944	*Henry Yevele.* London: Batsford, 1944
Harvey, J.H., 1985	Henry Yeveley and the nave of Canterbury Cathedral, *Canterbury Cathedral Chronicle,* **79** (1985), 20-32
Jope, E.M., and Dunning, G.C., 1954	The use of blue slate for roofing in medieval England, *Antiq. J.,* **34** (1954), 209
Leach, R., 1978	An investigation into the use of Purbeck Marble in medieval England. 2nd ed., Crediton: privately published, 1978
Robinson, E., 1988	Gravel-stone in Middlesex churches: what's in a name?, London Archaeologist, **5**.14 (Spring 1988), 367-71
Rutton, W.L., 1893	Sandgate Castle, AD 1539-40, *Archaeol. Cantiana.,* **20** (1893), 228-57
Tatton-Brown, T.W.T., 1980	The use of Quarr stone in London and east Kent, *Medieval Archaeol.,* **24** (1980), 213-15
Tatton-Brown, T.W.T., 1981	The Trinity Chapel and Corona Floors, *Canterbury Cathedral Chronicle,* **75** (1981), 50-56
Tatton-Brown, T.W.T., forthcoming	The buildings and topography of St Augustine's Abbey, Canterbury, *J. Br. Archaeol. Assoc.,* forthcoming
Toke, N.E., 1930	The Opus Alexandrinum and sculptured stone roundels in the retrochoir of Canterbury Cathedral, *Archaeol. Cantiana.,* **42** (1930), 189-221
Willis, R., 1845	*The architectural history of Canterbury Cathedral,* London: Longman, 1845, repr. in *The Architectural History of some English Cathedrals,* Chichley: Minet, 1972
Willis, R., 1868	The architectural history of the conventual buildings of the monastery of Christ Church in Canterbury, *Archaeol. Cantiana,* **7** (1868), 1-206
Woodruff, C.E., 1911	A monastic chronicle lately discovered at Christ Church, Canterbury, *Archaeol. Cantiana,* **29** (1911), 47-84
Woodruff, C.E., 1933	The rebuilding of the south-west tower of Canterbury Cathedral in the fifteenth century, *Archaeol. Cantiana,* **45** (1933), 37-47

Chapter 6

Rubbish Recycled: A Study of the Re-Use of Stone in Lincolnshire

David Stocker, with Paul Everson

Throughout the whole of the period between the 10th and 20th centuries a large percentage of stone obtained from demolished buildings and other redundant structures has been taken into a cycle of re-use in further buildings or structures. This paper identifies some patterns visible within that process and concludes that almost all cases of re-use can be discussed under one of three general headings: casual, functional and iconic. These categories of re-used stone are analysed in some detail. Although the paper takes its evidence from Lincolnshire, it is probable that similar conclusions could be reached in most areas, whether well supplied with good quality building stone or not. Although the study originated in work on the Anglo-Saxon sculpture of Lincolnshire, all periods and types of cut stone are considered in the discussion.

Introduction

This paper has its origins in a study for the British Academy of Anglo-Saxon carved stone in the historic county of Lincolnshire which has been undertaken by the authors during recent years (Everson & Stocker forthcoming). Our work has involved a detailed study of the history of some 500 pieces of stone, looking not only at their use as sculpture in the Anglo-Saxon period but also at the way they have been re-used between then and now.

We have tried to sort these Anglo-Saxon stones according to the way in which they have been re-used, but to understand any underlying rules governing these re-uses we have found that the Anglo-Saxon evidence needs to be supported by case studies both from other periods and from different types of feature, architectural as well as sculptural. As a result, in this paper we shall be using examples of all types of stone cutting, from the Roman period to the present day.

The choice of Lincolnshire, obviously, has not been made because of the relative value of the evidence it contains. The county is an entirely arbitrary division petrologically, within which there is a supply of good freestone in the Jurassic ridge, the Lincoln Edge, which runs up its western side and where there is evidence for stone-digging in almost every parish. The county does not include the famous early quarries at Barnack but there are many others which have produced stone of similar types and quality, of which the most famous are around Ancaster and Lincoln. The limestones from this ridge have provided the great majority of the county's quality stone, but there are several other poorer stones available which have been used locally for building since the Roman period: blue lias, Spilsby and its related sandstones, and chalk (Wilson 1958; Swinnerton & Kent 1949). These lesser materials are quite often used for architectural features as well as for walling, but clearly, because of their relatively short useful life, they are much less valuable for re-use as anything other than rubble and it is for this reason that they play little further part in this paper.

A considerable proportion of the stone released by the demolition of buildings over the past two millennia has gone both for reduction to lime for spreading on clay fields and to be used simply as hardcore for roads and paths (see Stocker 1990, for example), but a great deal of this material has also been re-used in other buildings and this paper is devoted to the re-use of stone in new buildings and to the mechanisms which have governed the procedure.

Broadly speaking, there have been three categories into which most cases of the re-use of stone in buildings can be placed: casual re-use, functional re-use and iconic re-use. The mechanisms at work have apparently been the same at all periods up until the present.

Casual re-use

This category consists of cases where the original function of the stone is disregarded in its new use. It is much the most often seen and can be exemplified in many hundreds of building foundations excavated in recent years, although such casual re-use can also be observed in many more building fabrics where no detailed work has taken place.

Most stone which is casually re-used is not chosen with much care and is very often re-used in a completely haphazard way as rubble. It is often quite impossible to tell if a piece of rubble has been re-used more than once; there may be subtle signs – the presence of an earlier mortar, for example, or some clear tooling evidence – but as a rule a feature or detail in the wrong place is the indication that a fabric contains re-used stone. In fact many more buildings than we acknowledge are probably built of undistinctive re-used rubble and the recent detailed studies at St Mary Bishophill Junior in York and at Brixworth have shown that a high percentage of walling rubble of such early buildings can be re-used material (Briden & Stocker 1987; Sutherland & Parsons 1984).

In addition to such undistinctive walling material, which on close inspection turns out to have been re-used, there are a very large number of examples of buildings re-using stone which retains cut faces from its original use. Such primary cut faces are often concealed during re-use, and have come to light only during restoration work, often during the 19th century. In 1875 the south aisle fabric of the church at Bracebridge near Lincoln was taken down and found to contain at least 27 whole or partial grave markers and covers dating from the 10th to the 13th centuries (*AASRP* 1875, xi-xiii; Everson & Stocker, forthcoming). All of these pieces seem to have been turned inwards during their re-use in the 13th-century fabric and their presence was unsuspected (illustration 25). This process of 'turning-in' of old stone so that its decorated face is towards the core appears to be an absolutely standard technique.

25. Casual re-use: the south aisle wall of Bracebridge church. During rebuilding in 1875, this wall was found to have fragments from at least 27 medieval graveyard monuments built into it, none of which had been visible previously.

Turning-in does not necessarily require that the stone be recut, but stones re-used in this way have often been trimmed square. At Cranwell an important 10th-century monument, related to the so-called hogbacks and originally about 2m long by 0.75m across, was cut up, probably by saw, into six regularly sized ashlars. The weathering on the cut faces shows that, when re-used, the newly cut faces were outwards and it would have been hard to spot these pieces amongst the other ashlars in the wall in which they were discovered in 1902-03 (*AASRP* 1904, lxv). Occasionally technical information about such recutting processes survives. One of the late pre-Conquest gravemarkers re-used in the 13th-century rebuilding of St Mark's church in Lincoln has been carefully scored around the middle to allow it to be broken into two convenient building stones with a single mallet blow (Stocker 1986, no.IV/9, 78). In this case the final blow never came, leaving us with a rare illustration of a somewhat cruder method than that at Cranwell for producing less regular squared stone quickly. Even more crude is another technique, also illustrated at St Mark's, and suggested by quite small patches of calcination on the surfaces of some of the larger slabs (Stocker 1986, nos. I/30, II/14, II/45). It is possible that these patches are entirely accidental, but, because they often occur across fracture lines, they may be evidence that the stone has been broken up by lighting a fire on its surface and then dousing it to crack the stone in the rapid change of temperature. This technique would be easy and quick, but would result only in irregular chunks of rubble for re-use.

For obvious reasons, it is not possible to make a comprehensive analysis of walls constructed wholly of turned-in stones, but fortunately there is a very large number of structures which re-use stone in such a way that its earlier use is apparent in its new setting. Dr Buckland has hinted at the extent to which the church towers of the late 10th and 11th centuries around the Humber are built with re-used Roman material (Buckland 1988; see also Morris 1976; and Rodwell & Rodwell 1982 for the evidence from Barton-on-Humber). At Winteringham in north Lincolnshire, for example, some of the stones in the west tower can be positively identified as re-used Roman blocks, including a number of sections of tegulation from a major Roman building and at least one altar. These distinctive stones can tell much about the Roman buildings they came from, but there are many more stones in the Winteringham tower which are revealed as being from Roman buildings by the presence of lewis holes and cramp sockets.

The Roman stone re-used in north Lincolnshire towers is not only distinguishable by means of its cut and carved features, but also by its distinct petrology. Much of this stone is gritstone from the Pennine fringe, a stone greatly favoured in the later Roman period and exported throughout the Ouse/Humber river system, but because it was never in such vogue again, its presence may itself indicate re-used Roman stone. In the case of Broughton, Dr Rodwell has suggested (in a lecture to the Horncastle Weekend on Church Archaeology, 1983) that the banding of Roman blocks in distinct petrological groups in the western stair turret is a consequence of the arrival of stone at the site for re-use in different cart loads. It is unclear whether such loads came from different Roman sites and whether such loads came all the way, or only the final leg, by cart.

The topic of the redistribution of Roman gritstones around the Humber basin in the later pre-Conquest period requires a proper study, but for the present we can note a number of churches of the late 10th, 11th and 12th centuries in the northern parts of Lincolnshire which re-use Roman gritstone and which lie in close proximity to the likely transportation routes for such second-hand material, the rivers of the Humber system. (Examples are at Alkborough, Barton-on-Humber, Broughton, Burton Stather, Whitton, Winteringham and there are certainly other sites as well.)

This re-use of Roman material is not confined to gritstones in churches near the Humber. The detailed work done on Lincoln city churches in recent years has shown that few of those which preserve 11th-or 12th-century fabric do not also re-use Roman stone casually. This re-use is much more difficult to detect when there is no petrological distinction between the re-used material and the new stone, which (in contrast to the Humber shore) is the situation in the limestone areas of the county. Casual re-use of Roman stone has been detected in excavations of the 11th-century phases of both St Mark's and St Paul's churches and it can be observed in the 11th-century belfry of St Peter-at-Gowts (Gilmour & Stocker 1986, 85) and the 12th-century St Mary's Guildhall.

It is easy to show, then, that there is a considerable re-use of Roman building stone between the later 10th and 12th centuries. It seems to be less common, however, after the 12th century and by the 13th century it is more common to find 11th-century pieces being re-used. Our catalogue of late pre-Conquest sculptures shows that a majority of them were re-used as building stones in 13th-century fabrics: thirteen were re-used in 11th- and 12th-century fabrics, seventeen in 13th-century fabrics and only six in fabrics of the 14th century. Even so it is not really possible as yet to correlate the rise in the re-use of pre-Conquest stone with the presumed exhaustion of supplies from Roman buildings.

By the later medieval period it is most common to find 12th-century fragments being re-used, on a small scale, for example, in the case of the 12th-century tympanum re-used in the footings of the late 14th-century chancel at Whaplode, or – on a more spectacular scale – the great new nave of Crowland Abbey, built soon after 1405 (Moore 1861), which was constructed on foundations made of the architectural fragments of its 12th-century predecessor. In the post-medieval period the pattern is no different. Buildings very often contain casually re-used stone from redundant buildings in the vicinity and, naturally, most of those buildings were about 200 years old. It should be no surprise, then, that the majority of the stone casually re-used in post-medieval fabrics appears to be later medieval rather than earlier. By the early post-medieval period, of course, dissolved monasteries were major sources of supply and there are many cases similar to the 17th- or 18th-century cottages adjacent to Barlings Abbey, the fabrics of which were full of moulded stones which had been casually re-used.

It was during a second iconoclasm at the cathedral in 1644 that many of its monuments and fittings were demolished, but once again this rubble was re-used by Sir Christopher Wren's masons during the rebuilding of the cathedral library in 1673-74. The recent repair work on the library has produced many fragments from late medieval monuments which had been re-used in the wall core of the library, whilst the north wall can be seen to contain a number of large structural pieces presumably from the same source.[1]

These examples show that casual re-use of stone is widespread and occurs in Lincolnshire at all periods between the late 10th century and the post-medieval period. We should, now, try to isolate some of the specific factors which have affected the re-use of stone within this 'casual' group.

First, there is the effect which stone type has on the pattern of its re-use. Clearly stones with certain petrologies are likely to be of more use for some tasks than stones of different type. In the north-east of the county, particularly, church fabrics are predominantly of the poor local materials, chalk or Cretaceous sandstone. In these areas, clearly, good building stone will be valued and indeed the fabrics of these churches often contain limestone blocks from the Lincoln Edge. Such limestones are often used as lintels and for other structural purposes. A clue to the origin of some, if not many, of these limestones can be seen for example at Croxton, where the building material is otherwise chalk. Here many of the architectural features (i.e. buttresses and embrasures) are made from cut-down grave covers and the north-west buttress has no less than eight pieces of grave cover in it. Similarly, almost all of the late-medieval architectural features in the west tower re-use funerary monuments of various types dating from the 12th to the 14th century. The best stone here, well away from the limestone ridge, seems then to have been imported by individual parishioners for their tombs, and only once those tombs were redundant was the valuable stone carefully cut up and sparingly re-used at critical points in the building. This re-use of grave covers of imported oolite at structurally critical points in the fabrics of churches in the east and north-east of the county is so common as to be almost the rule. Although this sort of re-use is quite sophisticated it can still be seen as 'casual' rather than 'functional' re-use as the stones have been selected merely for their petrology and not for their functional characteristics (i.e. they have not been selected for re-use because they were originally grave covers).

The Viking-Age cross shaft at Crowle on the Isle of Axholme is unique amongst the Anglo-Saxon sculpture of the county, as it is cut on a gritstone column. We have no proper evidence, but what has already been said about such gritstone in the northern part of the county may suggest that it too could be a re-used Roman column. However, whether Roman in origin or not, the stone was chosen for a cross shaft in the 10th century at least partly because of its colour and texture. A more critical consideration in this case, however, may have been the great length of the stone which made it potentially useful as a shaft, and this factor – the size and shape of the stone – is a second important consideration affecting casual re-use. The Crowle shaft may be, therefore, a case of pre-Conquest re-use of Roman stone selected partly for size, but a more certain example is the large Roman block re-used as a grave marker from Lincoln Cathedral. The Roman origin of the stone in this case is quite evident from the lewis hole in one face, which would probably have been filled with plaster during its late 10th-century re-use.

There are numerous similar examples of selection of Roman stone for size. Warwick Rodwell's work at Barton-on-Humber showed how the quoins relied on the availability of long Roman stones (Rodwell & Rodwell 1982, 294 etc.), and several other early quoin stones betray their Roman origins with cramp and lewis holes. Other Lincolnshire examples of the 11th and 12th centuries include those at Burton Stather, Whitton and Winteringham.

Of course pre-Conquest cross shafts themselves, when cut up, make useful quoin stones because of their proportions: another example of a selection for size. There are six cases known to us: Blyborough, Creeton, Kirkby Underwood, Normanton, North Rauceby, Ruskington.

Cross shafts are also of convenient size and shape for re-use as lintels, and we have firm evidence that seven of our Lincolnshire examples have been re-used in this way at some time during their history (Barrowby 2, Castle Bytham 1, Creeton 1, Harmston 1, Hougham, Crowle, Winterton). At Barrowby, Hougham and Winterton these stones are still in place as lintels. In addition we must consider a further three examples (Bassingham 2, Crowland St Guthlac's Cross, and Northorpe) where the evidence for such re-use is confined to a trimming along one side, which could be to allow a door or shutter to close or could equally be a chamfer cut to decorate the stone when re-used in a plinth course. Several of the stones in the county study have been re-used as plinths (Bicker, Blyborough 4 & 5, Eagle 1) and at Broughton (no.4) and Corringham (no.9) Anglo-Saxon grave covers have been re-used as the footings for arcade piers. At Great Hale and Glentworth similar monuments have been re-used in monolithic jambs, whilst grave covers at Mavis Enderby, Miningsby and Cammeringham have all been re-used as thresholds. Once again all these pieces have been selected for re-use in these positions because of their appropriate size.

The practice of re-using graveyard monuments for such purposes continues through the medieval period. Within the county we have at least five examples of grave covers being re-used in Norman tympana, either undecorated ones, as at Upton, Howell or Springthorpe, or sculpted ones as at Haltham-on-Bain and Little Bytham. Later in the medieval period, 13th- and 14th-century monuments are also re-used in this way, for example at Buslingthorpe, where the lintel over the west tower window re-uses a fine incised grave cover of a priest (Greenhill 1986, 32). A real oddity, though, is the re-use of a late Anglo-Saxon cross head at Harmston to light the inserted late-medieval tower stair. Here the cross head forms the complete frame of the window and the light is admitted through the interstices between the cross arms and the rim – a case of ingenious selection of a stone for its shape.

Selection for size was also responsible for the re-use of an enormous 11th-century grave cover as a bridge in the parish of Howell (*AASRP* 1870, 234) and the re-use of the famous Romanesque sculpture of St Paul at Lincoln Cathedral as culvert cover (Zarnecki 1988; Willson Collect., portfolio D, f.32). At least two important stones were selected for their size and shape as the supports for chimneys in the early post-medieval period. The memorial to Blanche de Wake who was buried in the Greyfriars at Stamford was found supporting a cottage chimney by Christine Mahany in 1966 (Hartley & Rodgers 1974, 64-65). And the spectacular reredos from an altar of St Catherine was found supporting a chimney in uphill Lincoln in 1796 (*Gentleman's Magazine*, 67/II, (1797), 650-51).

Casual re-use also describes those objects which are used for a purpose akin to their original but which is not quite what was originally intended. This group of pieces is quite large and occupies a grey area on the boundaries between the casual and functional re-use categories. An excellent example lying on the boundary between the two categories is provided by the fine 11th-century cross shaft at Stoke Rochford. The shaft was evidently re-used in the fabric of the medieval church at North Rochford, which was itself demolished in the 1840s. On its rediscovery, the shaft was repaired (it had been broken into three sections) and re-erected in the landscaped parkland which Christopher Turnor was creating around his house, Stoke Rochford Hall (Davies 1913, 130). However, this was not a straightforward functional re-use as a Christian shaft because the top was recut as a pyramid to become another 'antique' object to be glimpsed as an eye-catcher in the distance. This is almost a re-use for its original function (as a memorial shaft) but not quite.

The more versatile components of architecture, capitals, bases and such like, are often re-used in this way: the 12th-century capitals re-used as corbels supporting the Perpendicular north aisle roof at Sibsey are examples representative of many in the county. Also within this group we should include at least four kitchen mortaria which have been re-used as fonts. The one at St Leonard's Kirkstead could have been taken from the kitchen of the neighbouring Cistercian monastery to provide a font once the medieval chapel had been raised to parish status and given baptismal rights after the Dissolution. In this case, in fact, there may be grounds for calling this an 'iconic' re-use: the mortar may have been re-used in preference to any other suitable bowl because of its former monastic associations. Although we can speculate about such a process at Kirkstead, however, it is less clear how the mortaria at Normanby by Spital and Langton St Margaret came to be used for the same purpose. At Walesby, although we know that the original font was taken for use as a horse-trough in the 1560s (Hodgett 1975, 171), we cannot be sure about the motives which governed its replacement with a kitchen mortar.

Finally the casual re-use category should include a number of examples where stone has been re-used decoratively. The Perpendicular clerestory of Redbourne church contains shaft sections (probably of 13th-century date) set on end and arranged in a pattern of crosses in between the windows. It is not clear how common such decorative re-uses of stone are in the medieval period; certainly there do not appear to be very many authentic examples in Lincolnshire, but with the dissolution of the monasteries the decorative re-use of stone fragments seems to have become quite widespread. For example, one of the 17th- or 18th-century cottages at Barlings had a splendid boss set decoratively in the gable,[2] whilst at St Mary's, Barton-on-Humber, Hougham, Old Clee and Wrawby are examples of a decorative re-use quite often seen: sections of tracery from the restoration of windows turned upside down and used as pinnacles and finials.

Functional re-use
The functional re-use category consists of those pieces which have been re-used for the purpose for which they were originally cut: doorways re-used as doorways, for example, or windows re-used as windows. As with the casual re-use category, this is not a phenomenon confined to particular periods but is rather something which has occurred throughout the history of stone building.

Dr Rodwell has suggested that the tower arch at Barton-on-Humber, like much of the rest of the tower, is not only made of re-used Roman stone, but that a whole arch has been carefully removed from a defunct Roman building and re-assembled here (Rodwell & Rodwell 1982, 294). In fact this practice of re-using entire Roman archways in Anglo-Saxon buildings may be relatively common. Baldwin Brown suggested that the arches at Escomb church (Co. Durham) and Corbridge (Northumberland) were reset Roman ones (1925, 140-45), and the same has been suggested subsequently in several other cases (eg. Market Overton, Leicestershire, formerly Rutland (Taylor & Taylor, 1965, 412); St Mary Bishophill Junior, York (Briden & Stocker 1987, 98)). In Lincolnshire, the tower arch at Alkborough appears to belong to this group (illustration 26). First, the voussoirs here are very skilfully and accurately cut when compared with all the other embrasures – the quality of this architectural feature is quite out of character with the remainder of the tower. Secondly, the extrados of the voussoirs are all cut to a single line. This is essential in archways of more than one order but most unusual in those of one order only. As the tower arch is of only one order this precision in the extrados is best explained by the theory that the arch comes originally from a different structure of more than one order. Thirdly, the impost blocks at Alkborough are undoubtedly Roman, although whether they were originally intended for this impost position is debatable. They are, at least, unequivocally re-used from a major Roman building, as is the length of trellis decoration near the base of the archway, which has nevertheless entered the literature as a piece of Anglo-Saxon interlace (Davies 1926, 7).

26. Functional re-use: the tower arch of Alkborough church. This is one of several tower arches in Lincolnshire and Yorkshire which are probably reset Roman arches.

Barton-on-Humber and Alkborough are the only really clear examples of re-used Roman architectural features in the county (although the 11th-century tower arches at Broughton and Great Hale both have voussoirs with a similar uniform extrados), but it is possible that the mid-wall shaft in the 11th-century south belfry opening at Glentworth has a Roman origin. Like one or two other key features in this tower, it has an unusual petrology and there was a major Roman villa in an adjacent field. The re-use of Roman architectural shafts for exactly this purpose is known at the contemporary tower of St Mary Bishophill Junior in York (Briden & Stocker 1987, 103-07) and a Roman origin for the Glentworth shaft might help to explain its odd eliptical cross-section, although it is easy to overstate the evidence for a Roman origin in this case.

Re-use of medieval architectural features in later buildings is by now well documented and Lincolnshire provides as many cases as other counties. A good example is the fine mid 12th-century door of the Augustinian priory at South

Kyme, which was reset in the mid 14th-century south aisle. Christine Mahany's work at Stamford Castle has suggested that the three fine early 14th-century doors from the castle hall had been rebuilt in their present position early in the post-medieval period, although they had originally been set on approximately their present site (Mahany forthcoming); the west door of the church at Burton-by-Lincoln seems to have been re-assembled from the remains of a fine 12th-century door in 1678, whilst the Romanesque west door of Benniworth church was moved here, from elsewhere in the building, by James Fowler in 1875 (*AASRP* 1873, xiii-iv; Pevsner & Harris 1964, 208, 190). But these cases are far from exceptional: there are many other examples at all periods.

Windows almost certainly have had the same mobility, although the problems of identifying the correct date of a wall in which a window is set means that authentic cases of moving windows in the medieval period are more difficult to spot. An original window in the south aisle at Strubby was reset in the new building in 1857 and is a representative example of the many re-uses of monolithic window heads, although a more famous case is that of the fine late-medieval oriel taken from the town house of the Sutton family in Wigford to Lincoln Castle in 1849 (Hill 1948, 168 & n).

Arcades are sometimes re-used as arcades; at Sibsey, for example, the component parts of the Romanesque arcade were clearly reset when the Perpendicular clerestory was added, with extra sections in the piers to double its height. Again such resetting of arcades in the medieval period is probably not uncommon and it is possible to identify other cases in Lincolnshire, at St George's, Stamford, Belton in Axeholme, Pinchbeck and perhaps Sutterton, but the problem is always detection. In the 19th and 20th centuries, of course, such re-use of structural arches became widespread and, although many examples could be cited, that at Withern is particularly remarkable as the Perpendicular nave arcades may have been re-used on new lines within a nave which is otherwise almost wholly of 1812. Mostly, re-used arcade arches derive from buildings on or adjacent to the site, but occasionally arches prove quite mobile, as in the case of the arch into the transept at Keddington church which evidently came from the ruins of the Cistercian abbey of Louth Park some two miles away (Pevsner & Harris 1964, 283).

Capitals and similar components of architectural features are, of course, even more mobile than the whole features of which they are parts and so it is no surprise to count large numbers of capitals, re-used functionally as capitals, in new settings, either within their original building or in a new one. Sometimes they are used for purposes very similar to those for which they were originally cut, as in the capital block from St Hugh's crossing tower at Lincoln Cathedral which was built c.1200 and which collapsed in 1237. The tower was quickly replaced by the present structure but several fragments from the old tower were re-used in the new, and this large double capital was reset in the south transept west clerestory in a position similar to that for which it was originally cut.

Finally the point should be made that it is not only architectural features which get re-used in this functional way. There is a monument to a late 16th- or early

17th-century lady, perhaps a member of the Rigdon or Burrell families, in Dowsby church which belongs to a small group of late 16th-/early 17th-century effigies which are recuttings of medieval monuments. This is, of course, merely the logical extension of the practice of recutting and re-using grave covers and slabs for which we have evidence throughout the later medieval period (Lincolnshire examples include stones at Dunsby, St Giles, St Paul and St Peter-at-Gowts in Lincoln, and Skillington). The case of the Dowsby effigy is only distinguished from these other examples because of the relative complexity involved in curtailing a long 14th-century gown on the three dimensional sculpture and in carving a waisted bodice within its original drapery.

Iconic re-use

One should probably see the case of the Dowsby effigy simply as a functional re-use, undertaken for reasons of convenience and cost, into which no additional message should be read. But, against this functional explanation we have the parallel and famous case of a similar appropriation of medieval monuments by Lord Lumley at Chester-le-Street church in County Durham, which had a more profound purpose. Lord Lumley was renowned at the court of James I for his interest in his lineage and was constantly promoting the antiquity of his family (King James is reputed to have quipped 'I did na' ken that Adam's ither name was Lumley'). Consequently Lumley sent out agents to ruined monastery sites to procure effigies with which he liked to think himself connected (Parry 1981, 134; Pevsner & Williamson 1983, 127) and some of these effigies were recut in the same way as the Dowsby monument. Lord Lumley was re-using stones as a way of legitimising his family. Re-uses of stone in this way form the third category with which this paper is concerned. Any stone would not suit Lord Lumley's purpose: it was important that these were particular stones, which brought with them particular associations, because he was employing their very antiquity in a didactic or iconic way to demonstrate the antiquity of his family.

Such iconic re-use of stone is much the least common mechanism which one can identify at work in Lincolnshire but it is also much the most interesting. Iconic re-use becomes quite widespread in the 19th century, but there are probably some genuine early cases. For example, there is a group which appears to represent the iconic re-use of Roman sculpture in the 11th century.

The most straightforward of these cases is the famous re-used Roman gravestone set close to eye level south of the west door in the tower of St Mary-le-Wigford, Lincoln. The Roman inscription is unremarkable (*Dis manibus*, etc.), but there is an unusual Anglo-Saxon dedicatory inscription squeezed into the gable over the Latin panel (*Ertig me let wircean 7 fios godian christi to lofe 7 sce marie*). Although the panel has been greatly discussed, no one has asked why the builders of one of the most impressive parish church towers of its date in eastern England should have wanted to place their dedicatory inscription on an old and broken stone which hardly has the room for it. No suggestion that they were short of large pieces of flat stone suitable for inscriptions will do. After all, if they were only interested in the stone as a writing tablet they could have turned it around and used the back. Surely the viewer is meant to take a message from the placing of a new inscription above the Roman one and the message is clear: the kudos of the Roman world is being appropriated for church use. Further credibility is given to such a suggestion by the observation that, unusually, the inscription runs backwards from the bottom to the top of the space available. Although there might be alternative explanations for this curious layout, the most satisfactory is that the designer wanted to have the single word 'Mary' at the top of the stone visibly dominating the Latin inscription. We can suggest, therefore, that the placing of such a carefully arranged English Christian inscription over the pagan Latin one is a deliberate attempt to show the domination of the latter by the former. In the same way, instead of having Roman monuments demolished, Pope Gregory I in one age (Sherley-Price & Latham, 1968, 86-7) and Sixtus V in another (Ackerman 1982) thought it more effective to have altars or crosses put in and on them and so 'convert' them. Similar adaptations of Roman objects for Christian

use is, of course, well documented throughout the Middle Ages, and we propose that the St Mary-le-Wigford example is an iconic re-use of a Roman inscription and a minor 11th-century example of the Christianisation of the Roman past (see Panofsky 1939, 18-31; Panofsky 1944; Oakeshott 1959).

A second example of such iconic re-use may be provided by the seated figure reset in the west face of the tower of St Peter-at-Gowts, Lincoln, which although sometimes claimed as Anglo-Saxon is very probably of Roman origin (illustration 27). However, as reset here in the public 'façade' of the church, it is clearly intended to represent Christ in Majesty or perhaps St Peter. In one sense, of course, this could be viewed as a functional re-use; the 11th-century builders were in need of a sculpture, this piece happened to be available and they thought it a close enough resemblance to what they wanted. This does not sound very convincing, however, and it seems more likely that the sculpture was perceived in the 11th century as Christ/St Peter, whether it

27. Iconic re-use: the 'Majesty' figure in the tower of St Peter-at-Gowts, Lincoln. This is probably a Roman monument which has been re-used because of its perceived resemblance to a Christ in Majesty.

was known to be Roman or not, and its display in this prominent position represents a deliberate attempt on the part of the builders to associate the new tower with the reverence with which the sculpture was viewed at that time. This can only be described as iconic re-use.

There may have been an almost exactly parallel iconic re-use of a Roman panel at the church of St Martin in Lincoln. The panel was drawn in the mid-18th century, but the church was demolished in 1876-77 and the panel lost (Hill 1948,142-3) so, intriguing though it is, we can know little about the case and it would be unwise to make any strong claims for it.

Awareness of the possibility that early stonework might be re-used in this iconic way encourages a search for examples at later dates. At first sight the re-use of an Anglo-Saxon shaft at Hougham appears just another casual re-use of a shaft as a lintel over the later medieval south door, having been selected in the late Middle Ages because of the size and shape of the stone. Such considerations must have played their part. However, there are hints that there is more to this case. The decoration has been carefully selected for its symmetry vis-à-vis the door, and the borders of the panels have been carefully removed to leave the interlace standing out in low relief. The stone has been reset in this wall with considerable thought and care so as to suggest that there has been an attempt to display the old stone. The reasons behind such a wish for display can only be guessed at, but it is entirely possible that it was intended to associate the new church building with earlier Christian uses of the site. Furthermore, the symbolic and even superstitious importance of the entrance to the medieval church may have affected the decision to re-use the stone in this position.

Certainly the church itself had an appreciation of the symbolic, if not the superstitious, power which could adhere to stones which had been used for certain ritual purposes, and such beliefs may have led to their being re-used in iconic ways. Fonts, for example, having been consecrated and having held sacramental water, were considered to be endowed with special properties (for example, Thomas 1973, 33, 40-41, etc.), and there still is an elaborate procedure surrounding the disposal of redundant fonts. At Ewerby the 12th-century font has been used to provide a podium for its 14th-century successor, not one suspects merely because this was convenient but because the new font would be legitimised by its standing on the old. Several accounts exist of early fonts being buried in the floors of churches below their successors, including those at Folkingham and Cabourne in Lincolnshire (*AASRP* 1857, 248; *AASRP* 1871, lxxvii; Bond 1908, 127, 131, 278), and the curious case at Bassingham should also be considered in this context, even though without further archaeological information it cannot be discussed with confidence. At Bassingham a large later 10th-century cross shaft was carefully hollowed out (presumably between the 11th and 13th centuries) to form a trough, complete with drain. The trough was subsequently buried in the nave of the church where it was discovered during restorations in 1861. At this time the trough was described as a cross shaft which had been re-used as a font in the 12th or 13th centuries and which had then been buried in the 14th century, in this consecrated ground, to avoid desecrating it by breaking it up

(Cole 1897, 387). It is perhaps somewhat unlikely that this trough would have served as anything other than a temporary font, but it could be seen as an example of a sacrarium or 'holy rubbish bin' of the type recently defined by Parsons (1986). Whether a font or a container for the debris of ritual, however, a case can be made for this as an example of an iconic re-use of the early monument as a specialised receptacle. Its secondary purpose would have been given greater impact by the fact that it was made from a re-used monument.

Allied to the fonts which have evidently been treated with reverence because of their original function we must also consider cases such as that at Mavis Enderby, where a 12th-century pillar piscina has been carefully re-used as a holy water stoup by the south door in the 15th century. One explanation to account for the survival of so many pillar piscinas which had been superseded by wall-mounted models would be that many pillar piscinas were subsequently used as stoups precisely because they were viewed as having been sanctified by their original use (for piscinas generally see Parsons 1986; Jessiman 1958). One should probably also consider in this context the motives of the 85-year-old owner of Southorpe Grange, Northorpe (or possibly his executors), when he (or they) re-used a pre-Reformation altar stone for the ledger stone over his vault in 1602 (Greenhill 1986, 92).

It is possible that potency was also accorded to certain stones which carried a depiction of the cross. There are several well known examples of the iconic re-use of early crosses in later church fabrics in Yorkshire (for example at Hovingham, Londesborough and Middleton), and the re-use of crosses from 12th-century grave covers in the north tympanum of the belfry opening at Horbling is probably a minor Lincolnshire example of the same thing. However, it seems possible that many depictions of the cross in stone were treated with special care. This is a difficult idea to explore, but it does appear on superficial inspection that a disproportionate number of cross heads from grave covers and markers seem to survive relative to fragments from other parts of such covers and, furthermore, these cross heads are sometimes re-used in what may be iconic ways. Such use is made of cross heads from two grave covers in an aumbry in the north wall at Thornton-le-Moor, whilst the back panel is formed by a fragment of 11th-century interlace (which, although it has no representation of the cross, one could argue was seen as an 'ancient Christian' object and therefore endowed with a residual sanctity).[3] A very similar use is made of cross heads from 12th- and 13th-century covers in the piscinas in the 14th-century chancel and north aisle at Wilsford. Again it is possible to account for these arrangements by saying simply that these flat slabs are ideal for such purposes, and their earlier use is irrelevant. However, if this is the case, we have to ask why these slabs have been recut to preserve the crosses intact and then why have they been re-used this way round rather than reversed (for popular and superstitious uses of the cross in the late medieval and early post-medieval periods see Thomas 1973, *passim*). It seems clear that the builders of these piscinas and aumbries were intending the cross heads to be seen. The reasoning behind the re-use of these crosses in this way can only be guessed at, but it is clear that such depictions of the cross were sometimes treated with special care and we must presume are here re-used in an iconic way.

Further credibility is given to such analyses by the remains of the piscina at Carlby. Here an 11th-century grave cover has been cut up in the later medieval period and the section bearing the cross head has been turned upside down to have a piscina bowl cut in its reverse side. This could be quite accidental, but the drain hole for the bowl passes carefully through the middle of the cross underneath. This conjunction of features is less likely to be accidental in view of the very similar cross from a small cover at Frisby-on-the-Wreake, just over the county border in Leicestershire, which has also been re-used in a piscina and also has a drain passing exactly through the centre of the cross.

We can produce, therefore, a small body of evidence to support the contention that some crosses from early memorials were treated with especial respect in the later medieval period and that respect sometimes led to their being re-used in an iconic way.

The header tank for the water supply of 16th-century Lincoln, known as St Mary's Conduit, was installed in the early 1540s, and it may well represent a rather different example of iconic re-use of stone. We know a great deal about the construction of this tank, and the system which went with it, because a relevant City Council minute book survives and, from an analysis of that book and the building itself, it has been suggested that the conduit head was built out of stone taken carefully from the chantry chapel of Ranulph Kyme, a famous mayor of Lincoln, and re-erected in this showy way (Stocker 1990). The City Council could have built a plain tank and they could have chosen dozens of other buildings from which to pillage their stone, yet they went to considerable trouble to acquire this particular building (which was attached to the Whitefriars' church) and then to re-erect parts of it in this distinctive, public way. Although we cannot demonstrate it with certainty, it is possible that this was a gesture on the part of the Council to ensure that the memory of one of their more distinguished ancestors continued to be marked after the dissolution of his chantry, only now in this modern, secular fashion. This case, then, looks rather like the iconic re-use of stone on a civic scale.

In the post-medieval period, as both documentary and archaeological evidence survives better, it becomes possible to identify many more examples of stones being re-used in an iconic way, providing legitimation for individuals and institutions of all sorts. The church at Minting in Lincolnshire is one of many 19th-century buildings which have reset displays of early sculpture in their walls to demonstrate and commemorate the tradition of Christian activity in the parish. At Aisthorpe and Waddingworth early sculpted stones are re-used as date-stones commemorating the rebuilding of the churches in 1867 and 1807 respectively – iconic re-uses which invite comparison with the re-use of the Roman inscription in the dedication stone of St Mary-le-Wigford's tower and which stress the continuity of such patterns of re-use over a period of some 800 years. Such cases (and there are many of them) are clear iconic re-uses of stone to give new buildings an important symbol of their inheritance.

One quite common associated phenomenon is the transport of fragments from ruined abbeys to restored Victorian parish churches, out of a desire that the parish church of the 19th century should be physically associated with the monastery of

the medieval period. In Lincolnshire we have already seen this process at work
at Keddington and it can also be seen at Revesby, Stixwold and Southrey – all
examples where the ancient stone has been re-used iconically in the new fabric.
There are many more examples where monastic masonry has been brought into
a nearby church for preservation. The legitimation of a new parish church by re-
using stones from ruined monasteries is best seen in Lincolnshire at Wold Newton,
where the (evidently High-Church) rector who oversaw the rebuilding in 1862
seems to have travelled around many Lincolnshire monastic sites literally picking
up worked stone which he then had reset as brackets to support statues of saints
in his new building. Interestingly, not all of the pieces he picked up came from
the monastic buildings on these sites: there is, for example, a console from
the grand early 17th-century house which replaced the monastery at Thornton
(Roberts 1984). Had the rector of Wold Newton known that this was a secular
piece, he would surely not have reset it in its position of honour.

Such re-uses as these modern cases represent can be understood in much greater
detail than we have attempted here, usually because there is some direct or
circumstantial written evidence which casts light on the motives for re-use.
Clearly there is an antiquarian background to many 19th-century examples, and
such cases will provide a fascinating study which is, however, well beyond the
scope of this paper. This present study can only be a preliminary step, describing
these complex motivations for the re-use of stone only in general terms, even
though (where the documentation survives) each case appears distinctive. For the
present we do not propose to divide these iconic re-uses further, but instead we
can give a modern example which illustrates the complex variety of motives
behind the re-use of ancient stone, which we can discover only where full
documentation has survived. This is at Toft-by-Newton, where two fragments
from a 10th-century cross shaft were reverently built into a monument commemorating the rector's wife in 1944. The stones (which had already been recut for
re-use during the later Middle Ages) were being re-used functionally, for their
original purpose, that is they were being once again set upright to mark a burial.
But in this case there were also important considerations which would allow the
re-use to be described as iconic: they were objects of Christian devotion, antiquarian and scholarly interest and – bearing in mind the date at which they were
erected – they were specifically 'English' objects suggestive of a long national
history. All these ideas were ones with which the bereaved rector wished his
monument to be associated, yet they would be unknowable without the surrounding direct and indirect documentation.

Conclusion
With very few exceptions (for example the Elloe Stone and the Brattleby cross),
the stone which has been catalogued for the Anglo-Saxon Corpus in Lincolnshire
has been re-used in one of three ways, either casually, functionally or iconically,
and furthermore virtually all re-uses of cut stone from the Roman period to the
modern can be described by reference to one or other of these three categories.
There can be little doubt that Lincolnshire is typical: our own observations

suggest that the same processes of re-use are in operation elsewhere in the country, and this paper could have been illustrated with examples from almost any county.

There remains, however, one major issue, central to the theme of this volume, which must be addressed: the whole question of how these patterns of the re-use of stone relate to the known patterns of activity in the stone quarries. Is there any truth in the often made assumption that during periods when the quarrying industry is quiescent, the re-use of stone becomes more intensive (see, for example, Jope 1964, 97-98)? The question is complex, but on the whole we have not found much direct evidence to support the assumption in the Lincolnshire sample. All three types of re-use of stone occur at all periods and it is certainly not possible to demonstrate satisfactorily that there was more re-use of stone during the pre-Conquest period, when it is often presumed that the quarrying industry was inactive, than there was during the later medieval period, when the quarrying industry was in full production. Proof of such an assertion requires a very much more detailed study than we have undertaken here and, indeed, given the limitations in the survival of the evidence, it may never be possible. However, rather than point to one particular period when stone re-use was more frequent than another, the lesson from this study of the Lincolnshire evidence is rather that the re-use of stone has been common over the whole period from the 10th century to modern times. Stone was always too valuable a resource to be wasted, even in a stone-rich county, and making maximum use of stone involved re-using it over and over again.

Notes

1) I am grateful to Mr P.R. Hill for access to the site during these restorations to make these observations. Those items of medieval stone removed are now in the cathedral lapidarium.

2) This well known cottage was unexpectedly demolished in 1984, although one of the two fine later 14th-century decorated bosses was recovered and is now in store at the Trust for Lincolnshire Archaeology.

3) The date of the arrangement now visible in the aumbry at Thornton-le-Moor is relatively modern, but there are good reasons for thinking that the component stones were originally arranged in a similar way.

BIBLIOGRAPHY

Unpublished Work

Willson Collect.   The Willson Collection of Manuscripts, Society of Antiquaries of London, MS 786

Published Works

AASRP 1857   *Assoc. Archit. Soc. Rep. Pap.* **4** (1857): Reports
AASRP 1870   *ibid.*, **10** (1870): Fragments

AASRP 1871   *ibid.*, **11** (1871): Reports
AASRP 1875   *ibid.*, **13** (1875): Reports
AASRP 1904   *ibid.*, **27** (1904): Reports
Ackerman, J., 1982   The Planning of Renaissance Rome, *Rome and the Renaissance: the City and the Myth*, ed. P.A. Ramsey, 3-17. Medieval and Renaissance Texts and Studies, **18**, Binghampton, NY: Centre for Medieval and Early Renaissance Studies, 1982

Bond, F., 1908   *Fonts and Font Covers*. London: Oxford University Press, 1908
Briden, C.M., and   The Tower of the Church of St Mary Bishophill Junior, *St Mary*
    Stocker, D.A., 1987   *Bishophill Junior and St Mary Castlegate*, ed. P. Wenham *et al.*, 84-146. The Archaeology of York 8/2, London: Council for British Archaeology, 1987

Brown, G.B., 1925   *The Arts in Early England*, **2**: *Anglo-Saxon Architecture*. 2nd ed., London: Methuen, 1925

Buckland, P., 1988   The Stones of York – Building Materials in Roman Yorkshire, *Recent research in Roman Yorkshire*, ed. J. Price *et al.*, 237-87. British Archaeological Reports, Br. Ser. **193**, Oxford, 1988

Cole, R.E.G., 1897   Notes on the Ecclesiastical History of the Deanery of Graffoe, *Assoc. Archit. Soc. Rep. Pap.*, **24** (1897), 381-448

Davies, D.S., 1913   Ancient Stone Crosses in Kesteven, *Lincolnshire Notes and Queries*, **12**/5 (Jan. 1913), 129-50

Davies, D.S., 1926   Pre-conquest Carved Stones in Lincolnshire, *Archaeol. J.*, **33** (1926), 1-20

Everson, P., and   *The British Academy Corpus of Anglo-Saxon Stone Sculpture*, **5**: *Lincoln-*
    Stocker, D.A.,   *shire*
    forthcoming
Gilmour, B.J., and   *St Mark's Church and Cemetery*. Archaeology of Lincoln **13**/1, Lon-
    Stocker, D.A., 1986   don: Council for British Archaeology, 1986
Greenhill, F.A., 1986   *Monumental Incised Slabs in the County of Lincoln*. Newport Pagnell: Coales, 1986

Hartley, J.S., and   *The Religious Houses of Stamford*. Stamford Survey Group Report **2**,
    Rogers, A., 1974   Nottingham: University Department of Adult Education, 1974
Hill, J.W.F., 1948   *Medieval Lincoln*. Cambridge: University Press, 1948
Hodgett, G.A., 1975   *Tudor Lincolnshire*. History of Lincolnshire, **6**, Lincoln, 1975
Jessiman, I. McD., 1958   The Piscina in the English Medieval Church, *J. Br. Archaeol. Assoc.*, ser. 3, **20-21** (1957-58), 53-71
Jope, E.M., 1964   The Saxon building stone industry in Southern England, *Medieval Archaeol.*, **8** (1964), 91-118

Mahany, C.,   *Excavations at Stamford Castle.*
    forthcoming
Moore, E., 1861   Crowland Abbey, *Assoc. Archit. Soc. Rep. Pap.*, **6** (1861), 20-27
Morris, R.K., 1976   Kirk Hammerton church, the tower and the fabric, *Archaeol. J.*, **133** (1976), 95-103

Oakeshott, W., 1959   *Classical Inspiration in Medieval Art*. London: Chapman & Hall, 1959
Panofsky, E., 1939   *Studies in Iconology*. New York: Oxford University Press, 1939
Panofsky, E., 1944   Renaissance and Renascences, *Kenyon Review*, **6** (1944), 201-36
Parry, G., 1981   *The Golden Age Restor'd: The Culture of the Stuart Court*. Manchester: University Press, 1981
Parsons, D., 1986   Sacrarium: ablution drains in early medieval churches, *The Anglo-Saxon Church: Papers . . . in honour of Dr H.M. Taylor*, eds. L.A.S. Butler and R.K. Morris, 105-20. Res. Rep. **60**, London: Council for British Archaeology, 1986

Pevsner, N., and   *Lincolnshire*. The Buildings of England, Harmondsworth: Penguin,
    Harris, J., 1964   1964.

Pevsner, N., and Williamson, E., 1983 — *County Durham*, 2nd ed. The Buildings of England, Harmondsworth: Penguin, 1983

Roberts, D.L., 1984 — John Thorpe's drawings for Thornton College, the house of Sir Vincent Skinner, *Lincolnshire History and Archaeology*, **19** (1984), 57-63

Rodwell, K., and Rodwell, W., 1982 — St. Peter's Church Barton-on-Humber: Excavation and Structural Survey 1978-1981, *Antiq. J.*, **42** (1982), 283-315

Sherley-Price, L., and Latham, R.E. (eds), 1968 — *Bede: A History of the English Church and People*. 2nd ed., Harmondsworth: Penguin, 1968

Stocker, D.A., 1986 — The Sepulchral Fragments, in Gilmour & Stocker 1986, 55-82

Stocker, D.A., 1990 — Archaeology and the Reformation: a case study of the redistribution of building materials in Lincoln, 1520-1560. *Lincolnshire History and Archaeology*, **25**, (1990), forthcoming

Sutherland, D.S., and Parsons, D., 1984 — The petrological contribution to the survey of All Saints' church Brixworth, Northamptonshire: an interim study, *J. Br. Archaeol. Assoc.*, **137** (1984), 45-64

Swinnerton, H., and Kent, P.E., 1949 — *The Geology of Lincolnshire*. Lincoln: Ruddock, 1949

Taylor, H.M., and Taylor, J., 1965 — *Anglo-Saxon Architecture*, 2 vols. Cambridge: University Press, 1965

Thomas, K., 1973 — *Religion and the Decline of Magic: Studies in Popular beliefs in sixteenth- and seventeenth-century England*. Harmondsworth: Penguin, 1973

Wilson, V., 1958 — *East Yorkshire and Lincolnshire*. British Regional Geology, London: HMSO, 1958

Zarnecki, G., 1988 — *Romanesque Lincoln: the sculpture of the Cathedral*. Lincoln: Honywood, 1988

Chapter 7

Burnt Stone in a Saxon church and its Implications

Diana S. Sutherland

The distribution of burnt stone in the fabric of All Saints' church, Brixworth, provides evidence of conflagration in situ *where coherent areas of masonry have been affected; but the more widespread occurrence of isolated burnt blocks at random throughout the building points to the use of reclaimed stone as standard practice here in successive phases of middle and late Saxon building.*

The fabric of All Saints' church, Brixworth

The well-known parish church of All Saints, Brixworth, in Northamptonshire, comprises a large nave, choir and clerestory mostly dating from the 8th and perhaps the 9th centuries (illustration 28); the lower part of the west tower represents a remnant of the original narthex, and the lower levels of the apse and ambulatory may perhaps be assigned to the same period, as can the extensive remains of the porticus, subsequently demolished, that have been revealed by excavation (Audouy, 1984). A substantial part of the present building thus consists of middle Saxon masonry. The stair turret and tower rising above the 4m of earlier narthex, with the remnants of Saxon work in the apse (rebuilt in the 19th century by the Reverend C.F. Watkins), date from a major reconstruction in the late Saxon or possibly early Norman period, 11th or perhaps early 12th century (Parsons 1978; Sutherland & Parsons 1984, table 1).

A petrological survey carried out in the last few years by the Brixworth Archaeological Research Committee, under the direction and supervision of David Parsons, has gathered much valuable information about the use of batches of stone in successive stages of the building (Sutherland & Parsons 1984). An extraordinarily varied collection of stone is found in the lower courses of the early masonry, up to 4m above the ground, including several different kinds of igneous rocks from Leicestershire: microdiorite from the hills south-west of Leicester such as Croft and Stoney Stanton, the dioritic rock known as mark-fieldite, banded volcanic ashes (tuffs) and Swithland slates from Charnwood Forest north-west of Leicester, and rocks from Mountsorrel north of Leicester. Other non-local stone found in these early batches at Brixworth includes Triassic and Carboniferous sandstones from the north or west, and Jurassic limestone thought to be from the Towcester area. Here is a mixture of at least twelve different types of stone from five or more separate distant sources, in masonry only 4m high. The local glacial drift does not contain this assemblage of stone and the lower church masonry is more reasonably explained as re-used material,

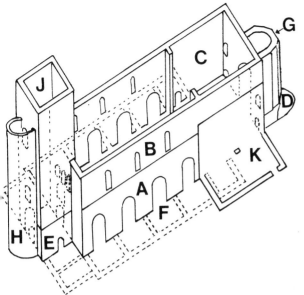

28a. Diagrammatic plan and elevation of All Saints' church, Brixworth (based on an axonometric drawing of Parsons 1978b). A-F are essentially Anglo-Saxon, including some 19th-century reconstruction (such areas are indicated by dashed outlines in later detailed figures of elevations): A = nave; B = clerestory; C = choir; D = ambulatory; E = central compartment of narthex, forming the base of the tower; F = porticus (south side conjectural, north side excavated). G-J are late Saxon or early Norman: G = apse (possibly Saxon rebuilding of an earlier apse; much of the present apse is 19th-century); H = stair turret; J = tower (the upper part of which is 14th-century). Most later medieval features omitted; K = existing Verdun Chapel (c.1300) as modified in the 19th century, shown in outline only.

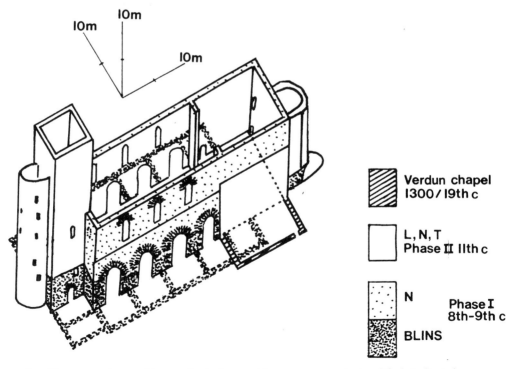

Verdun chapel
1300/19th c

L, N, T
Phase II 11th c

N
Phase I
8th-9th c
BLINS

28b. The same view, with petrological assemblages, very much simplified, indicated on external walls and plans of the demolished porticus and narthex. Materials (given in the key) are coded as follows: B = brick; L = Jurassic limestone; I = igneous and associated rocks from Leicestershire; N = varieties of Northampton Sand; S = Triassic and Carboniferous sandstones; T = tufa.

probably from at least two sources: Roman Leicester (where existing masonry closely resembles the Leicestershire assemblage at Brixworth) and, judging by the textures of various limestones, perhaps Towcester. A sandstone bearing a Latin inscription (Sutherland & Parsons 1984, 51; Hassall & Tomlin 1985, 324), and carved Roman architectural fragments found in excavations at Brixworth (Blagg 1978), together with the large quantity of Roman brick used for arches and bonding courses, confirm the link with Roman sources. Indeed the architectural features at Brixworth bear such a striking resemblance to the standing Roman walling at Leicester, each with their brick arches supported on large sandstone blocks, that one could reasonably suggest that the 8th-century Saxons were making a deliberate attempt to copy the architectural example and construction methods of the Romans, even perhaps attempting to dismantle, transport and re-erect an actual Roman building.

Amongst the exotic material in the lower assemblage is a certain amount of local stone, varieties of the Northampton Sand making up an estimated 29% of the masonry. Does this represent material quarried nearby, augmenting the stone brought in from a distance? Moreover, does the dramatic change from the exotic lower assemblage (at about 3 to 4m above ground level) indicate the point when, perhaps for a new building season, stone was obtained entirely from local quarried sources instead of bringing reclaimed stone from afar? Examination of the Northampton Sand blocks both in the lower assemblage and above suggests that the answer is probably not so simple. The Northampton Sand walling, particularly above 4m, is by no means homogeneous; unlike, for example, the 19th-century facing along the base of the north side of the nave, which is a recognisable batch of shelly ironstone (coded N_8 in the survey), the Saxon walling consists of part-courses and single blocks of any of nine different rock-types belonging to the Northampton Sand. Although a large quarry in the Northampton Sand Formation (Ironstone and overlying Variable Beds) could supply perhaps four or five varieties from the successive strata, some pattern of reasonably uniform batches would be expected; and a quarry on the scale of, say, Duston (north-west of Northampton) in the 19th century is not an appropriate model for Saxon Brixworth. For the stone to be newly quarried one would need to postulate the working of many small pits around Brixworth. The possible extent of primary stone extraction is assessed below.

Even a brief examination of the external fabric at Brixworth reveals a great number of stones affected by burning. Along the north elevation of the nave, for example, above the offset that once may have supported an aisle roof, is a continuous band of deeply reddened stone, seven courses high, broken only by the 19th-century patching where a post-Saxon medieval window was removed (illustration 29). This band of reddening was, without doubt, caused by the burning *in situ* of an adjacent roof. A few years ago, a barn wall in another Northamptonshire village, composed of similar stone also from the Northampton Sand, was reddened in this way by the burning of the adjacent thatched roof in a fierce blaze lasting a few hours. Here the reddening affected the wall in contact with the glowing thatch and below, but not above it (colour plate IV).

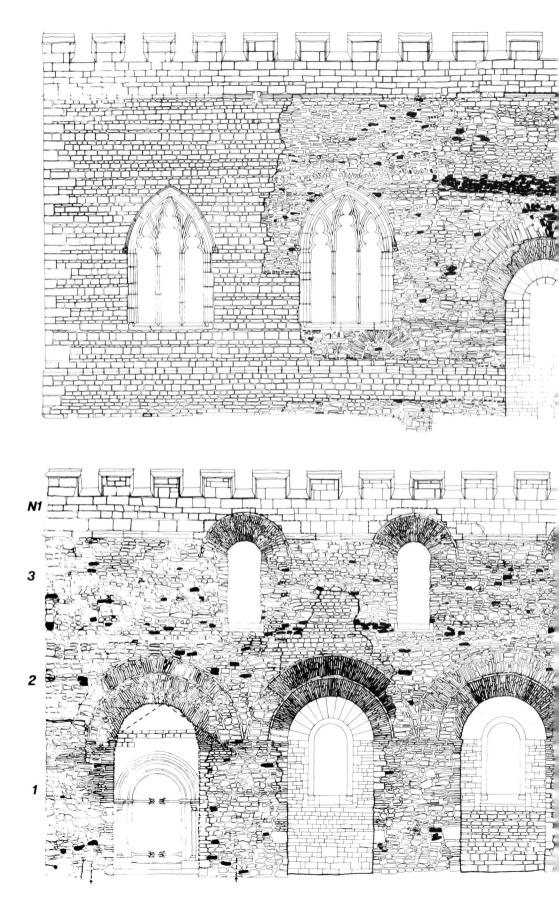

3

2

1

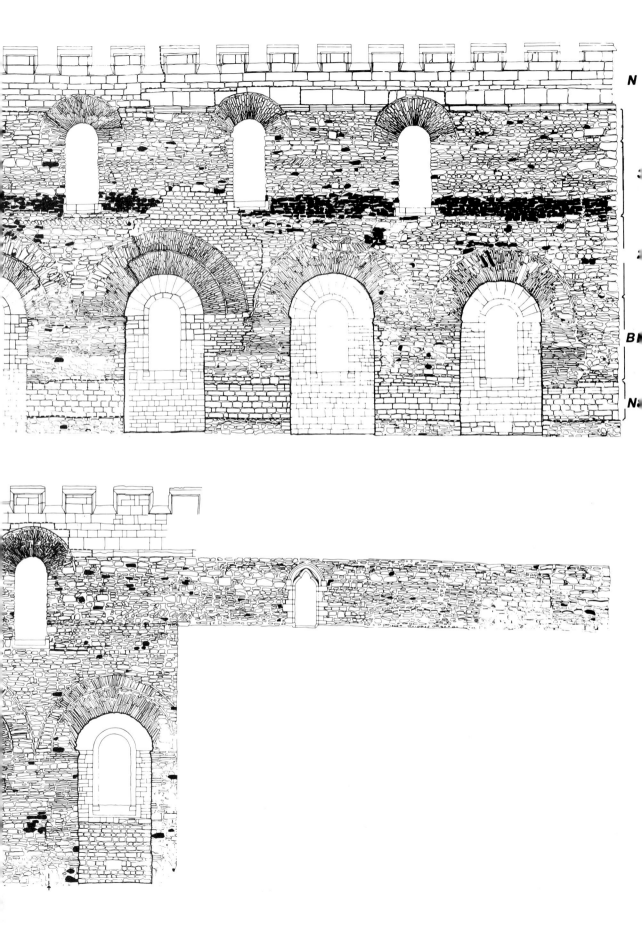

N

B

N

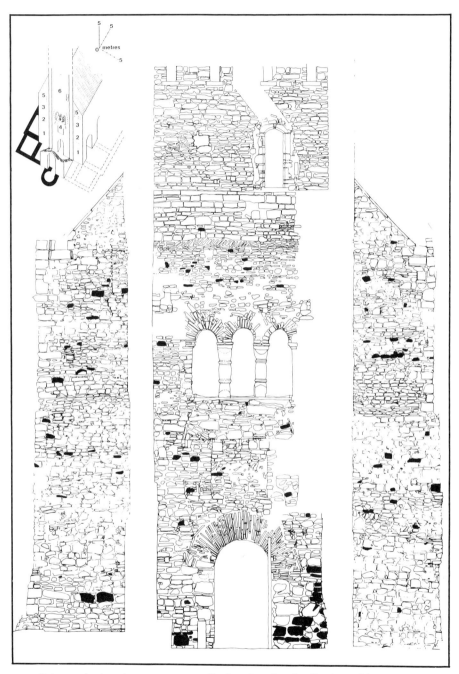

31. Brixworth church, west nave wall, showing the distribution of burnt stone.
Inset: numbers in outlined areas refer to successive stages of building: 1-3 = Phase I
(?8th-9th centuries); 4 = Phase II reconstruction; 5 = upper-level renovation,
possibly but not necessarily related to Phase II; 6 = upper-level
reconstruction of the tower area (14th century).

Comparison suggests that the Brixworth aisle roof may have been made of thatch having the thickness of the reddened stone.

On the south elevation of the nave, where there is a similar offset, there is little obvious sign of burning, but the petrological survey has shown a discontinuous band of reddening three or four courses high (illustration 30), particularly notice-able in the central section (where it is broken by an area of 19th-century patching). Perhaps the roof of this aisle for the most part collapsed soon after the start of the blaze, hanging long enough in the central section to cause more intense reddening of the wall. In the inside of the tower, the west nave wall shows a patch of burnt stone (limestone as well as Northampton Sand) perhaps caused by the burning of fallen timbers (illustration 31).

Many types of stone are affected in this way by burning, the reddening being caused by the oxidation of even small quantities of iron minerals to red-brown ferric oxide. The ferruginous rocks of the Northampton Sand show it particularly well, but so too do pale limestones, which can become quite pink. The igneous rocks in the lower assemblage do not show any obvious signs of burning, nor in general do the Triassic sandstones which are red with ferric oxide to start with, although enhanced patchy reddening has been detected in some of them low in the west nave wall.

Apart from the areas of burnt stone which can be ascribed to burning *in situ*, on every wall there are many other stones reddened by burning, most of them randomly distributed and occurring as isolated blocks surrounded by stones unaffected in any way by fire. The burning of these individual blocks cannot have occurred *in situ*, and it has to be inferred that the stones were already burnt at the time they were incorporated into the building. The distribution of these burnt stones is interesting, and relevant to an assessment of sources of stone in the early medieval period.

The middle Saxon building

The four walls of the nave, choir and clerestory (illustrations 29-32) can be considered as a group, in terms of assemblages or architectural levels common to each.

1: The lowest assemblage

This is best seen in the west wall of the nave, where there appears to have been little subsequent reconstruction at this level (though Professor Rosemary Cramp has suggested that the carved limestone cross fragment to the south of the tower, being probably of 8th- or 9th-century date, is intrusive [Sutherland & Parsons 1984, 61, table 1]). The assemblage consists of brick, limestone, igneous and associated Leicestershire rocks, Northampton Sand and other sandstones (B-L-I-N-S). There are a few burnt blocks in addition to those apparently affected by burning at ground level inside the tower (to the right of the doorway in illustration 31). Two are red sandstones (north of the tower) which may previously have been burnt, but which in any case are not local, and are certainly reclaimed material. The other random burnt blocks at this level are Northampton Sand.

The nave piers of the north wall, where they are unaffected by 19th-century work (illustration 29), also contain a few burnt blocks of Northampton Sand. The south wall includes burnt blocks of at least three types of Northampton Sand, and two types of limestone, all of them randomly distributed. Burnt blocks of Northampton Sand and Jurassic limestone were also found in the excavated porticus to the north.

At foundation level, in the area excavated by Audouy in 1981-82, the mortared aggregate mostly consists of small broken pieces, up to 100mm, of sandy ironstone ('N'); only one piece was found burnt. The otherwise uniform appearance suggests that this could have been freshly dug local stone. Towards the west end, however, the foundations of porticus and narthex include conspicuous amounts of limestone and brick with occasional igneous lumps amongst the ironstone, indicating that batches of assorted reclaimed stone were already on site.

2: Second-level nave masonry

Above the first assemblage is a marked petrological break, but no evidence of a roof, or of burning at this level. The masonry continues with varieties of Northampton Sand, devoid of any exotic igneous rocks, sandstones or limestones. The remarkable change in rock-type can be traced all round the nave and choir at a height of almost 4m above ground at the west end, approximately 3m in the choir area to the east.

The upper limit of this second-level assemblage is taken at the level of the clerestory offset that marks the aisle roof, although there is no obvious petrological break here; as a reference line it can be traced between offset levels each side of the west wall of the nave, and along the south nave as far as the Verdun chapel externally; along the north nave the offset terminates against the upstanding choir wall, but the reference line is continued arbitrarily through the choir at the same

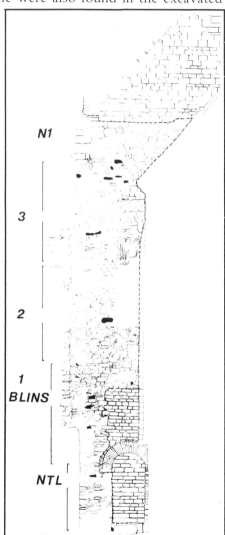

32. Brixworth church: stone survey of the east choir wall, of which only the area south of the apse is pre-19th-century, showing burnt stone. The restored area is indicated by a dashed outline. To the left is part of the wall of the 14th-century Verdun Chapel.

level as far as the rebuilt section in the north-east corner. On the east choir wall, south of the apse, the arbitrary level is taken at the same height, which is more or less level with the springing of the arch head of the window (illustration 32).

Excluding the areas known to be rebuilt by Watkins in the 19th century, the different rock-types in the second assemblage are distributed as follows (figures in percentage):

N   (mixed-type sandy and/or calcareous ironstone, or unspecified), 70.2-
       42.4
N_3 (more obviously calcareous), 33.5-19.1
N_1 (ferruginous sandstone), 7.8-1.0
N_5 (crinoidal, calcareous, flat), 5.3-2.0
N_6 (N with calcite seams), 4.8-1.0
N_4 (dark, ferruginous), 3.9-0.4
$N_{5'}$ (a ferruginous variety of N_5), 3.5-1.8

and only rare N_7 or N_8.

The west nave wall contains 14 separate, recognisably burnt stones; most are 'N', one N_3, and one N_5. Even if the distribution of N_4 is taken into consideration (N_4 being dark and oxidised and possibly including some that are burnt), there is no grouping that might obviously be related, say, to the burning of a narthex roof.

The north elevation (illustration 29) contains over 90 burnt stones in the second-level assemblage below the clerestory. Some of them occur in clusters above three of the arcade openings (the fourth having been rebuilt), and could perhaps be regarded as related to the time of burning of the aisle roof. Nevertheless, there are also sufficient random burnt blocks to suggest that batches of stone used for the building included many that were already burnt. The south elevation (illustration 30) contains some 18 isolated burnt stones at this level. In the east choir wall, only part of which remains in its pre-Watkins condition, one stone (N) is burnt at the level of assemblage 2.

Around the nave and choir at this level, there are equal numbers burnt of N and N_3, a few of N_5, and one N_8. The inclusion of the few N_4 at this level does not alter the pattern significantly.

3a and b: The third-level (clerestory) assemblages
Architecturally the next level is defined as the clerestory up as far as a region of modified masonry under the parapet. Petrologically it is not as uniform as it might appear, there being all kinds of Northampton Sand, fairly well coursed, but consisting of assorted batches of different-sized blocks and varied assemblages. There is a case for dividing it into two, the upper half being recognised by the incoming of conspicuous amounts of $N_{5'}$, a dark variety of N_5, often in large blocks. The division is fairly distinct on the north and west walls, where it is recognisable at 16.5m above the reference datum, but on the south wall the batches are rather different, with an area of masonry characterised by much

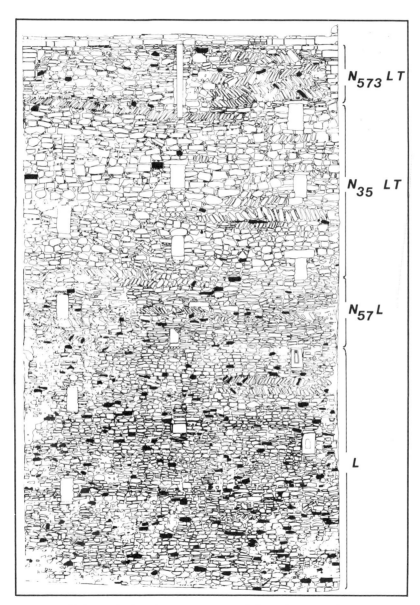

N_{573} L T

N_{35} L T

N_{57} L

L

33. Brixworth church: stone survey of the stair turret, showing distribution of burnt stone.

calcareous sandy and oolitic N_7 at middle clerestory level, and $N_{5'}$ coming in higher up, more irregularly.

For this assorted masonry to be freshly quarried stone, a number of pits would have to have been in work. However, the distribution of burnt stone in the clerestory, apart from aisle roof levels, points to the continuing use of batches that included already burnt stone. All varieties of Northampton Sand occur as random burnt blocks, with the possible exception of N_6. N_6 is a mixed-type ironstone having seams of crystalline calcite, and is known to occur within 200m south of the church where it may well have been dug. Perhaps it should be noted, however, that blocks without visible calcite seams would be coded 'N', and since many of these are burnt, N_6 could have the same history of re-use.

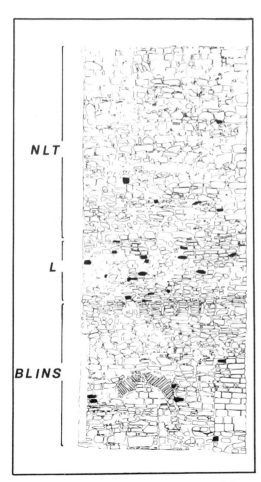

34. Brixworth church: stone survey of the north elevation of the tower, showing burnt stone.

The Phase II reconstruction

Much later, in perhaps the 11th century, the masonry of the narthex was raised to form the tower, the stair turret being built against it and the great west door partially blocked; the central arch over the west nave doorway was blocked and a new triple arch with baluster shafts inserted at a higher level. The new consignment of stone brought in for this work was Blisworth Limestone, which can be seen in the lower section of the stair turret. ('Blisworth Limestone' is the geological name for the rock once called Great Oolite Limestone which is widespread in south and east Northamptonshire – it is not restricted to Blisworth). It is a uniform batch of naturally varying limestone textures, and might well be thought to be newly quarried stone, except for the abundance of random burnt pink limestone (colour plate V; illustration 33). It is similar to limestone from south of Northampton. Above 15m above datum, the assemblage changes with the incoming of Northampton Sand in mainly flat blocks of calcareous, crinoidal and sandy types coded N_5 and N_7. In illustration 33 most of the burnt stone is limestone, but there is also burnt Northampton Sand: N_1, N_3, N_4, N_5 and N_7. Again, N_6 is not seen burnt. The foundations of the turret (excavated by

Audouy in 1981-82) consisted of very large blocks of N and N$_6$, roughly trimmed, overlain by pitched blocks of limestone that included burnt ones.

Above about 17m above datum, tufa makes its appearance in the turret construction. This very porous limestone was used extensively in this phase, for stair vaulting internally, and for quoins, window edging and walling in the tower and turret and similarly in the apse; it was also used in the new arch heads of the triple-arched opening in the west wall. There is no evidence so far of its having been burnt, nor any other indication of possible previous use.

The tower above the BLINS assemblage (of earlier date) is petrologically similar to the turret, and shows a similar pattern of burnt stone (illustration 34). Again, most burnt stones are limestone, but some Northampton Sand burnt blocks occur in the earlier BLINS assemblage and above.

In the Saxon remains of the apse and ambulatory at the east end, a few random burnt stones are recognisable; they are limestone and varieties of Northampton Sand: N, N$_3$ and a piece of N$_6$.

Discussion

The occurrence of assorted materials from different sources, some demonstrably of Roman origin, in the lower assemblage points to re-use of stone reclaimed from existing buildings or ruins, the rock-types indicating that the likely sources were up to some 30 miles (48km) distant. The presence of random blocks of burnt ironstone at this level suggests that even some of the local material is probably re-used. The Roman villa that lay less than 1km to the north, built partly of ironstone, may have furnished some local stone, including perhaps burnt blocks, but it is worth noting that the bricks of the villa are not the same as those in the church, and tufa, which occurs at the villa, is not found in the church until the later reconstruction of Phase II. There were no doubt other buildings existing locally, of which we have no record.

In view of the lengthy journeys undertaken to obtain stone in the initial stage of construction at Brixworth, it is reasonable to suppose that there was little organised quarrying locally at the time. North and west of the church the Northampton Sand at the surface is the pale, calcareous N$_5$; this is the natural rock that forms the floor of the ambulatory. It is scarcely seen in the lower masonry. The type that was used is sandy ironstone (N), as broken rock in the foundations, and as generally poorly shaped rubble in the masonry. Such rock could have been obtained by digging lower on the western valley slopes, where surface outcrops would be poor in quality and suitable only for rough rubble. Some 200m south of the church the rock is ironstone with calcite seams, a source of N$_6$; but, though during excavation for roadworks there was some indication of former quarrying here, N$_6$ is rare in the lower masonry. It appears in the second assemblage onwards, and is much in evidence in Phase II. There is therefore little evidence of 'quarrying' in the Northampton Sand when the building began in about the 8th century; perhaps there was merely some superficial 'digging' of ironstone for foundations and rubble.

In successive stages of construction of the nave (8th or 9th century) there is still little indication that quarrying was undertaken to any great extent. If the stone immediately surrounding the church (N_5) were being exploited, one would expect whole courses or areas of N_5 masonry to appear in the building (as one sees in field walls today). But N_5 occurs only as random blocks in assorted masonry, and isolated blocks of N_5 are burnt. The same observations apply to most other varieties of Northampton Sand obtainable within about 3 miles (5km) of Brixworth.

Where, for example, there is some evidence for a 'batch' of stone, as with $N_{5'}$, the presence of burnt blocks argues against its being newly quarried. The possibility of actual quarrying of building stone by underground mining, involving firing methods in the manner described by Agricola for metalliferous mining, is unlikely; there is no evidence of such methods at this time, for example, at Raunds (Cadman, below, Ch. 12). It is far more likely, particularly in view of the mixed nature of the assemblages, that the stone is re-used from previous buildings. Many of the rock-types in the third-stage assemblage (with $N_{5'}$) are to be found near Boughton, 3 miles (5km) to the south; but the buildings being robbed may not necessarily have been at the site of the original quarrying.

Some of the arguments for persistent reclamation are summarised as follows:
1) the absence of homogeneous courses or batches of particular rock-types
2) the presence of mixed rock-types from several sources in single courses of masonry
3) the assorted sizes of blocks in single and adjacent courses
4) the presence of random, isolated burnt blocks of almost all kinds of Northampton Sand.

It is not easy to judge how much of the Northampton Sand may have been dug for use alongside the reclaimed material in the nave assemblages; perhaps one can assume a limited amount of continued digging of 'N' and the introduction of freshly dug 'N_6'. What is surprising is that when the Phase II reconstruction was carried out, in perhaps the 11th century, reclaimed stone was used yet again. Though the material was not a mixed batch of stone (it was initially a uniform assemblage of limestone for the stair turret), and the blocks were of similar size, they were not local, and they were very much burnt. When Northampton Sand was brought in, some of these blocks were also burnt, presumably re-used. However, in this phase, there is evidence that selection of stone for particular functions may have involved deliberate quarrying. In the setting of huge blocks of N_6 in the foundation of the turret and for the ambulatory steps, and the extensive use of tufa for the vaulting of the staircase (as well as the triple-arch heads, and elsewhere) there is no indication that either the tufa or the N_6 is secondhand. There appears to have been purposeful quarrying on a significant scale in Phase II. Alongside this was the continued practice of employing reclaimed stone for general walling, quite acceptable for any wall that was to be concealed in rendering. It is clear that from middle Saxon times stone blocks became a highly valued commodity; lengthy transportation was undertaken, and re-use of material from obsolete buildings was normal procedure; a practice which of course continues to the present day.

ACKNOWLEDGEMENTS

The work of the Brixworth Archaeological Research Committee was instigated by the Rev. J.N. Chubb, and further encouraged by his successor the Rev. A.J. Watkins and by the Parochial Church Council, to all of whom we are grateful. The outline stone drawings were prepared by Kathleen Harman from 1:10 site drawings, and reproduced by the Central Photographic Unit of the University of Leicester.

BIBLIOGRAPHY

Audouy, M., 1984	Excavations at the church of All Saints, Brixworth, *J. Br. Archaeol. Assoc.*, **137** (1984), 1-44
Blagg, T.F.C., 1978	A decorated Roman cornice from Brixworth, Northamptonshire, *J. Br. Archaeol. Assoc.*, **131** (1978), 110-12
Hassell, M.W.C., and Tomlin, R.S.O., 1985	Inscriptions, *Britannia*, **16** (1985), 324
Parsons, D., 1978a	Barrel-vaulted staircases in England and on the continent, with special reference to Brixworth church, Northamptonshire, *Zeitschrift für Archäologie des Mittelalters*, **6** (1978), 129-47
Parsons, D., 1978b	Past history and present research at All Saints' church, Brixworth, *Northamptonshire Past and Present*, **6** (1978), 61-71
Sutherland, D.S., and Parsons, D., 1984	The petrological contribution to the survey of All Saints' church, Brixworth, Northamptonshire: an interim study, *J. Br. Archaeol. Assoc.*, **137** (1984), 45-64

Chapter 8

Ballast and Building Stone:
A Discussion

P. C. Buckland and Jon Sadler

Maritime trade in the Old World has often been elucidated by considering the distribution of archaeological finds from particular centres. Many of the principal commodities were of low density and required the ballasting of ships. Saleable ballast, frequently stone or other building materials, was widely dispersed as a result of this. The evidence for the movement and use of building stone in the classical, medieval and later periods is reviewed. The identification of stone from both shipwrecks and archaeological sites, although seldom examined, provides a potential source of archaeological information about trading contacts.

'Then there was the launching full of difficulty; there was shifting of ballast above and below until two thirds was submerged'

Utnapishtim's account of the *Flood* to Gilgamesh, 3rd millennium BC
(Sandars 1960)

Introduction

It is perhaps inevitable that, in the study of building material, most attention has been given to those sources which produce the best ashlar (e.g. Arkell 1947; North 1930), to the neglect of the less obvious materials, which often form the bulk of structures and may be the only aspect remaining in the robber trenches and cobbled surfaces of archaeological sites. Rarely has such debris been retained or drawn to the attention of the all too infrequently consulted geologist. Yet, in the maritime context, the cobbles, rubble, sand and gravel provide a potential source of information about trading contacts after the principal commodities have long since decayed. Many of the trade items of the classical and medieval world, from stockfish to silk, were of low density and shipment of any quantity required the ballasting of ships with sufficient heavy materials to ensure stability, a practice equally necessary when a vessel was travelling without cargo. As McGrail (1989) has recently pointed out, the greater the freeboard, the more the need for ballast in the hull of the ship and, from the earliest development of boats with some superstructure, a knowledge of ballast requirements must have formed an essential part of the mariners' art. The earliest archaeological evidence comes from the Bronze Age wreck off Cape Gelidonya, southern Turkey, where, in addition to a cargo of copper ingots, 116kg of ballast stones were recovered (Bass 1967). The ingots themselves need not have been the primary merchandise, forming, like the wrought iron bars of later classical Mediterranean wrecks (Gibbins & Parker 1986,

114

290–93), and the cast iron of the sailing ships engaged in the post-medieval Baltic trade (Hildebrand 1960) excellent saleable ballast. It is this latter category which is pertinent to the stone trade.

Despite the suggestion that ballast, saleable or otherwise, is essential to all ships with substantial freeboard, contemporary references are so sparse that its use has been questioned by several modern authors. Briggs (1976) wholly dismisses ballast as a factor in stone distribution in England. Morrison (1976) doubted whether the Greek trireme was ballasted except when either being towed without its crew or when damaged, although the recent replica did require ballasting for its sea trials (McGrail, personal communication). In contrast, Foley and others (1982) suggest a ballast figure of 13,100kg, 40% more than the wooden weight of the vessel. Rouge (1981) states that the ships of the Ancient World, with their only moderately protruding keels and rather flat bottoms, would have to be loaded with ballast. Similar problems exist with medieval shipping. Christensen (in Granlund 1970) argues that most Nordic ships managed without ballast, taking it on board only in bad weather, rather a difficult action in mid-Atlantic. In part, however, interpretative problems relate to confusion between warships and merchantmen; in the later medieval period the two functions coalesce, with the need for heavily armed merchant shipping and the development of the cannon. Classical trade was not carried out in triremes, nor was the Norse Atlantic route the preserve of longships (Marcus 1980).

The classical world

Both Greek and Latin have words for ballast, ἕρμα and *saburra* respectively, and some hint of the scale of movement is indicated by the existence of a guild of ballast handlers, *Saburrarii*, at Rome's port of Ostia (Laures 1986), where the provision of loads for ships returning to their ports, having delivered cereals, olive oil and other consumables, must have been a continual problem. Although post-medieval sources show that sand (Lindroth 1957), even earth (Leslie 1890), was often used, its tendency to go thixotropic when disturbed in a wet condition, and problems in handling meant that it was not a preferred material. Sand is referred to at Ostia (Rouge 1981, 69) but stone, either worked or rubble, had the advantage of being potentially salable at the other end. Rocks from the Campania and Rome's demolition debris might therefore be expected to form a proportion of Sicilian, Cyrenaican and Nile Delta Roman deposits. During periods of urban expansion, however, the pattern of movement may be obscured by the re-export of marbles and other decorative stones brought from a variety of sources through Rome. The early 3rd-century AD Punta Scifo wreck from near Crotone, southern Italy, loaded with Asiatic marble and alabaster (Pensabene 1978), presumably reflects a loss during importation but it is tempting to see in the Mahdia wreck, a 1st-century loss off the coast of Tunisia, with its 270 tonnes of marble (Casson 1960), a grain ship returning in saleable ballast. Italian marble, principally Carrara, is apparently rare in North Africa. At Lepcis Magna, Proconnesian marble from the Bosphorus is the most frequent (Walda & Walker 1984) and the Rome connection might have to be sought in smaller, less commonly examined materials. Peacock's recent study (1980a; 1986) of the distribution of Roman millstones from Orvieto in Umbria provides a useful indication of the movement of an ideal salable ballast item, presumably shipped down the Tiber for loading at Ostia. Similar relationships in terms of ballast must have existed between Athens and her granaries in the Crimea. Part of the available space would have been occupied by finished goods and the export of Pentelic marble to the Black Sea colonies may have occurred but less obvious materials must also have been involved.

The continual need to retrim loads by replacing sold cargo with additional ballast during coastal shipping and trading would impose a secondary redistribution pattern. The wreck from Cavalière bay, Var, southern France, of the end of the 2nd century BC, with a small cargo of amphorae and heavily ballasted with 'volcanic stone' (Liou 1975), may represent a coasting vessel approaching the end of its voyage, but a better indication of the cosmopolitan nature of classical coastal trading is provided by the contents of the Le Dramont D wreck from the same region, with materials from Syria, Cyrenaica (?), the Aegean, Italy and Spain (Parker 1980a); associated ballast movements, evident in wreck assemblages and on-shore coastal archaeology, have yet to be studied. Material from ballast accounts for some otherwise enigmatic occurrences of artifacts. Roman coins from the south coast of Iceland (Eldjárn 1974) probably came from medieval or later wrecks rather than Roman ones. The presence of sherds of samian, initially from Roman Gaul, in the ballast of a 17th-century wreck off Bermuda (Noel Hume 1982) argues for caution in the interpretation of casual finds!

Querns or millstones have considerable advantages as ballast for not only are they likely to be eminently salable at the destination, but they may also be of a fairly standard size, easily handled and their shape made them unlikely to shift in the event of a storm. They are therefore not infrequent finds from wrecks. Twenty-nine millstones, probably from the island of Nisyros, off the south-west point of Turkey, weighing 1,650kg, topped out with cobbles and sand, formed the ballast of the 3rd-century BC Kyrenia wreck from northern Cyprus (Katzev 1980). A wreck of *c*.150-140 BC, containing Campanian amphorae from off the Catalonian coast of Spain, was ballasted with twelve millstones, ten of local lava from Ampurias, one from Agde in southern France and another from Etna (Williams-Thorpe & Thorpe 1987); the range of rocks might suggest the trimming of loads from ballast wharves. In Roman Britain, the presence of an unfinished Millstone Grit topstone of a quern in the Blackfriars, London, boat, otherwise loaded with Kentish Rag (Marsden 1967), is best explained in terms of trimming ballast. In more general terms, the ease with which Niedermendig lava querns from the Middle Rhine penetrated the eastern English markets, particularly in the Roman period (Peacock 1980a), geographically more easily served by Pennine Millstone Grit products, could be the result of the subsidy provided by ballast transport. The more direct use of this rock as ballast is suggested by its apparent incorporation in the footings of the precinct wall of the Temple of Claudius in Colchester (Hull 1958, 169). Ballast has provided an explanation for the suite of

Cornish, Channel Island and Breton rocks incorporated in 1st-century structures at the Fishbourne villa on the Sussex coast (Sanderson, in Cunliffe 1971). The paucity of likely exports from the Channel Islands must have inevitably resulted in ships travelling in ballast but a direct connection between the Islands and Fishbourne need not be argued, the whole assemblage being the end result of a complex of shipping and ballast movements. The high-sided ships of the Veneti of Brittany, described by Caesar (III, 13), would have required considerable ballast and their trading activities, both across the Channel and beyond, should be as detectable in the rocks of pre-Conquest sites like Hengistbury Head (Cunliffe 1987) as in their pottery (Peacock 1971).

As much ballast would merely have been dumped, the accumulation, over several thousand years of trade, of a wide suite of rocks in coastal sediments is inevitable. The problem of interpretation in the archaeological context around Britain is complicated by the reworking of the deposits of Quaternary glaciation, tills, fluvioglacial gravels, ice-rafted debris and dropstones. The mix of 'erratics' in, for example, Chesil Beach, the tombolo along the Dorset coast (Arkell 1949) must include much former ballast and the presence of far-travelled rocks in Flandrian coastal sediments should not be used uncritically in support of theories of glaciation (cf. Kellaway *et al.* 1975). The point has been effectively considered by Kidson and Bowen (1976) in relation to the English Channel.

The Fishbourne villa assemblage is not restricted to rocks from either side of the Channel and two cobbles from Neronian to early Flavian deposits are of a foraminiferal limestone of Mediterranean origin (Sanderson, in Cunliffe 1971). In contrast with the water-worn pebbles, a wide range of worked decorative stones from northern France and the Mediterranean occurs. Such finds are not confined to the atypical palace site at Fishbourne, occurring as *opus sectile* work on a number of villas (Clarke 1983, 211), as well as at major urban centres, at London (Pritchard 1986), Colchester (Crummy 1984), Lincoln (Dunham, in Coppack 1973) and York (Buckland 1988a). Between these sites, practically the whole range of decorative stones which occurs in Rome, from Egyptian Porphyries and Asiatic marbles to Greek, Italian and North African marbles (Gnoli 1971), is represented and much must reflect conscious deliberate import rather than adventitious disposal of saleable ballast. The few battered fragments from York, however (Buckland 1988a), may be the result of incidental ballast movement. Lynn (1984), in reviewing Irish occurrences of porphyry, has also raised the possibility of such small pieces being post-Roman pilgrims' curios and Stevenson (in Curle 1982, 46) has made a similar suggestion for examples from Scotland.

On a more local basis, the occasional use of Jurassic limestones in York has been interpreted as a result of ballast off-loading (Buckland 1978; 1984). More perplexing is the incorporation of blocks of barytes in the core of the fortress wall near the Multangular Tower, York (Buckland 1988b). Naturally, the mineral occurs as gangue in lead veins and the nearest source would be in the Yorkshire Dales (Dunham 1974). As lead is likely to have been moved downstream in relatively small, flat-bottomed lighters, it is unlikely to have arrived in ballast from that source and a more remote source is probable. Massive barytes-witherite

veins have been worked from the Coal Measures of the East Durham Coalfield
(Smith 1980) and the identification of coal from the same source at Hibaldstow
in north Lincolnshire (Smith, in Buckland 1988a) would support this connection.
As Conrad's (1902) narrator, Marlow, knew, cargoes of coal can have disadvan-
tages, but corn from Lincolnshire and the Vale of York, as well as the Fens (Frere
1967, 276), may have been exchanged at South Shields or Wallsend for saleable
ballast, either coal or building materials. In eastern England, particularly East
Anglia, lacking good building stone, ballast must always have had a ready
market, although the plethora of glacial erratics makes interpretation of individual
archaeological finds particularly hazardous and routine identification of all stone
from an excavation is unlikely without the provision of a resident geologist.

Medieval and later evidence

The collapse of the centralised economy during the 5th century and subsequent
decline, or at least change in character, of urban settlement (cf. Esmonde Cleary
1989) left massive reserves of stone which were widely redistributed both as
ballast and building materials through the medieval period (Lanciani 1899). In
the Mediterranean context, it becomes difficult to distinguish between the two
categories but the one relevant wreck which has been published, that of *Mar-
zememi B* from the south-eastern tip of Sicily, may have been loaded with a
complete 6th-century Byzantine prefabricated pulpit (Parker 1980b). In northern
Europe, within the former Empire, re-use of stone for building was perhaps the
norm until available sources were used up. York appears thus to have remained
the quarry for much of its hinterland until Thomas of Bayeux's cathedral (Phillips
1985) swallowed up most that remained in the late 11th century (Buckland 1988a).
The use of Millstone Grit for quoins and jambs in such churches as Barton-on-
Humber, S. Humberside, in the late Saxon period certainly reflects the re-use of
Roman materials, presumably from York, but, in view of the efforts made to
avoid freestone quarrying at both Brixworth, Northamptonshire (Sutherland &
Parsons 1984) and Kirby Grindalythe, North Yorkshire (Buckland 1988a), with
long distance overland transport, it is unnecessary to regard this merely as ballast
movement.

The paucity of medieval documentary references to the use of ballast compared
with the frequency of later mentions has led to its use being regarded as a late
innovation. Many of the late references, however, relate to unusual sets of
circumstances associated with the stockfish trade. In terms of building materials,
Leland's near contemporary comment (*c.*1535-43) upon Hull is most pertinent:

> At such tyme as al the trade of stokfisch for England cam from Isleland to Kingeston, bycause
> the burden of the stokfisch was light, the shipes were balissed with coble stone brought out
> of Isleland, the which yn continuance pavid al the town Kingeston througout (Toulmin-
> Smith 1964, **1**, 49).

The floruit of Hull's involvement in these fisheries was during the 15th century
(Carus-Wilson 1954) and its impact on the streets should be evident in its
archaeology. The need for fish in Catholic Europe was considerable and contacts
were not confined to those between Hull and Iceland. Earlier, the focus of the

fisheries had lain off the coast of Norway and its ballast must be mixed with the erratics of many east coast beaches and walls, for the trade involved many ports between Newcastle and Dunwich (Carus-Wilson 1954, 128). King's Lynn's involvement is suggested by the high frequency of Scandinavian metamorphic and igneous rocks in its structures (Clarke & Carter 1977, 440) and the same port was also involved in Iceland (Carus-Wilson 1954, 129). That ballasting was necessary in the other direction is evident from two finds from trawls off Iceland. Flint paramoudra are known from Breidafjördur in the west and off Skogar on the south coast. Although the former was regarded as an erratic (Thórarinsson 1966), both are more likely to have arrived in Icelandic waters as ballast (Buckland 1988c). The absence of urban centres and the dispersed nature of settlement in Iceland would have provided limited markets in relation to the apparent volume of the fisheries and only the merchants, which included those of Bristol as well as east coast ports (Carus-Wilson 1954), might expect to take saleable items in addition to ballast to trade for stockfish; the occasional piece of Nottingham alabaster for a church in Iceland (Nordal 1986) must have provided a welcome outward load. As the return loads of ballast are likely to have been largely of basalts and hyaloclastites (cf. Einarsson 1971), they should be easily recognisable in the archaeological context.

Apart from King's Lynn, ballast has rarely been recognised in medieval archaeological contexts. Peacock (1980b) noted both Isle of Wight and Breton material from Saxon Southampton and Renn (1960) has suggested that ships returning in ballast from campaigns in France c.1103-12 provided material for the keep at Wareham, Dorset. In Ireland, Waterman (1970) has observed that, whilst Dundry Stone from the Jurassic of Somerset was imported in quantity, some of the lesser occurrences of this and other alien rocks may be the result of ballasting. The coastal distribution of some building materials could also relate to saleable ballast. Jope and Dunning (1954) have discussed the use of Cornish roofing slate along the south coast and have also noted the presence of slate from Fumay in the Ardenne at the deserted medieval village of Hangleton, Sussex. Caen stone, which first appears in the early Roman palace at Fishbourne (Sanderson, in Cunliffe 1971), was widely employed in southern England from shortly after the Norman Conquest (Clifton-Taylor 1987, 23). During the reign of William I, the loss of 14 out of a fleet of 15 ships importing Caen stone is recorded (Brown *et al.* 1965, 465; Gem 1987). Again ballast import must have supplemented such direct purchase, the latter sometimes involving intermediary workshops. The Neville Screen in Durham Cathedral was carved in London from Caen stone in 1372, shipped and assembled locally (Dunham & Dunham 1956-57).

The extent of medieval trade in commodities like dried fish, wool and cloth, which would have required ballast to stabilise boats, is evident from the port books of such centres as Bristol (Carus-Wilson 1954), but many lesser ports once had extensive connections. In one year (1409-10) over 200 ships left Bordeaux for England to such ports as Dartmouth, London, Hull, Bristol, Fowey and Plymouth, bringing not only wine (Carus-Wilson 1954, 34) but also sufficient ballast. The few wrecks of the period which have been examined provide little information of the quantities involved. A cog, lost off Vijby, Zealand, in *c.*1377 was ballasted with Cornish rocks (Weeks 1978) and the Graveney boat from Kent of AD 944 ± 30 contains fragments of one or more unfinished Niedermendig lava querns, again interpreted as ballast (Fenwick 1978). The only published quantitative information comes from a replica of a post-medieval ship, which lies at the upper end of the size range of earlier vessels: Baker's (1983) *Mayflower* of 180 tonnes deadweight required 133 tonnes of ballast. In contrast, discussion with the crew of the replica knarr *Saga Siglar*, which sailed successfully from Norway to North America and beyond via Shetland, Tórshavn, Reykjavk and Godthåb in 1984 (cf. Crumlin-Pedersen 1986), suggests that the 45-tonne boat required 16 tonnes of ballast, or equivalent in weighted cargo. A few finds from Iceland indicate some transport of stone. Norway ragstone hones and soapstone bowls are widely scattered, as they are elsewhere in medieval Europe (Moore 1978) but the find of two complete mullions of the former, from the Eidsborg quarries in southern Norway, in southern Iceland (National Museum of Iceland, unpubl.) suggests the transport of the rock in unmanufactured form as ballast, for which these regular elongate blocks would have been ideal. About 50 Eidsborg hones formed part of the cargo of the Klastad ship, wrecked off the coast of Norway in the 12th or 13th century (Christensen 1970). In Norse Greenland, although Lindroth (1957) has suggested that ships on the infrequent voyages from Europe would have had sufficient commodities, particularly iron, to preclude the need for ballast, it is tempting to see in the Igaliko Sandstone hones, which turn up in the Western Settlement, above Godthåb (Roussell 1936, 181; 1941, 251, 258), a result of the need to take on ballast, having disposed of part of their cargo at Gardar, in the Eastern Settlement, close to the source of the rock.

Brick, like millstones, had considerable advantages as ballast and seems first to have been used as such in the Roman period, when the products of north Italian brickyards appear in Dalmatia (Wilkes 1979). In northern Europe, in the post-medieval period, the Dutch East India Company ballasted many of its boats out with construction materials for Batavia, present-day Jakarta. Eight thousand bricks from Overijsselsde Steen in Holland and 37 tonnes of stone prefabricated as a Tuscan portico were recovered from the *Vergulde Draeck* (Green 1973; 1980; Pearson 1974), wrecked off Western Australia in 1656, and similar material occurs in two Shetland wrecks, the *Haan* of 1640 and the *Kennemerland* of 1664 (Forster & Higgs 1973). Earlier, Dutch brick must have been the ballast of many ships engaged in the wool trade with Flanders. Clifton-Taylor (1987, 212) notes a shipment of over 200,000 bricks in 1278 to the Tower of London, and Flemish brick was imported into East Anglia in the 14th century (Knoop & Jones 1933, 7). Although Hull had begun to use locally manufactured bricks by the early 14th century, saleable ballast imports of brick and tile are likely to have continued into the post-medieval period, when the earliest pantiles in Britain also came from the Low Countries (Clifton-Taylor 1987). Brick, however, also had a functional use in shipping. The galley of Henry VIII's great warship the *Mary Rose*, which capsized in 1545, was lined with over 2,000 bricks; its ballast, whose stowage probably contributed to the sinking, was of flint and sand (Rule 1982, 107).

The value of ballast as a relatively cheap source of building materials usually led to its rapid dispersal into the ports and it is only in unusual sets of circumstances that its presence was noticed. A ballast cargo is evident in the alleged gold ore with which Martin Frobisher returned from Baffin Island in 1578. A contemporary, William Camden, comments caustically, 'which stones, when neither Gold nor Silver nor any other metall could be extracted from them; we have seen cast forth to mend the High-ways' (Stefansson 1938). Hogarth and Roddick (1989) have recently located some of Frobisher's 'gold ore' amongst beach cobbles in southern Ireland, where one of his ships was wrecked on the return journey in 1578. In the 17th century, the Newfoundland fisheries succeeded those off Iceland and, in the absence of permanent settlement, vessels had problems in ballast disposal, resulting in several ordinances against the fouling of harbours with ballast (Lindroth 1957, 157-58). Both in the scale of movement and the size of ships, the Newfoundland trade, often triangular with Iberia, and returning in ballast to south-west English ports, bears comparison with later medieval Europe. In 1618, Sir Richard Whitbourne comments of the Newfoundland harbours, 'frequented by English near 40 in number, almost spoiled by casting out their balast and presse stone into them' (Lindroth 1957, 158). In Europe, much of this material, from the Roman period to the adoption of salt water ballast tanks in the late 19th century, would have been absorbed in the building trade.

Conclusion

In an interesting comparison between late Roman and later medieval trade, Fulford (1978) suggests that the entire trade between Bristol and Ireland would leave no archaeological trace; Waterman's study (1970) of building stone in southern Ireland implies otherwise. Careful examination and identification of stone from archaeological excavations and studies of standing buildings may reveal unexpected trading connections, although the effects of multiple glaciation in northern Europe and the reshipment of ballast are likely to cause interpretational problems. Keith and Simmons (1985, 416-17) have commented that 'stone ballast is the most thoroughly ignored object category in shipwreck archaeology. Research, however, should not be restricted to wrecks and coastal localities. Navigation brought sea-going vessels far inland; in the case of England, this occurred to the extent that Lincoln in 1205 ranked fourth, after London, Boston and Southampton, in taxes levied by King John upon ports (Barley 1936). The rock of a site might have significance far beyond the humble cobble that it is.

ACKNOWLEDGEMENTS

This paper had a curious beginning in a study of the origins of the faunas of North Atlantic islands (Buckland 1988c) and owes much to discussion with a wide range of specialists in diverse fields. Particular thanks are due to J. Collis, P. Foster, D. Gilbertson, Prof. S. McGrail, Prof. N. Pounds and E. Wright for picking up a few additional 'unconsidered trifles' and to Joan Buckland and Mave Torry for typing.

BIBLIOGRAPHY

Arkell, W.J., 1947   *Oxford Stone*. London: Faber, 1947

Arkell, W.J., 1949   Erratics in Dorset shingle beaches, *Proc. Dorset Nat. Hist. Archaeol. Soc.*, **70** (1949), 125

Baker, W.A., 1983   *The Mayflower and other Colonial Vessels*. London: Conway Maritime Press, 1983

Barley, M., 1936   Lincolnshire Rivers in the Middle Ages, *Archit. Archaeol. Soc. Co. Lincoln*, **1** (1936), 1-22

Bass, G.F., 1967   Cape Gelidonya: a Bronze Age Shipwreck, *Trans. American Phil. Soc.*, ser 2, **57** (1967), 8

Briggs, C.S., 1976   Cargoes and Field Clearance in the History of the English Channel, *Quaternary Newsl.*, **19** (1976), 10-16

Brown, R.A., Colvin, H.M., and Taylor, A.J., 1965   *The History of the King's Works*, **1**. London: HMSO, 1965

Buckland, P.C., 1978   Building Stones, *Riverside Structures and a Well in Skeldergate and Buildings in Bishophill*, by M.O.H. Carver, S. Donaghey and A.B. Sumpter, 40-44. Archaeology of York **4** (1), London: Council for British Archaeology, 1978

Buckland, P.C., 1984   The 'Anglian' Tower and the Use of Jurassic Limestone in York, *Archaeological Papers from York Presented to M.W. Barley*, ed. P.V. Addyman and V.E. Black, 51-57. York: York Archaeological Trust, 1984

Buckland, P.C., 1988a   The Stones of York: Building materials in Roman Yorkshire. *Recent Research in Roman Yorkshire: Studies in honour of Mary Kitson Clark* ed. J. Price, P.R. Wilson, C.S. Briggs and S.J. Hardman, 237-88. British Archaeological Reports, Br. Ser., **193**, Oxford, 1988

Buckland, P.C., 1988b   The Stones of York, *Geology Today*, **4** (1988), 171-75

Buckland, P.C., 1988c   North Atlantic faunal connections – introduction or endemics?, *Entomologica scandinavica Suppl.*, **32** (1988), 7-29

Caesar   *Gallic War*, transl. H.J. Edward. Loeb Classical Library, London: Heinemann, 1917

Carus-Wilson, E.M., 1954   *Medieval Merchant Venturers*. London: Methuen & Co., 1954

Casson, L., 1960   *The Ancient Mariners*. London: Victor Gollancz, 1960

Christensen, A.E., 1970   Klastadskipet, *Nicolay*, **8** (1970), 21-24

Clarke, G., 1982   The Roman Villa at Woodchester, *Britannia*, **13** (1982), 197-228

Clarke, H., and Carter, A., 1977   *Excavations in King's Lynn 1963-1970*. Society for Medieval Archaeology, Monograph **7**, London, 1977

Clifton-Taylor, A., 1987   *The Pattern of English Building*. 4th ed., London: Faber & Faber, 1987

Conrad, J., 1902   *Youth*. London: Blackwoods' Magazine

Coppack, G., 1973   The Excavation of a Roman and Medieval Site at Flaxengate, Lincoln, *Lincolnshire Hist. Archaeol.*, **8** (1973), 73-114

Crumlin-Pedersen, O., 1986   Aspects of Viking-Age Shipbuilding, *J. Danish Archaeol.*, **5** (1986), 209-28

Crummy, N., 1984   The stone architectural fragments, in P. Crummy, *Excavations at Lion Walk, Balkerne Lane, and Middleborough, Colchester, Essex*, 28-29. Colchester Archaeol. Rep. **3**, Colchester: Colchester Archaeological Trust, 1984

Cunliffe, B.W., 1971   *Excavations at Fishbourne 1961-1969*, **2**: *the finds*. Res. Rep. Soc. Antiq., **27**, London: Society of Antiquaries, 1971

Cunliffe, B.W., 1987   *Hengistbury Head, Dorset*, **1**: *the prehistoric and Roman settlement 350 BC-AD 500*. Oxford University Committee for Archaeology, Monograph **13**, Oxford, 1986

Curle, C.L., 1982	*Pictish and Norse Finds from the Brough of Birsay 1934-74.* Soc. Antiq. Scot., Monograph Ser. **1** Edinburgh, 1982
Dunham, K.C., 1974	Epigenetic Mineral, *The Geology and Mineral Resources of Yorkshire*, ed. D.H. Rayner and J.E. Hemingway, 293-308. Leeds: Yorkshire Geological Society, 1974
Dunham, M., and Dunham, K.C., 1956-57	The Stone of the Neville Screen in Durham Cathedral, *Durham Univ. J.* ser.2, **18** (1956-57), 47-50
Einarsson, Th., 1971	*Jardfraedi.* Reykjavk: Mal og Menning, 1971
Eldjárn, K., 1974	Fornthjód og Minjar, *Saga Islands*, **1**, ed. S. Lindal, 101-52. Reykjavk: Hd´slenzka bókmenntafélag, 1974
Esmonde Cleary, S., 1989	*The Ending of Roman Britain.* London: Batsford, 1989
Fenwick, V., 1978	*The Graveney Boat.* British Archaeological Reports Br. ser. **53**, Oxford, 1978
Foley, V., Soedel, W., and Doyle, J., 1982	A trireme displacement estimate, *Int. J. Naut. Archaeol. Underwater Explor.*, **11** (1982), 305-18
Forster, W.A., and Higgs, K.B., 1973	The Kennemerland, 1971, *Int. J. Naut. Archaeol. Underwater Explor.*, **2** (1971), 291-300
Frere, S.S., 1967	*Britannia.* London: Routledge & Kegan Paul, 1967
Fulford, M., 1978	The interpretation of Britain's late Roman trade: the scope of medieval historical and archaeological analogy, *Roman shipping and trade: Britain and the Rhine provinces*, ed. J. du Plat Taylor and H. Cleere, 59-69. Res. Rep. **24**, London: Council for British Archaeology, 1978
Gem, R., 1987	Canterbury and the Cushion Capital: a Commentary on Passages from Goscelin's De Miraculis Sancti Augustini, *Romanesque and Gothic: Essays for George Zarnecki*, ed. N. Stratford, 83-101. Woodbridge: Boydell & Brewer, 1987
Gibbins, D.J.L., and Parker, A.J., 1986	The Roman wreck of *c.*AD 200 at Plemmirio, near Siracusa (Sicily): interim report, *Int. J. Naut. Archaeol. Underwater Explor.*, **15** (1986), 267-304
Gnoli, R., 1971	*Marmora Romana.* Rome: Edizioni dell'Elefante, 1971
Granlund, J., 1970	*Kulturhistoriskt Lexicon för nordisk medeltid fron vikingatid till reformationtid*, **15**. Marmo: Allhens, 1970
Green, J.N., 1973	The wreck of the Dutch East Indiaman the Vergulde Draeck, 1656, *Int. J. Naut.Archaeol. Underwater Explor.*, **2** (1973), 267-89
Green, J.N., 1980	Western Australia, a New Maritime Museum, *Int. J. Naut. Archaeol. Underwater Explor.*, **9** (1980), 81-84
Hildebrand, M.K.G., 1960	Exportation du fer et navigation en Baltique, *Le Navire et l'Economie maritime du Nord de l'Europe du Moyen-Age au XVIII siecle*, ed. M. Millat, 111-20. Ecole Pratique des Hautes Etudes, VIe section, Paris, 1960
Hogarth, D.D., and Roddick, J.C., 1989	Discovery of Martin Frobisher's Baffin Island 'ore' in Ireland, *Canadian J. Earth Sci.*, **26**, 1053-60
Hull, M.R., 1958	*Roman Colchester.* Res. Rep. Soc. Antiq., **20**, Oxford: University Press, 1958
Jope, E.M., and Dunning, G.C., 1954	The Use of Blue Slate for Roofing in Medieval England, *Antiq. J.*, **34** (1954), 209-17
Katzev, M.L., 1980	A cargo from the age of Alexander the Great, *Archaeology under Water*, ed K. Muckelroy, 42-43. London: McGraw-Hill, 1980
Keith, D.H., and Simmons III, J.J., 1985	Analysis of Hull Remains, Ballast, and Artifact Distribution of a 16th Century Shipwreck, Molasses Reef, British West Indies, *J. Field Archaeol.*, **12** (1985), 411-24
Kellaway, G.A., Redding, J.H., Shephard-Thorn, E.R., and Destombes, J.-P., 1975	The Quaternary history of the English Channel, *Phil. Trans. R. Soc. Lond.* ser A, **279**, 189-218

Kidson, C., and Bowen, D.Q., 1976   Some comments on the history of the English Channel, *Quaternary Newsl.*, **18** (1976), 8-10.

Knoop, D. and Jones, G.P., 1949   *The Mediaeval Mason*. Manchester: University Press, 1949

Lanciani, R., 1899   *The Destruction of Ancient Rome*. Handbooks of Archaeology and Antiquities, London: Macmillan, 1899

Laures, F.F., 1986   Roman maritime trades, *Int. J. Naut. Archaeol. Underwater Explor.*, **15** (1986), 166-67

Leslie, R.C., 1890   *Old Sea Wings, Ways and Words in the Days of Oak and Hemp*. London: Chapman and Hall, 1890

Lindroth, C.H., 1957   *The Faunal Connections between Europe and North America*. New York: J. Wiley & Sons, 1957

Liou, B., 1975   Cavalière bay, Le Lavandou (Var), *Int. J. Naut. Underwater Explor.*, **4** (1975), 376.

Lynn, C.J., 1984   Some Fragments of Exotic Porphyry found in Ireland, *J. Irish Archaeol.*, **2** (1984), 19-32

McGrail, S., 1989   The Shipment of Traded Goods and of Ballast in Antiquity, *Oxford J. Archaeol.*, **8** (1989), 353-58

Marcus, G.J., 1980   *The Conquest of the North Atlantic*. Woodbridge: Boydell Press, 1980

Marsden, P.R.V., 1967   *A Roman Ship from Blackfriars, London*. London: Guildhall Museum, 1967

Moore, D.T., 1978   The petrography and archaeology of English honestones, *J. Archaeol. Sci.*, **5** (1978), 61-74

Morrison, J., 1976   The Classical Tradition, *Archaeology of the Boat*, ed. B.Greenhill, 155-73. London: Adam & Charles Black, 1976

Noel Hume, I., 1982   *Martin's Hundred*. London: Gollancz, 1982

Nordal, B., 1986   Skrá um enskar alabastursmyndir frá miðöldum sem vardveist hafa á Islandi, *Árbok hins´slenzka fornleifafelags*, **85** (1986), 85-130

North, F.J., 1930   *Limestones: their Origins, Distribution and Uses*. London: T. Murby, 1930

Parker, A., 1980a   Roman merchantmen rediscovered, *Archaeology under Water*, ed. K. Muckelroy, 52-53. London: McGraw-Hill, 1980

Parker, A., 1980b   A ships' graveyard off Sicily, *Archaeology under Water*, ed. K. Muckelroy, 60-61. London: McGraw-Hill, 1980

Peacock, D.P.S., 1971   Roman Amphorae in Pre-Roman Britain, *The Iron Age and its Hill-Forts*, ed. M. Jesson and D. Hill, 161-88. Southampton: University Archaeological Society, 1971

Peacock, D.P.S., 1980a   The Roman millstone trade: a petrological sketch, *World Archaeol.*, **12** (1980), 43-53

Peacock, D.P.S., 1980b   The stones, *Excavations at Melbourne Street, Southampton, 1971-76*, ed. P. Holdsworth, 75. Res. Rep. **33**, London: Council for British Archaeology, 1980

Peacock, D.P.S., 1986   The Production of Roman Millstones near Orvieto, Umbria, Italy, *Antiq. J.*, **66** (1986), 45-51

Pearson, C., 1974   The Western Australian Museum Conservation Laboratory for marine archaeological material, *Int. J. Naut. Archaeol. Underwater Explor.*, **3** (1974), 295-305

Pensebene, P., 1978   A cargo of marble shipwrecked at Punta Scifo near Crotone (Italy), *Int. J. Naut. Archaeol. Underwater Explor.*, **7** (1978), 105-18

Phillips, D., 1985   *Excavations at York Minster*, **2**: *the Cathedral of Thomas of Bayeux*. London: HMSO, 1985

Pritchard, F.A., 1986   Ornamental Stonework from Roman London, *Britannia*, **17** (1986), 169-90

Renn, D.F., 1960   The Keep of Wareham Castle, *Medieval Archaeol.*, **4** (1960), 56-68

Rouge, J., 1981   *Ships and Fleets of the Ancient Mediterranean*. Middletown: Wesleyan University Press, 1981

Roussell, A., 1936   Sandnes and the Neighbouring Farms, *Meddelelser om Gronland*, **88**.3, 1936

Roussell, A., 1941   Farms and churches of the medieval Norse settlement of Greenland, *Meddelelser om Gronland*, **89**.1, 1941

Rule, M., 1982   *The Mary Rose*. London: Conway Maritime Press, 1982

Sandars, N. K., 1960   *The Epic of Gilgamesh*. Harmondsworth: Penguin, 1960

Smith, F.W., 1980   The Mineralisation of the Alston Block, *The Geology of North East England*, ed. D.A. Robson, 89-96. Newcastle upon Tyne: Natural History Society of Northumbria, 1980

Stefansson, V., 1938   *The Three Voyages of Martin Frobisher*. London: Argonaut Press, 1938

Sutherland, D.S., and   The Petrological Contribution to the Survey of All Saints' church,
    Parsons, D., 1984   Brixworth, Northamptonshire: an Interim Account, *J. Brit. Archaeol. Assoc.*, **137** (1984), 45-64

Thórarinsson, S., 1966   Hvadan mundi vera sá stóri steinn? *Nátturúfraedingurinn*, **36** (1966), 42-47

Toulmin-Smith, L., 1964   *The Itinerary of John Leland in or about 1535-1543*. London: Centaur Press, 1964

Walda, H., and Walker,   The Art and Architecture of Lepcis: marble origins by isotopic
    S., 1984   analysis, *Libyan Stud.*, **15** (1984), 81-92

Waterman, D.M., 1970   Somersetshire and other Foreign Building Stone in Medieval Ireland, *c*.1175-1400, *Ulster J. Archaeol.*, **33** (1970), 63-75

Weeks, J., 1978   Vejby, Zealand, *Int. J. Naut. Archaeol. Underwater Explor.*, **7** (1978), 237-38

Wilkes, J., 1979   Importation and Manufacture of Stamped Bricks and Tiles in the Roman Province of Dalmatia, *Roman Brick and Tile*, ed. A. McWhirr, 65-72. British Archaeological Reports, International ser., **68**, Oxford, 1979

Williams-Thorpe, O., and   Els origens geologics dels molins Romans de Pedra del Nord-Est
    Thorpe, R.S., 1987   Catalunya, *Vitrina* (spring, 1987), 56-57

Chapter 9

The Quarrying of Stone Roofing Slates and Rubble in West Yorkshire during the Middle Ages

Stephen Moorhouse

Documentary and archaeological evidence for the medieval stone slate (thackstone) and rubble quarries in West Yorkshire are used to examine the location of the quarries against the geological background. The number of quarries and their lifespan are also considered, along with such questions as which levels of society were using the stones for what purposes, on which buildings they were used and the distances over which they travelled. Reasons are suggested for the use of different materials on the roofs of different buildings within the same complex. The importance of rubble quarries is also considered, and where and why the rubble was used.

Introduction

The extensive use of medieval stone roofing slates is well known from original roofs surviving on medieval buildings and their presence on excavated medieval sites. As in other aspects of medieval construction, the most detailed studies of the documentary sources for stone slate quarries are by L.F. Salzman (1923, 88-90; 1967, 232-33) and Knoop & Jones (1933; 1938; 1967, 67-70). Although wide ranging, the studies have illustrated general trends and have given the impression, primarily through the kind of documents being used, that stone roofs were restricted to the buildings of the landed classes, and that quarries were few in number. Detailed work at a local level, using primarily manorial court rolls, manorial account rolls, minor place names and occupational names shows that small quarries were numerous in the medieval landscape and that, in some regions, houses at peasant level were frequently covered with stone slates. The documents make it clear that quarries were often opened up specifically to provide rubble for a variety of uses. This paper examines the combined evidence within the geographically small but geologically diverse area of modern West Yorkshire. The thoughts expressed are not intended as definitive statements, but merely suggestions as to where further work, currently in progress by the author, might produce some rewarding results.

Previous work on stone slate in the region has been limited. Despite the wealth of albeit scattered documentary evidence for the quarrying and use of slates in the Middle Ages, C.H. Vellacott's otherwise detailed and exhaustive accounts of other aspects of medieval crafts and industries in the Victoria County History is restricted, when discussing stone slates, to one short paragraph for the whole of the historic county of Yorkshire (Vellacott 1912, 379). The working practices of the Elland Flag slaters and their tools are covered in an important paper by James Walton on the English stone slaters (Walton 1975). Otherwise, the literature is confined mainly to the repetition of facts and opinions of earlier writers, much of which is based on tradition rather than hard, historical facts.

Geological background

West Yorkshire is rich in a variety of building stones, ranging from the different sandstones in the central part of the county to the limestones down the eastern side (illustration 35). Despite this ready supply of building stone, most medieval buildings in the area at all social levels were of timber, a fact which owes more to fashion than the availability of building materials. While the building and

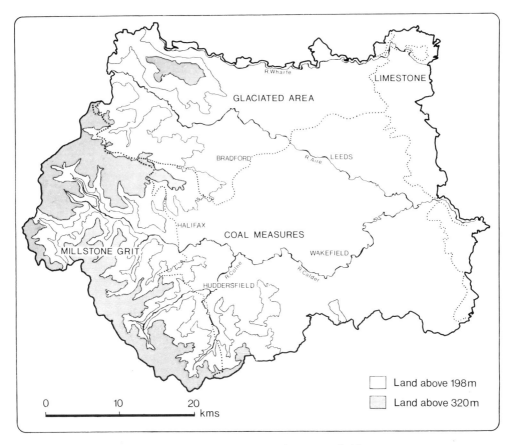

35.   Geology and relief of West Yorkshire.

repair sections of manorial accounts suggests that more medieval stone buildings existed than actually survive, the overwhelming evidence is that, apart from churches, monastic houses and some manor houses and bridges, all other structures in the region were built of timber. This view is supported by building stone from within the now defunct modern county being much sought after for important medieval buildings elsewhere in the country. The important quarries at Huddlestone, Stapleton and *Thevesdale*, bordering the eastern part of the modern county, supplied large quantities of building stone for York Minster, Selby Abbey, Eton College and Westminster Abbey (Salzman 1967, 131-32). Magnesium limestone was supplied in vast quantities for York Minster from unlocated quarries in Bramham township from the 14th to the 16th century (Raine 1859, *passim*). Stone called 'Pontefract stone' was much sought after in southern England (Salzman 1967, 131). Stone did not become a common local building material until the later 16th century, when a change in the layout and form of the domestic house took place, responding to changes in social needs (Moorhouse 1981, 803-05; Giles 1986). Many of the existing timber buildings were simply given a veneer of stone, giving the impression today from outside that they were built in the 16th or 17th centuries. While archaeology, surviving medieval buildings and in particular manorial accounts show that stone was used commonly for padstones beneath principal posts, as sill walls, and even half height walling for timber superstructures, the overwhelming use of stone in the region during the Middle Ages was as a roof covering.

Stone roofing slates and their quarries

While the extent of suitable sandstone defines the area within which stone slate quarries can be expected, it is the various strands of documentary evidence which give us a clue as to their location and frequency. Salzman's monumental survey of medieval building practices and materials presented a one-sided picture gained by studying mainly building and repair accounts. These provide a wealth of detail for the different types of roof coverings, the buildings on which they were used, the detailed procedures and sequences for laying the roof covering, and occasionally the quarry sources. Such documents cover the buildings mainly of the seignorial classes upwards. Court rolls are useful for the lower social orders, through licences obtained for extraction, but mainly through fines for illegal taking of stones without licence (see Table 9.1). These cases provide perhaps a glimpse only of the many occasions when small-scale quarrying took place without manorial consent. Court rolls also provide details for the extensive use of stone slates on the houses of the peasantry, buildings which must have been of sufficient stature to withstand a heavy stone roof, a point which is discussed further below.

One particularly useful and previously underused source is minor place- and field-names used and recorded in the Middle Ages. Names containing the elements *delf* and *quarrelle*, both meaning 'quarry', are particularly common across the county. The apparent absence of large numbers of stone structures (with the exception of churches), the widespread use of wood for most building purposes and the well documented use of stone slates, suggests that many of these quarries were for stone slates, or, in the language of the documents, 'thackstones'. Occasionally this can be confirmed. The name *le stondelf* is not uncommon, and simply refers to a stone quarry without specifying the use of the stone. A series of late medieval Rastrick deeds is more explicit. The same piece of land was exchanged three times: in 1399 it was referred to as *Stonedelfts*, in 1410 as *le Stone delft*, but in 1400 as *at Sclaftonedelffe*, confirming beyond doubt the function of the quarry (Moorhouse 1981, 810). Unhappily, this kind of confirmation is only rarely found. The probable reason why so few of these names have survived on estate or more recent maps, or through oral tradition, is that the quarries were short lived, used for one particular building or perhaps for a few years and then abandoned. The short-lived 15th-century quarry excavated at *Hillam Burchard* (discussed below) was deliberately backfilled, was not evident on the surface because of later activity over its site, and was not recorded as a minor place-name.

Occupational names can also be helpful, although they have to be used with caution. The names *sclater* and *theaker* refer to people who put the covering material on the roof. The first clearly refers to a person working with slates, and in the eastern Pennines it can be assumed stone slates, because of the overwhelming documentary evidence for locally quarried 'thackstones' and the absence of true slates in the archaeological record in the region. Theaker means a roof coverer. The frequency of the occupational names in the region, the overwhelming evidence for stone slate roof coverings and the origin of the name suggests that some, if not most, of the people called 'le theaker' were stone roof coverers, a suggestion which is supported by their distribution in areas of documented stone slate quarrying. There is a variety of names related to the extraction of stone. People called 'le hewer' occur in the townships of Stanley, Flockton and in Wakefield itself. More specifically, a Walter Stanhewere occurs in a late 12th-century Horsforth grant (Lancaster & Baildon 1904, 76, no. 101), significantly in a small area of the Aire valley where many types of stone objects were quarried throughout the Middle Ages (Moorhouse 1991). Other names have been noted only once, such as Richard le Stonpotter who, in 1337, was fined 6d. for illegal pasturing in Hipperholme township, a township also the heart of an important stone extraction industry during the Middle Ages (Table 9.1; Moorhouse 1991); Richard was most likely a maker of stone mortars. Despite the number of people bearing occupation names related to stone extraction, and the variety of such names, none can be specifically related to the digging of stone slates.

Location of thackstone quarries

West Yorkshire contains a varied geology, which has concentrated particular quarrying processes to certain areas of the county. The distribution of thackstone quarries is shown in illustration 36, and is predictably restricted to the Coal Measure sandstones, where the laminated beds are easily accessible. The quality varied greatly; then, as now, the most sought-after was the Elland Flagstone. These beds were exploited where they outcropped and were most easily obtained

TABLE 9.1

LOC. ON ILLUS. 36	QUARRY SITE	WHERE USED	DATE	PURPOSE OF REFERENCE	SOURCE
1	Alverthorpe	—	1339	tenant fined for breaking *yakstone* and inquisition found *thakstone* taken illegally	YAS MD759, pp.22, 58
2	Ambler Thorn	—	1523	*Ambler Delphs* reported as being in good order	Walton 1975, p.41
3	Booth Town	Halifax	1379	16 cartloads of *sclatestone* taken illegally	Turner 1893, p.103
4	Bramley	Rothwell	1356	slate for manorial stable	PRO DL29/507/8226
	Bramley	Methley	1384/5	see Table 9.2	—
5	Calverley	—	1448	tenant fined for taking *thakstone* without licence	YAS MD130/15/1448
6	Elland	—	1515	John Savile pays rent for *sclatestone delve*[1]	NRO/DDSR 227/105
7	Featherstone	Methley	1435-6	see Table 9.2	—
8	*Hillam Burchard*	—	15th c.	excavated quarry complex: see illus. 37-41	—
9	Hipperholme[2]	—	1314	Thomas del Northend[3] pays rent of 3d. for *thakstones*	Lister & Ogden 1906, p. 45
	Hipperholme	—	1332	John del Bottom fined 6d. for digging stone on the lord's bond land for roofing	Walker 1981, p. 215
	Hipperholme	—	1336	two tenants fined 6d. each for digging stones for roofing their houses	YAS MD225/1336, m. 14d.
10	Manningham	Manningham	1339	two tenants fined for digging stones on bond land in Manningham to cover their houses	BCR 1, p. 10, 12
11	Mickle Moss	—	1446	Richard Waterhouse fined for illegally taking *thakstone* at Mickle Moss (*Mykelmosse*)	YAS MD225/1446, m.2v
12	Northowram[4]	Southowram	1524	Richard and Robert Bayrestawe paid 12d. for taking slatestones out of Northowram[5]	Walton 1975, p. 41
13	Pudsey	Methley	1458/9	see Table 9.2	—
14	Rastrick	—	1331	Bate de Rastrick dug up *thakston* from highway in Rastrick	Turner, 1893, p. 72
	Rastrick	—	1400	property leased at *Sclaftonedelffe*[6]	Moorhouse 1981, p. 810
	Rastrick	Kirklees Priory	1416	Prioress of Kirkless bought *thackstones* from a Rastrick quarry	Walton 1975, p. 41
	Rastrick	—	1419	Thomas Duke of Rastrick and his son took 16 loads (*panstres*) of *thackstones* without leave	Turner 1893, p. 114
	Rastrick	Methley	1450/1	see Table 9.2	—
15	Rothwell	Rothwell	1373/4	2 cartloads of *sclatston* for 2s.10d.	PRO DL29/507/8227
16	Shadwell	Thorner	1393/4	400 *sclattstan* bought	WYAS/L/MX/Man/Accts, no. 9
	Shadwell	Thorner	1423/5	two purchases of *sclatston*, one without details for a barn, the other 12 waggonloads for 4s.	WYAS/L/MX/Man/Acctx, no.13
17	Snydale	Methley	1386/7	See Table 9.2	—
18	Small Clough[7]	Oakenshaw	1447	tenant at Oakenshaw fined for illegally taking *thakstones* at *Smalecloghhege*	YAS MD225/1447, m.6v
19	Thorner	Pollington	1465/6	9 waggonloads of stone called *sclatston*	WYAS/L/MX/Man/Accts, no.17
20	Woodhouse (Leeds)	Rothwell	1399-1400	*sclatstons* bought	PRO DL29/507/8229
	Woodhouse (Leeds)	Leeds	1438-39	5 loads of *sclatston* for the hall of pleas	Kirkby 1983, p. 6
	Woodhouse[8] (Leeds)	Rothwell	1439-40	2 cartloads of *Sclatston* at 12d. a cartload	PRO DL29/507/8232

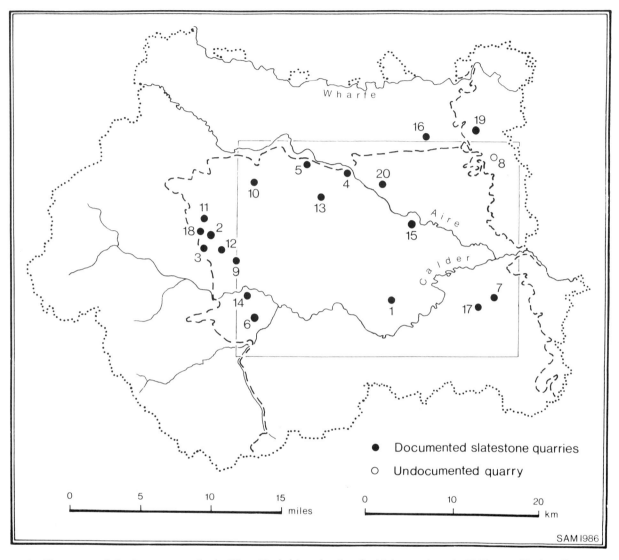

36. Documented thackstone quarries in West Yorkshire, details of which are given in Table 9.1. Broken lines indicate coal measures (see illustration 35). The inset shows the area of illustration 42.

Notes to Table 9.1.

1. The document is a rental of the manor of Elland, which included the townships of Elland cum Greetland and Southowram. The quarry, therefore, lay in one of these townships.

2. Hipperholme was the name given to a settlement, township and graveship in the manor of Wakefield. As the manor was administered through the graveships, references in manorial documents are likely to refer to the territory of the graveship. A piece of property described as lying

within Hipperholme could, therefore, lie in any of the constituent townships of Hipperholme, Northowram, or the southern part of Shelf. Northowram is the most likely, as quarrying is well documented there during the Middle Ages (see note 4 below).

3. This reference occurs in the 1314 extent of the manor of Wakefield, where rents are grouped together under their respective graveships (see note 2 above). Although listed under the graveship heading of Hipperholme, Thomas took his name from a small lost medieval settlement of *Northend* in Northowram township (Moorhouse 1981, 606), and the manor court rolls show that he held most of his property in Northowram township. It is likely, therefore, though not certain, that the quarry for which he paid rent lay in the vill of Northowram, where there was a concentration of thackstone quarries during the Middle Ages (see note 4 below).

4. Northowram contained an important thackstone quarrying industry during the Middle Ages. Some references to quarrying in the township are almost certainly lost under the general graveship heading of Hipperholme, in which Northowram lay (see note 2 above). A number of sites where illegal quarrying took place in the township are given by name: Ambler Thorn, Booth Town, Mickle Moss and Small Clough all lay within a small area on the north western edge of the township, where the Elland Flags outcrop conveniently.

5. Richard and Robert took their name from a now lost medieval settlement called Bairstow, which lay on Beacon Hill in the northern part of Southowram township, adjacent to the manor of Wakefield in the north, and bordering the important quarrying centre in Northowram (Faull & Moorhouse 1981, map 25). The wording of the entry shows that the slates were quarried in Northowram township but used elsewhere, probably at Bairstow in Southowram.

6. This is one of three deeds which refer to the stone quarry, but only this one specifies it as a 'slate stone quarry' (Moorhouse 1981, 810).

7. The 15th-century quarries may be those now abandoned to the east of and above Small Clough Farm on the edge of the valley, in precisely the position described by the 1447 place-name. The court roll entry is incomplete, for there is a gap left for the Christian name of the tenant from Oakenshaw; no other people are involved, as suggested in Turner 1893, 120.

8. The slates were bought from *Ledys Wodhouse*, leaving no doubt as to which of the many Woodhouses was intended, for roofing various buildings in the 'castle' (*infra castrum*).

---

along a north–south line to the east of Halifax. Predictably, this is where the greatest concentration of quarry sites lay, including the well-documented industries in Northowram, Hipperholme, Southowram, Elland and Rastrick townships (illustration 36; Table 9.1).

Sandstone slates were also exploited down the east side of the county. A combination of documentary and archaeological evidence suggests that sandstone slates were extracted from beneath the limestone. In 1465-66 nine waggon loads of stone called *sclatston* were quarried in Thorner for use at Pollington, in present-day Humberside (no. 19 in Table 9.1 and in illustration 36). It is possible that the unlocated quarry may have lain over the Coal Measure sandstones, for the western part of the township does not lie on the limestones.

Archaeological evidence comes in the form of a complete thackstone quarry excavated on the site of the deserted medieval settlement of *Hillam Burchard* in 1981 (Moorhouse forthcoming [a]). The quarry was an unexpected find, for it was not visible within the earthworks of the site, nor was it detectable through geophysical survey over its site. Excavation showed that the latest occupation of the site had occurred over the deliberately filled in quarry, thus obscuring its position. On excavation it turned out to be a rectangular quarry cut into the eastern side of a small shallow valley which opened out into the Cock Beck (illustrations 37 & 41). It had been cunningly cut so that a minimum of limestone

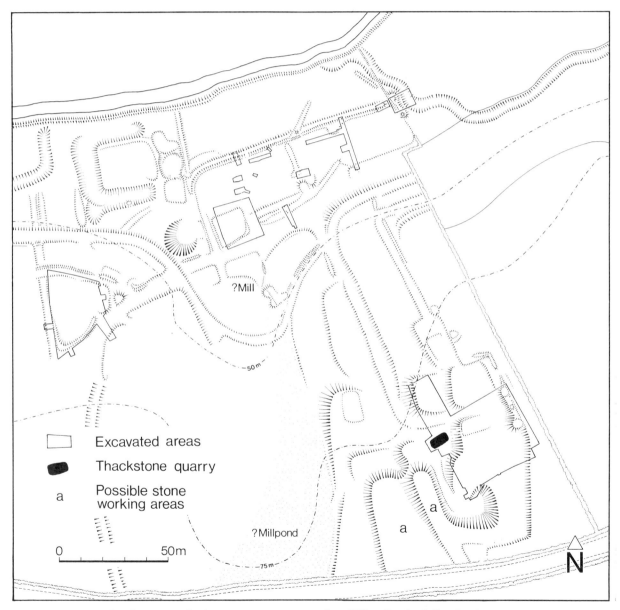

37. Location of 15th-century thackstone quarry excavated at *Hillam Burchard* (for details see illustration 41).

38. View along the length of the excavated thackstone quarry at *Hillam Burchard*, looking east, with the post position for the possible crane behind the vertical scale (scales in 0.5m divisions).

39. View along the length of the excavated thackstone quarry at *Hillam Burchard*, looking west (scales in 0.5m divisions).

40. View of the north-east corner of the excavated thackstone quarry at *Hillam Burchard*, showing how the blocks of sandstone were quarried, from which the stone slates were split (scales in 0.5m divisions).

capping had to be removed before reaching the sandstone beds. The stone was cut out in rectangular blocks approximately 1.5m square, varying in depth from 0.2m to 0.5m. The means of separating the blocks from the bed was not identified, for no tools were recovered in the deliberate fill, nor were there any signs of splitting on the quarry sides. The blocks appear to have been lifted out by means of a movable tripod crane, for which the only surviving evidence appears to have been a large single post-hole on the narrow eastern uphill side of the quarry (illustrations 38-41).

Working of the stone block appears to have taken place to the south of the quarry. Initial ploughing of the field revealed substantial quantities of laminated sandstone scatters on the platform marked *a* in illustration 37. At the time the quarry was unknown and it was assumed that the plough had disturbed natural sandstone beds. A large open working area would be essential for splitting the stones, especially if they were weathered over the winter for frost fracturing; natural lamination by frost action was more effective and efficient than splitting by wedge. Large terraced areas exist adjacent to medieval quarry sites at Broadbottom, in the Calder valley, and at West Hall, Nesfield, in the Wharfe valley (Moorhouse 1991). Unfortunately, the significance of the platforms at *Hillam* was not appreciated until the end of the excavation and it was not possible to excavate them. There was no evidence for the working of stones in the large excavated area within which the quarry lay. It seems likely that all the quarry-related activities with their associated buildings may lie on the group of terraced platforms downhill and to the west of the quarry (illustration 37), a feature which does not fit happily into the otherwise symmetrical plan of the earlier, abandoned settlement.

The quarry fill contained large quantities of thackstone waste, which revealed the process of shaping the slates from the laminated sandstone. Unfortunately, the material was discarded before the analysis was carried out. A wide range of shapes and sizes was evident, including a variety of sizes of the ubiquitous circular sandstone discs which are so common on sites of most periods in the north of England.

Distribution of the slates
Two sources of information can reveal the distances over which the slates travelled for their use: geology and documents. While large quantities of medieval thackstones have been found on a number of excavations within the county, such as the large numbers from Kirkstall Abbey near Leeds, they have not yet been examined petrologically. A programme of work is planned for the future.

Of greater potential is the documentary evidence. In particular, account rolls often record the repairs or reconstructions of manorial buildings. Often the repair of stone-covered roofs is mentioned, with occasionally the source of the slates. Unhappily, the number of quarry sources given for the thackstones is far exceeded by entries which simply record the purchase of the slates. It is often possible to show that slates were obtained many miles from the place where they were to be used. In some cases it can be shown that a landlord would quarry stone on one

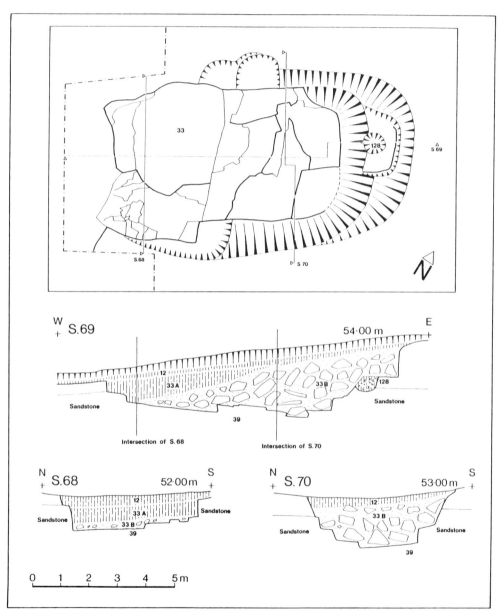

41. Plan and section of the 15th-century thackstone quarry at *Hillam Burchard* (for location see illustration 37).

part of his estate and move the stones for use on another of his centres elsewhere (Moorhouse 1991). This appears to have happened in 1465-66 when Thomas Metham had some slates quarried on his manor of Thorner for use at his other residence at Pollington, 20 miles to the south-east (Table 9.1, no. 19). The sources recorded for stone slates for the manor of Methley between 1384-85 and 1458-59 illustrate the distance over which slates could travel (illustration 42; Table 9.2).

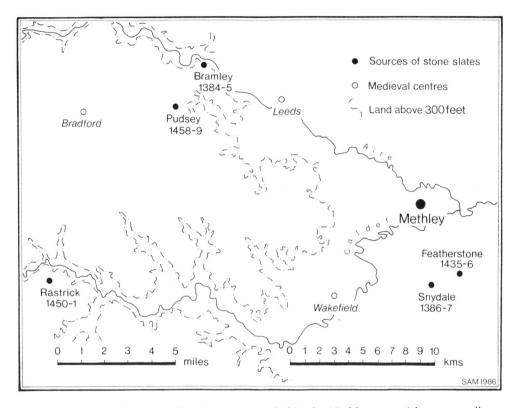

42. Location of sources of thackstones recorded in the Methley manorial account rolls, details of which are given in Table 9.2 (compare illustration 36).

All sources have been extracted from the accounts surviving between 1373-74 and 1463-64, while there have been many references, almost annually, which simply record the cost without giving the quarry source. Table 9.2 gives details of each purchase where the source is given. The two earliest entries reveal a picture common elsewhere. Where slates were brought from some distance away, the cost of carriage often exceeded that of the stones, a reflection of the quality of the slates and the trouble that some people would go to for better quality stones. Significantly, the high quality Elland Flagstones were purchased in 1450-51 from Rastrick.

TABLE 9.2

DATE	SOURCE	NAME OF STONE	No. OF LOADS	COST OF LOAD	COST OF CARRIAGE	BUILDING IN MANOR
1385–86	Bramley	*thakston*	2	10d.	3s. 0d.	manor
1386–87	Snydale	*sklat[ston]*	5	8d.	2s. 1d.	manor
1435–36	Featherstone	stones	1	5d.	—	kitchen
1450–51	Rastrick	*sclateston*	11	22s.	—	manor
1458–59	Pudsey	*sclateston*	1	2s.	—	house at the church

A trawl of the documentary sources is beginning to suggest that some areas were formerly important. The sandstones south of Leeds were popular, with quarries in Woodhouse, Calverley, Bramley and Pudsey (illustration 36), with those at Bramley and Pudsey being used by customers from some distance away (Table 9.1). The quarries in Woodhouse, to the west of Leeds, appear to have been manorial quarries which supplied stones for the repair of manorial buildings in the honour of Pontefract.

Who used stone slates and what for?
Stone slates were used by all levels of society in the Middle Ages for a variety of purposes. The most obvious was for covering the roofs of houses. The best known are those of the manor, recorded through building and repair sections in account rolls. Although stone slates can be found on most types of building, some are particularly common. The hall, kitchen and oven are the most obvious, but stables and barns are also mentioned fairly frequently (Tables 9.1 & 9.2). Other types of document can be helpful. The 1358 extent of the manor at Calverley lists the buildings of the manorial complex and states that the oven is roofed in stone (Moorhouse 1981, 599). It was not uncommon to find contemporary buildings in the same complex with roof coverings of different materials (e.g. Yarwood & Marriott forthcoming).

While account rolls cover the buildings of the landed classes, court rolls and private charters reveal that stone slates were also used on the buildings of the lower levels of society, that is of the peasants. Offences in court rolls frequently show villein tenants being fined for illegally taking thackstones (e.g. Table 9.1). While some of these stones may have been for commercial re-sale rather than for roofing their own buildings, three references have been found which record specifically that the stones were for covering the villeins' own houses. Two are particularly instructive: in a Bradford manor court in 1339 two villein tenants living in the township of Manningham were fined for digging stones to cover their houses, while in a Wakefield manor court three years earlier, two tenants were fined for an identical offence in Hipperholme township (Table 9.1, nos. 9 & 10). Repair clauses to copyhold property are also useful. In the Yeadon manor court for 29 July 1448 a tenant's responsibilities for maintaining a messuage included a house which was roofed 'with stones called *Sclatston*' (Price & Whittle 1984, 153). Occasionally, private charters can be useful, where they too include repair clauses. An unusual lease of 1432 contains specific details of a house to be built at Holdsworth, near Halifax. It is unusual in that it is written in both Latin and Middle-English. The building, a cruck structure of three bays, had to be covered *cum tegulis* – *Anglice, slatestons*, 'with tiles – in English, slatestones' (Moorhouse 1981, 807). Although scattered, the documentary evidence shows that stone-covered peasant houses were not uncommon.

The presence of a stone roof covering implies a permanent sturdy structure to the house frame below. Although stone-built medieval manor houses were more numerous than surviving examples suggest (see above), documentary evidence suggests that peasant houses were of timber. As such, they would have to be properly framed timber buildings, as is suggested by the wealth of indirect documentary evidence for their construction (Moorhouse 1981, 801-21). It is therefore likely that many, if not most, of the medieval peasant houses in the eastern Pennines were solid, if not substantial structures. The term 'peasant' described a very broad class of society which included a number of different types of tenure, even within the same manor, while it is clear from regular, heavy fines incurred by the same person in successive courts, that the status of the family into which people were born did not necessarily prevent them from acquiring property and wealth. Equally, both bondland and freehold land was acquired by villein and freeman alike: one of the most important late medieval timber-framed buildings in the county, Horbury Hall near Wakefield, was built by the Amayas family on copyhold land in the late 15th century. While burdened with the onerous manorial ties of serfdom, the medieval villeins in West Yorkshire manipulated the system to become wealthy men. It is against this complicated 'peasant' social structure that the wide variety of buildings in which they lived should be assessed.

One type of building, the barn, was common to all social levels, whether they formed part of the farm complex or lay out in the fields (Moorhouse 1981, 831-35). A number of late medieval timber-framed barns survive in the county but it is uncertain how many of their stone roofs are original. The recent re-roofing of the important barn at Stank Hall, Beeston, near Leeds, has shown the roof to have been replaced, probably during the 17th century when the barn was modified. While other roof coverings for barns are recorded in the documents, stone slates were particularly common. The accounts for the rebuilding of the tithe barn belonging to the rectory manor of Dewsbury at Hartshead in 1350-51 are particularly detailed in recording materials and the sequence of work, but simply record the cost of 15d. for stone slates and the carriage costs of 2s. (Moorhouse 1981, 834; Chadwick 1911, 381). Similarly, the barns of minor tenants were roofed in stone. The 1423-25 bailiff's building accounts for Thorner record the carriage of *sclatston* from Shadwell for a barn on the holding of William Cukschawe in Thorner (Table 9.1).

Stone slates were also used in the walls of buildings, where they replaced conventional wattle and daub, or 'stud and muntin' as an infill between the studs. Original stone slate infilling survives in a number of late medieval timber-framed gentry houses, such as Calverley Old Hall and Shibden Hall, but perhaps most spectacularly at the recently uncovered medieval walling at Sandal vicarage

44. Fleet Mills, Rothwell, showing the exposed shaped and set stone corework infilling the timber frame of the weir, of post-medieval date, lying above the truncated medieval weirs shown in illustration 45.

43. Wall of Sandal rectory, from inside, showing the original stone slate infill between the studs in the late medieval timber framing.

45. Fleet Mills, Rothwell, showing truncated remains of numerous medieval timber-framed weirs, with one exposed timber still in position and disturbed dressed and set stonework, which would have looked like that shown in illustration 44 before being disturbed.

(illustration 43). In all cases the position of the slates between original horizontal members of the frame shows that they could only have been inserted while the building was being erected. Fines in manorial court rolls for the illegal taking of stones from the walls of buildings suggests that thackstones may have been used lower down the social scale as a wall filler (Moorhouse 1981, 808-09). Such a suggestion is enhanced by the fact that medieval peasant buildings in the county were of timber. The stones taken from the walls of peasant buildings have, therefore, to be from something other than the main structure. The most likely suggestion is that stones infilled the walls of peasant houses, as they did higher up the scale.

Rubble quarries

During the Middle Ages, as today, rubble was in demand as foundation and backing material or corework. It was used chiefly in the cores of timber-framed dams attached to corn and fulling mills and forming part of fishponds. Account rolls make it clear that, although a variety of materials was used in the cores of many types of dam, the dominant material was roughly shaped but undressed stone or rubble. This was not simply tipped into the fill, but was, in the words of the documents, properly laid, often laminated with other materials as bedding agents (Moorhouse 1981, 712-16). Such medieval set stone corework has recently been uncovered in a series of superimposed medieval weirs at Fleet Mills on the River Aire (Moorhouse forthcoming [c]; illustrations 44 & 45). The well documented often annual destruction of dams and weirs attached to mills on major rivers must have created a constant and heavy demand for broken stones, and often quarries were opened up specifically as a source of rubble. The Leeds manorial accounts throughout the 14th and 15th centuries provide a wealth of information as to the large quantities of rubble required each year, what it was used for and where it was quarried from. References to the given sources of rubble stone from specific quarries are shown in illustration 46. In keeping with references to buying stone slates, there are many references in the Leeds accounts to buying stone corework for the various dams and weirs on the River Aire, but in only a handful of cases are the sources given, shown in illustration 46.

The quantities of rubble required can be gauged by repairs in 1400 when 170 cartloads of stone were bought from a quarry at Town End to fill in a breach 70ft (21.3m) wide in the corn mill dam. Documentary evidence suggests that there were well over 100 contemporary working water-powered mills in West York-shire between the 13th and 15th centuries. On all but the minor streams many were subject to annual damage, and in a few cases total destruction (Moorhouse 1981, 712-13, 716). The repairs of the dams and weirs to these mills would have created a strain not only on the provision of materials but also on the cost of paying people to carry out the repairs. Thus the customary repair of dams and weirs attached to certain holdings within manors had become common practice in the region by the mid-13th century, the date when adequate documentation commences. Most manors provided the material and sustenance, and the tenants

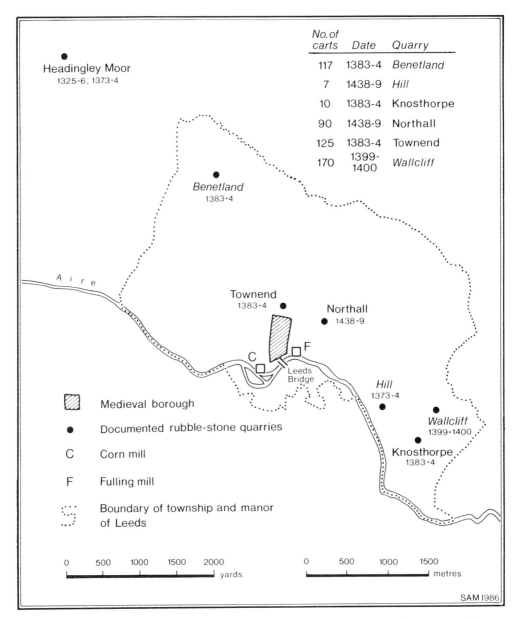

No. of carts	Date	Quarry
117	1383-4	*Benetland*
7	1438-9	*Hill*
10	1383-4	Knosthorpe
90	1438-9	Northall
125	1383-4	Townend
170	1399-1400	*Wallcliff*

46. Location of quarry sources for rubble recorded in the 14th- and 15th-century Leeds manorial accounts (sources: Le Parourel 1957; Kirkby 1983).

their labour, but the manor of Wakefield duties required the tenants *inter alia* to provide timber and stones, as well as their labour (Moorhouse 1981, 714-15).

Conclusion

The documentary evidence shows that both stone slates and rubble were subject to a wide and constant demand throughout the Middle Ages. The slates were used as a covering for many types of building at all social levels, but both the documentary evidence and surviving examples show that they were also used extensively as the infill between the studs in both external and partition walls in the buildings of all social classes. Carefully shaped rubble was used extensively as the properly laid core to a variety of dams and weirs. The breaching of weirs on major rivers could occur almost annually, creating a much greater demand for rubble than might at first appear. The many references to the purchase of stone roofing slates in manorial accounts, on an almost annual basis, and the many references to illegal extraction recorded in court rolls, suggest that those quarries which are documented either through minor place-names or as the sources of material are only a handful of the many which must have existed. The quarries which provided this material could lie on geologies where the suitable sandstone beds were not exposed, as seen at *Hillam Burchard*. It is also clear from the documents that many of these quarries were short-lived, again as we saw at *Hillam*. It will be demonstrated elsewhere that many quarries and mines were opened up within a field system and, when exhausted, were filled in and reverted back to cultivation (Moorhouse 1981): the whetstone quarry recorded from the 1260s in Calverley township had been under the plough well before the 1750s (Moorhouse 1991, 583, 584, n.3), while medieval ploughing overlies extensive quarrying of uncertain type to the south of Druid's Altar Lane, Bingley. What is clear is that the identifiable sources of stone slate and rubble known from documentary sources represent only a minute proportion of those which existed, an 'industry' which existed through many small, short-lived quarries operated by professional craftsmen, rather than a number of large quarry sites.

Postscript

This paper forms an earlier version of a chapter to appear in Moorhouse 1991, where the evidence for many of the statements made above is presented and discussed. Further evidence has been found for the importance of the stone slate quarrying in the later Middle Ages, and the rise of centres such as those at Bramley and Pudsey. Slaters ran their own quarries, often leased from the manor on recurring leases, and employed slaters to produce the slates whilst they were out contracting work, often up to 40 miles away. In contrast to movement by combined land and water transport found with building stone, stone slates were always moved around by cart and occasionally waggon. Slaters often worked in colonies of other craftsmen involved in the building trade, such as the masons, carpenters, theckers, bordewrights, wrights, smiths and more specialised iron-workers such as nailers.

ACKNOWLEDGEMENTS

I am grateful to John Hedges and the West Yorkshire Archives and Archaeology Joint Committee for permission to use illustrations 37-41 and 43 in advance of their publication, and to Bob Yarwood, Jenny Marriott and Martin Ecclestone for access to transcripts of medieval manorial accounts for Methley and Thorner in advance of their publication.

ABBREVIATIONS
(used mainly in Table 9.1)

BCR	Bradford court rolls: an interrupted series of transcripts and translations of courts held between 1339 and 1425 in four volumes held by West Yorkshire Archives Service/Bradford District Archives
NRO	Nottinghamshire Record Office
PRO	Public Record Office
WYAS/L	West Yorkshire Archives Service/Leeds City Archives
YAS	Yorkshire Archaeological Society

BIBLIOGRAPHY

Chadwick, S.J., 1911 — Account rolls of Dewsbury rectory, 1348-1356, *Yorkshire Archaeol. J.*, **20** (1911), 352-92

Faull, M.L., and Moorhouse, S.A. (ed), 1981 — *West Yorkshire: an archaeological survey to AD 1500*, 4 vols. Wakefield: West Yorkshire MDC, 1981

Giles, C., 1986 — *Rural Houses in West Yorkshire, 1400-1830*. Royal Commission on Historical Monuments, Suppl. ser. **8**, London: HMSO, 1986

Kirby, J. (ed), 1983 — *The manor and borough of Leeds, 1425-1662: an edition of documents*. Publ. Thoresby Soc., **57** (1981), Leeds, 1983

Knoop, D., and Jones, G.P., 1933 — The building of Eton College, 1442-1460: a study in operative masonry, *Ars Quattuor Coronatorum*, **46** (1933), 70-114

Knoop, D., and Jones, G.P., 1938 — The English medieval quarry, *Econ. Hist. Rev.*, **9** (1938), 17-37

Knoop, D., and Jones, G.P., 1967 — *The medieval mason: an economic history of English stone building in the later Middle Ages and early modern times.* 3rd ed., Manchester: University Press, 1967

Lancaster, W.T., and Baildon, W.P. (ed), 1904 — *The coucher book of the Cistercian abbey of Kirkstall.* Publ. Thoresby Soc., **8**, Leeds, 1904

Lister, J., and Ogden, J.H. (ed), 1906 — Poll Tax 2 Richard II, 1379: parish of Halifax in the wapentake of Morley with notes on the local return, *Halifax Antiq. Soc. Rep. Pap.*, 1906; text repr. from *Yorkshire Archaeol. J.*, **6** (1881), 287-306

Moorhouse, S., 1981 — The rural medieval landscape, in Faull & Moorhouse 1981, 581-850

Moorhouse, S., 1991 — *The quest for stone: medieval quarrying in West Yorkshire.* Yorkshire Archaeology, **4**. Wakefield: West Yorkshire Archaeology Service, forthcoming

Moorhouse, S., forthcoming (a) — Excavation at the deserted medieval settlement of *Hillam Burchard*, 1981, in Moorhouse forthcoming (b)

Moorhouse, S., forthcoming (b) — *Medieval settlement in West Yorkshire.* Yorkshire Archaeology, **5**, Wakefield: West Yorkshire Archaeology Service, forthcoming

Moorhouse, S., forthcoming (c) — The medieval corn mills in the manor of Rothwell, in Moorhouse forthcoming (b)

Price, G.R., and Whittle, S.J., 1984 — *A transcript of the court rolls of Yeadon 1361-1476 with the early rentals and accounts of Esholt Priory.* Draughton: privately published, 1984

Raine, J. (ed)., 1859   *The fabric rolls of York Minster: with an appendix of illustrative comments.* Publ. Surtees Soc., **35**

Salzman, L.F., 1923   *English industries of the Middle Ages.* 2nd ed., Oxford: Clarendon Press, 1923

Salzman, L.F., 1967   *Building in England down to 1540.* Corrected ed., Oxford: Clarendon Press, 1967

Turner, J.H., 1893   *History of Brighouse, Rastrick and Hipperholme.* Bingley: privately published, 1893

Vellacott, C.H., 1912   Quarrying, *Victoria history of the county of York,* ed. F.M. Page, **2**, 376–81. London: Constable, 1912

Walker, S.A. (ed), 1981   *Wakefield court rolls 1331-3.* Wakefield Court Roll Ser., Yorkshire Archaeol. Soc., 1981

Walton, J., 1975   The English stone-slater's craft, *Folk Life,* **13**, 38–53

Yarwood, R.E., and Marriott, J., forthcoming   A fourteenth-century manor site at Methley with a note on the contemporary landscape, in Moorhouse forthcoming (b)

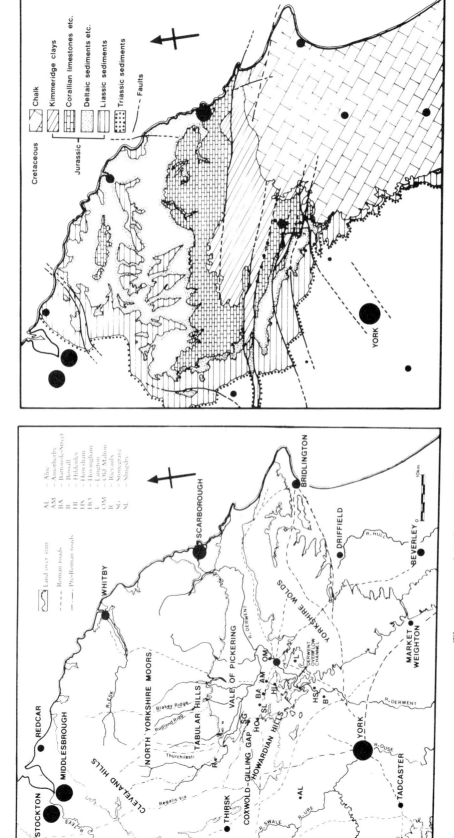

47. The area around Malton, East Yorkshire: (a) topography and communications; (b) geology.

Chapter 10

Hildenley Limestone: A Fine Quality Dimensional and Artifact Stone from Yorkshire

J. R. Senior

An interim survey of buildings and artifacts found in east Yorkshire indicates that a unique facies of Upper Jurassic (Oxfordian) limestone found on the Hildenley Estate, 2 miles (3km) WSW of Malton, North Yorkshire, has been quarried since c.AD 200. Although this fine quality stone has been used for dimensional masonry and for detailed sculptures since the Roman administration of Britain, it has been exploited only sporadically because the reserves of stone have always been small.

Introduction

The ancient quarry complex of Hildenley is situated some 2 miles (3km) WSW of Malton, North Yorkshire (SE 711 747), on the northern margins of the Howardian Hills (illustration 47). The quarries cover an area of *c*.7.75 hectares and consist of a pattern of pit quarries surrounded by heaps of stone waste (illustration 48a). A few more recent 17th- to early 20th-century quarries still have visible faces (illustration 48b & c).

Geographically Hildenley is situated on a fault-bounded Upper Jurassic limestone ridge which marks the southern margin of the Vale of Pickering (illustration 47). During the Devensian ice advance in the Late Pleistocene (20-18,000 BP) the low lying Vale of Pickering was the site of the ice-dammed Lake Pickering which was drained via the Derwent Gorge near Kirkham Priory. After the retreat of the Devensian ice the Vale of Pickering was left as a tract of low-lying and extremely marshy ground which the Cistercian community at Rievaulx started to drain soon after 1158 (Waites 1959, 490). Ancient track-ways tended to utilise the drier ridges because of the marshy Vale of Pickering, so the eastern branch of the Regalis Via which connected the western edge of the North Yorkshire Moors (Hambleton Hills) with the Yorkshire Wolds, followed the limestone ridge a little to the north of the Hildenley quarry complex. This same ridge-way was also used by the Romans for communications with the fortress at *Derventio* (Malton) (road 815 of Margary 1957, 155). Wade's Causeway, the Roman road from Aislaby (NZ 850 087) connected Whitby and the coastal signal stations with *Eboracum* (York) via *Derventio*; it transversed the North Yorkshire Moors and the Vale of Pickering (road 81b of Margary 1957, 156; Hayes & Rutter 1964) to Amotherby. Road 81b is thought by Hayes and Rutter (1964, 19) to have terminated at Amotherby, but earlier authors (Young 1817, 700; Elgee & Elgee 1933, 138) thought that the road

48. Limestone quarries at Hildenley, near Malton, East Yorkshire: (a) old quarry pits and waste heaps; (b) Home Farm quarry; (c) main quarry.

continued southwards towards the navigable River Derwent and Roman kiln fields of Crambeck (Corder 1928; SE 735 673), near the present site of Kirkham Priory. If Wade's Causeway did extend southwards from Amotherby as indicated by Elgee and Elgee along the trackways which still exist there today, then this Roman road cuts the western edge of the Hildenley quarry complex (illustration 49).

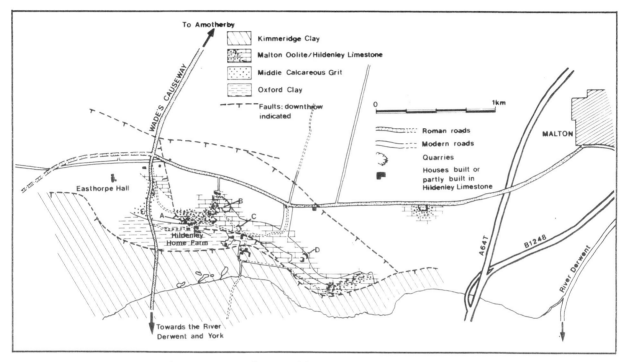

49.   The quarry complex at Hildenley, near Malton, East Yorkshire.

The geology of Hildenley Limestone

The Howardian Hills form the southern margin of an important fault graben structure which underlies the Vale of Pickering, the complexity of which is almost totally masked by Kimmeridge and Speeton Clays (Upper Jurassic to Lower Cretaceous), with a veneer of Pleistocene varved lacustrine clays and gravels (illustration 50). This economically important fault zone is a reflection of a much older and deeper basement fault structure which affects the region from the Pennines (the Craven Fault System), the Vale of York and the Vale of Pickering (the Howardian Hills Fault Belt) and off-shore down to the region of the Wash (the Dowsing Fault Line). The fault graben complex beneath the Vale of Pickering acts as a hinge-line system, effectively separating the Mesozoic Cleveland sedimentary basin from the Market Weighton Block – East Midland Shelf (Yorkshire

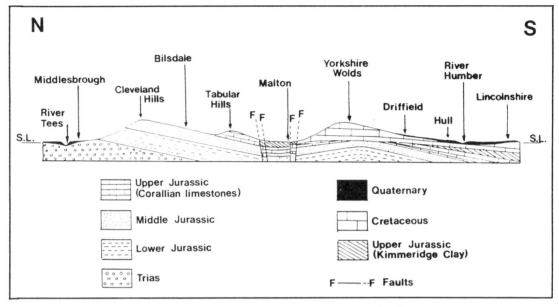

50. A structural sketch section across the Vale of Pickering.

Wolds – Lincolnshire Wolds). The Market Weighton Block acts as a structural 'high' because it is underlain by buoyant basement rocks, parts of which have been interpreted as granitoid in composition (Bott *et al.* 1978).

During the Oxfordian period (Upper Jurassic) this area (with the probable exception of the structural 'high' in the area of the Market Weighton Block) was covered by shallow tropical seas and the sediments deposited included calcareous sandstones (calcarenites), oolitic and reefal limestones (biosparites, bio-oomicrites and oosparites) and associated detrital talus deposits. The facies represented by these limestones and associated rocks in the Yorkshire Corallian are very variable and have been documented by Wright (1972) and Wilson (1933 & 1949). However, the very fine-grained limestones (biomicrites) found locally in the vicinity of Hildenley and North Grimston (the North Grimston Cementstone Member; Wright 1976, 130; SE 848 672) do not fit into the normal pattern of Corallian sedimentation in this region. It has been suggested by Wilson (1933, 502) and Kent (1980, 73) that the pure white limestone found at Hildenley represents fine-grained calcareous material washed off some nearby Upper Jurassic reef. This lagoonal facies interpretation does have some attraction but it does not entirely explain the restricted areal extent of the Hildenley Limestone; the presence of modified very fossiliferous Coral Rag deposits (Blake & Hudleston 1877, 372) in the upper sections at Hildenley; nor the apparent marginal interdigitation with oolitic limestones. Work in Western Europe, particularly in the area of the North

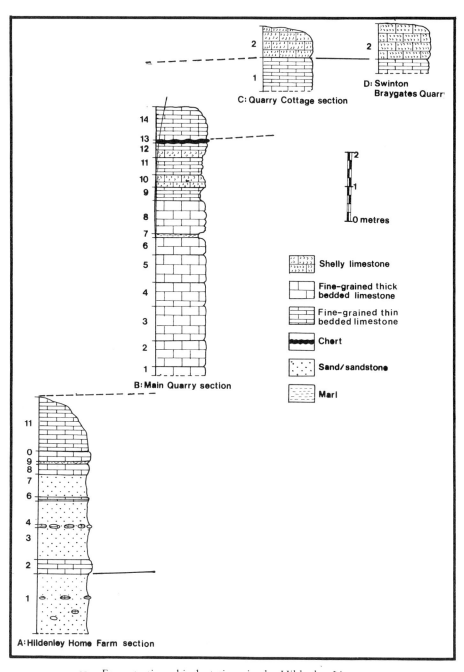

51. Four stratigraphical sections in the Hildenley Limestone.

Sea graben structures (Ziegler 1975) and the Wessex Basin (Jenkyns & Senior 1977), has shown that during the Jurassic Era many ancient basement fault systems were reactivated during the progressive opening of the North Atlantic. There is field evidence that syn-sedimentary fault movements also occurred during the Callovian to Oxfordian periods (Middle-Upper Jurassic) in the area now occupied by the Hambleton and Howardian Hills in Yorkshire. The restricted occurrence of fine-grained porcellaneous limestones of Oxfordian age at Hildenley and at North Grimston (illustration 47) might therefore also be interpreted as the sedimentary response to Upper Jurassic fault movements, where fine-grained material was swept off sea-floor 'highs' into adjacent, localised and slightly deeper fault bounded sea-floor basins. This would account for the areal restriction, the small volume of the Hildenley Limestone (illustration 49) and the interdigitation with normal oolitic sediments (Malton Oolite) at the margins of the deposit. After fault movement had ceased then a modified variety of the Coral Rag facies was deposited in the upper sections at Hildenley (illustration 51).

Sparse ammonite faunas from the Hildenley quarries suggest an Upper Densiplicatum Zone date for the Hildenley Limestone, which correlates with the Malton Oolite Formation and not the North Grimston Cementstones as suggested by Wright (1976, 133) which are of later Glosense Zone date (J.K. Wright in Cope 1980, 74). The occurrence of the North Grimston Cementstones, a similar fine-grained calcareous deposit, at a slightly higher stratigraphical position is not inconsistent with the concept that these faults were active over an extended period of time. Under similar fault-controlled sea-floor conditions the same sediment type may be deposited. The geology of the Howardian Hills area has been further complicated by later reversals on some of the faults in this asymmetrical hinge-line structure. A fuller account of the evidence for the fault control of sedimentary facies in the Middle and Upper Jurassic of the Yorkshire Basin will appear elsewhere.

Description of the Hildenley Limestone

Hildenley Limestone is a white to buff-white porcellaneous rock described by Barry *et al.* (1839) as 'resembling indurate Chalk'. It is very fine-grained (illustration 52a) and in thin-section contains up to 5% of the component *Rhaxella perforata* Hinde (illustration 52b), a rounded microfossil common in the Oxfordian limestones of Yorkshire (Sorby 1851). Body fossils occur sporadically in most of the beds exposed and these include the spines and plates of the echinoids *Paracidaris* and *Hemicidaris* (illustration 52c), *Nanagyra nana*, *Chlamys* sp. and *Nerinea* sp. Where the fossils have been partly silicified they stand out in relief on weathered buildings and quarry faces. In the vicinity of exposed minor faults some chertification of the limestones can be seen, but no chert has so far been noticed in the dimensional stone used for building purposes, so any chert-bearing limestones must have been discarded during dressing.

Four quarry faces are currently visible (illustration 51a-d), the limestones of the lower section (illustration 51a: Hildenley Home Farm) are arenaceous

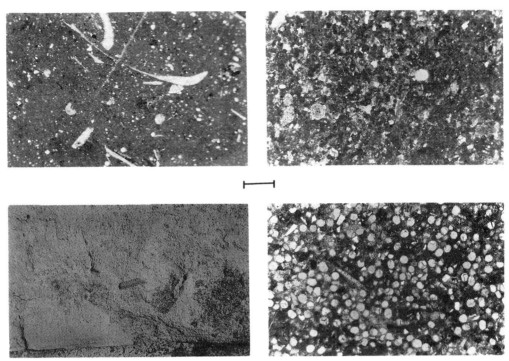

52. Hildenley Limestone sedimentology (scale = 1mm, unless otherwise indicated):
a. (*top left*) photomicrograph showing fine-grained limestone with microfossils and shell debris; b. (*top right*) occasional rounded fossils of *Rhaxella perforata* Hinde in limestone from the main quarry; c. (*bottom left*) fossiliferous ashlar of Kirkham Priory (scale = 10mm); d. (*bottom right*) *Rhaxella*-rich limestone from the Home Farm quarry.

(illustration 52d), grading upwards from the soft buff-coloured calcarenite sediments of the ?Birdsall Calcareous Grit Member or the Middle Calcareous Grit Member. The largest section, north of the stables and cottages complex (SE 7493 7100: illustration 51b), exposes the best fine-grained limestones which have been used extensively for dimensional and sculptural stone. The topmost beds, which probably locally represent the Coral Rag Member, also have a white biomicritic matrix but have much more shell content, including oyster beds, bivalve and echinoderm debris and occasional corals. These upper beds can be seen in the quarries at SE 7460 7134 and SE 7542 7070 (illustration 51c & d). Wilson (1933, 503) recorded that mudstones of the Upper Calcareous Grit Formation were formerly exposed at Hildenley overlying the Hildenley Limestone (Malton Oolite Member).

Hildenley Limestone is a good freestone capable of being worked in all directions and because it takes a fine arris it is an excellent stone for sculpture (illustration 58). However, because of the thin-bedded nature of this deposit, only stone up to 0.6m in thickness was obtainable from the quarries and much of the stone produced was less than 0.3m thick. In the *Report on the selection of Stone for Building the New Houses of Parliament*, Barry *et al.* (1839) noted that in the quarries the Hildenley Limestone showed extensive frost shattering. However, inspection of the stone used in the construction of various buildings indicates that this is not such an important consideration. Although very similar in appearance to Hildenley Stone, the fine-grained limestones of the North Grimston Cementstone Member are very prone to frost shattering and have apparently been used only rarely as a dimensional stone.

The exploitation of Hildenley Limestone

The following should be regarded only as an interim survey of the use of this geologically unique Oxfordian limestone, as inspection of buildings and museum collections of stone sculptures and artifacts continues to provide new data. So far I have seen no pre-Roman artifacts in Hildenley Limestone, but as a precaution future investigators should look very carefully at any Chalk-like stone artifacts found in the area around Malton.

Roman stone-work and artifacts

There is circumstantial evidence of Roman activity in the Hildenley area. Kitson Clark (1935, 19-20) records Roman burials at Hildenley, Crambeck and East Ness and notes that 'potteries at Crambeck on the Derwent and export of stone from Hildenley shows us a fairly busy neighbourhood. All this must be a response of Malton; which was a road centre for news and trade. . .' The Roman coffin burial at Hildenley (Kitson Clark 1935, 88) was found just south of Hildenley Hall and J.L. Kirk (quoted in Kitson Clark 1935, 88) suggests that 'the stone for the Malton Roman fort [probably] came from this Hildenley district. Inscriptions at Malton and Norton were on Hildenley limestone . . . The quarries have not yet been identified.'

However, there is little visible evidence to associate stone extraction from Hildenley with the building of the 'early' Roman fort. In his chronology of fort occupation at Malton, Corder (1929, 64-68) indicates that no stone was involved in the building of the pre-Agricolan vexillation fort of before AD 70, but the first stone gate was 'probably begun before Agricola's advance into Scotland and nothing more than the gate was completed before the troops were withdrawn for the Caledonian campaign'. Wenham (1974, 14) notes that the fort at *Derventio* was rebuilt in stone during the early part of the reign of Trajan (AD 98-117) and Corder (1929, 67) records good buildings of stone construction in Period 5 (*c.* AD 300-69). The use of stone in the construction of 2nd-to 4th-century *Derventio* was substantiated by Wenham's account of more recent excavation in Malton (1974). During the excavation of the *vicus* (1968-70) the remains of the 'Town House' were discovered, a lavish house with fine stone walls facing the road (the continuation of the Via Praetoria) with hypocaust heating of some rooms and the remains of fine mosaic floors. In this important house (dated AD 200 to 367), Wenham found one of a pair of finely carved door lintels, the 'Winged Victory',

53. Roman artifacts in Hildenley Limestone: (a) 'Winged Victory' from the excavations of the Town House of the vicus, *Derventio* (scale = 0.1m); (b) lathe-turned late 4th-century artifact from the well of the Langton villa, near Malton (scale = 0.1m); (c) railed sill from the basilica building of the Principia under York Minster (Crown Copyright, courtesy RCHME).

which on examination was found to have been sculpted in Hildenley Limestone (illustration 53a).

Examination of the Roman stone artifacts in Malton Museum and those now in the Yorkshire Museum has not verified the opinion of J.L. Kirk, cited by Kitson Clark (1935, 88) that the inscription stones from Malton were carved in Hildenley Limestone. Other locally available Upper Jurassic limestones can be recognised, notably Calcareous Grit, Malton Oolite and Coral Rag. Only one Roman inscription stone cut in Hildenley Limestone has been seen so far during this investigation; this, a fragment of altar (*RIB* 713) with part of a crudely carved figure and the letters CV, was found in the Orchard Field in 1943 and is now in Old Malton Priory church. This stone had been crudely recut to form the voussoir of an arch. During the 1926 and 1929-31 excavations of a Roman villa site at Langton (Corder & Kirk 1932), 2½ miles (4km) south of Malton (SE 814 674), a circular lathe-turned stone (no.1; later interpreted as a pewter plate mould: Goodall 1972, 34) was found 7.70m down the well of the settlement, between the dwelling house and the boundary south of the bath house (Corder & Kirk 1932, 49-50). Coin evidence suggests that the well was first dug or last cleaned out after AD 335 but had been used as a rubbish pit until the end of the occupation *c*.AD 400. This finely turned artifact in Hildenley Limestone (illustration 53b) was found in a late 4th-century context (Goodall 1972).

During the 1967-73 excavations of the *principia* beneath the crossing of York Minster two items of dimensional masonry in Hildenley Limestone were discovered, the largest and most important item being a sill with holes that once held metal railings. This sill (YM4; illustration 53c), whose original function is unknown, was found in the nave of the Roman basilica, having been moved from its original position in antiquity and re-used (D. Phillips, personal communication). A socketed voussoir block (Misc. 5) in Hildenley Limestone was also found.

Excavators of the Roman fort and *vicus* of *Derventio* do not seem to have taken a systematic interest in the types of stone used for dimensional masonry and artifacts, so it is difficult to assess how important the quarrying of Hildenley Limestone was during this period. The occurrence of quite large pieces of masonry in this material in the *principia* at *Eboracum* suggests that the stone was well known and liked. It is possible that further excavations in Malton and York may disclose more evidence of its use. The problem remains that after the Roman forts at both centres were abandoned they were systematically robbed of the ashlar by succeeding generations, so the Hildenley Limestone and other stone types used will indeed be incorporated in later buildings.

Anglo-Scandinavian ashlar and artifacts
There seems to be a 'rule of thumb' that stone is actively quarried and used in large quantities during periods of imperialistic expansion. Thus the opening of new quarries and cutting of stone associated with the Roman occupation of Britain

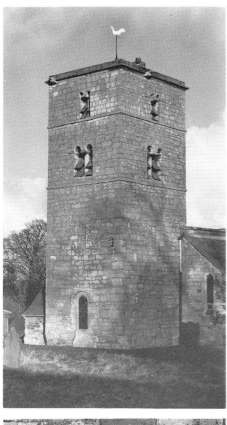

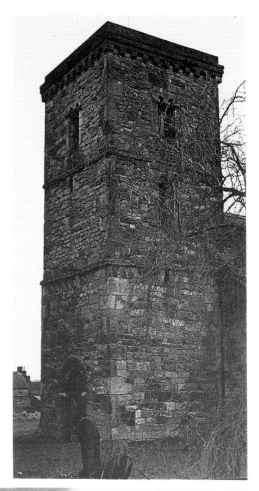

54. Use of Hildenley Limestone in pre-Conquest churches. 1. Appleton-le Street, near Malton: (a) tower,
(b) details of the ashlar; 2. Hovingham church, near Malton: (c) tower, (d) details of the belfry opening.

ceased when the infrastructure of Roman government broke down about AD 410 (Blair 1963, 159). In the next few centuries the Anglo-Scandinavian inheritors of North Yorkshire apparently used stone in only a relatively few of the more important buildings such as churches and for sculptures, and it is probable that this stone was largely robbed from Roman buildings. There is only a little evidence that Hildenley Limestone was being actively quarried between AD 410 and 1066.

Appleton-le-Street, near Malton (SE 735 736) has a late pre-Conquest church dedicated to All Saints with a square western tower with megalithic side alternate quoins and double belfry windows with plain square imposts (illustration 54a). The belfry window ashlar and many of the tower quoin stones are of Hildenley Limestone (illustration 54b), as are other parts of the tower fabric; other local stone types have been used as well. The construction of the western tower suggests that this may have been rebuilt using materials from an earlier building (church?). The 12th- and 13th-century remodelling of the church also includes re-used Hildenley Limestone. New Hildenley stone was used for the 13th-century west door frame.

The modified late Anglo-Scandinavian church at Hovingham, near Malton (SE 666 758), also dedicated to All Saints, has a square western tower (illustration 54c) with megalithic side alternate quoins, double belfry windows with chamfered imposts, double side windows and an upper door (Taylor 1977, 769). Many of the quoin stones are of Hildenley Limestone, as is the ashlar of the double side and belfry windows (illustration 54d) and some of the tower ashlar. The incorporation of 9th-century sculpture into the tower fabric suggests that this tower has been rebuilt, which is also indicated by the re-use of round-headed window lintels in Hildenley Limestone as quoin stones. Hovingham church is richly endowed with 9th- and 10th-century Anglo-Scandinavian sculptures and must have been an important ecclesiastical site.

Could the base of the square western tower of the church at Amotherby, near Malton (SE 751 735), be pre-Conquest in age? Virtually all the lower section of the tower has been constructed using Hildenley Limestone (illustration 55a).

A few Anglo-Scandinavian artifacts in Hildenley Limestone have been recognised so far. These include the 10th-century Anglian cross-head (OM2; illustration 55b) now in Old Malton church which could have been cut from Roman masonry from the *Derventio* fort or *vicus;* also a 10th-century cross-shaft fragment (YM12) found in the York Minster excavations of 1968-72.

A plain grave slab (YM43) and two stone coffins (one of a child), also from the York Minster excavations, were cut from the shelly limestones from the topmost horizons at Hildenley. The stone coffins (illustration 55c & d) were found in an 11th-century context, but possibly had been re-used (D. Phillips, personal communication).

The use of Hildenley Limestone for the window ashlar at Hovingham and Appleton-le-Street and for the grave slab and coffins of the York Minster excavations suggest that there may have been some quarrying activity at Hildenley during the late pre-Conquest period.

55.   Pre-Conquest ashlar and artifacts in Hildenley Limestone: (a) the tower of
Amotherby church, near Malton; (b) a 10th-century cross head (OM2) now in Old
Malton church; (c) coffin in coarsely fossiliferous Hildenley Limestone found in the
York Minster excavations (Crown Copyright, courtesy RCHME).

From the Norman Conquest of northern England to the dissolution of the monasteries (1070-1540)

With the conquest of northern England by another imperialistic regime it could be expected that there would have been reactivation of the quarrying industry at Hildenley, especially as the properties of this stone resemble those of Caen Stone, so favoured by Norman masons. However, if the account of the Harrying of the North (1069) attributed to Simeon of Durham is correct (Stephenson 1855, 551; 1987, 137) then the decimation of the peoples of Yorkshire by slaughter and famine probably postponed the reactivation of quarrying at Hildenley and other sites. By the early 12th century the qualities of this stone type had been rediscovered and it was put to good use as a fine building stone.

This renaissance in the use of Hildenley Limestone seems to have coincided with the founding of Kirkham Priory by Walter L'Espec in 1122 (also the founding benefactor of Rievaulx Abbey). This Augustinian establishment, dedicated to the Holy Trinity, was constructed on a possible pre-existing Roman site·at the head of navigation on the River Derwent, where it runs through the spillway channel cut during the late Devensian glaciation of Yorkshire. The priory is some $3\frac{1}{2}$ miles (5.5km) ESE of the Hildenley quarry complex. Hildenley Limestone was used for the ashlar in the 12th-century church and tower (1180). Stone from local quarries (notably Whitwell Oolite; also associated deltaic sandstone and iron-stones; Bajocian, Middle Jurassic) was used for the rubble arches, wall fills and less important walls. Hildenley Limestone was also used during the extensive early 13th-century rebuilding of the priory complex and for a 14th-century minor building programme (illustration 56a). There are many fine examples of carving in this limestone at Kirkham (illustration 56b & c).

Within 28 years of the founding of Kirkham, a priory of Gilbertine Canons was also founded at Old Malton, less than half a mile (0.5km) north of the Roman fort site of *Derventio*. Much of the priory was built in the late 12th and early 13th centuries using Hildenley Limestone ashlar (illustration 57a-c). Was all the limestone newly quarried or was it partly robbed stone from the remnants of Roman Malton?

After the dissolution of the priory in 1539, this building was robbed of much of its fine limestone ashlar and only a portion of the western façade with the nave arcades still remains. In *c.*1636 the residue of the building was walled and consolidated to form the parish church. Many of the contemporary houses and cottages in Old and New Malton were built using a fine white limestone!

The use of Hildenley Limestone in the fabric of the church of St Michael, Barton-le-Street, $4\frac{3}{4}$ miles (7.5km) WNW of Malton (SE 721 742), is almost contemporary with that of Old Malton Priory. This middle to late 12th-century church was totally rebuilt in 1871, using much of the original fine carvings in Hildenley Limestone (illustration 58a-c) and some newly carved Hildenley stone for good measure (illustration 58d). It is now difficult to ascertain the correct iconography of the remaining 12th-century sculptures as many seem to have been re-used out of context. Parts of the Romanesque doorway of the church of St Mary, Alne (SE 495 654) not only are stylistically similar to the carved stonework

58. Barton-le-Street church, near Malton:
(a)-(c) 12th-century sculptures in Hildenley
Limestone; (d) ?19th-century copy of a frieze
in Hildenley Limestone.

of Barton-le-Street, but in part are also manufactured from Hildenley Limestone. A complete survey of the medieval sculpture of these churches by J.T. Lang and the author will appear elsewhere.

The early to middle 13th-century cruciform parish church dedicated to St Botolph at Bossall, is situated $7\frac{3}{4}$ miles (12.25km) SW of Malton (SE 719 608) and $\frac{5}{8}$ mile (1km) from the River Derwent. Hildenley Limestone has been used for much of the original church, particularly the north and south transepts, the south walls of the nave, most of the interior and much of the corbel tables. Parts of the corbel tables, large portions of the west wall of the nave and the majority of the chancel have been later rebuilt using an inferior quality Calcareous Grit sandstone (Upper Jurassic).

The Cistercian monastery at Rievaulx near Helmsley (also founded by Walter L'Espec in 1131) had land holdings in the Vale of Pickering and therefore must have witnessed the construction of the priories at Kirkham and Old Malton. Therefore, it is not surprising to find the remnants of a well carved screen in Hildenley Limestone amongst the architectural remains from the Abbey.

Use of Hildenley Limestone from 1540 onwards
Following the dissolution of the monasteries, there seems to have been a general decline in the quarrying of Hildenley Limestone. Partly this was due to the availability of already dressed stone from the Kirkham and Old Malton sites. As has been already noted, Old Malton Priory was in a ruinous state by c.1636 and in need of consolidation; a large quantity of well cut stone from this building complex had been used in the construction of contemporary houses and cottages in the near vicinity.

There is a widely held view that the façade of Howsham Hall (built c.1619) was constructed from facing stone pillaged from Kirkham Priory. If this is correct, then the stone was certainly recut and the large Roman Doric and Corinthian columns at the front must have been cut from very large pieces of masonry. This Jacobean building is situated $1\frac{1}{2}$ miles (2.3km) south of Kirkham Priory (SE 736 631; illustration 59a).

This limestone was used in the construction of Slingsby Castle ($5\frac{1}{4}$ miles/8.5km WNW of Malton; SE 696 749). This Elizabethan-style house, whose architecture has been ascribed by Pevsner (1985, 347) to John Smithson, was built for Sir Charles Cavendish in the 1620s. Were the window mouldings and quoin stones (illustration 59b) freshly quarried from Hildenley or were they recut stone acquired from Kirkham or Old Malton?

Nunnington Hall, situated on the south bank of the River Rye some 8 miles (13km) NW of Malton (SE 670 794) was first built in the mid-16th century by Dr Robert Huicke, physician to Queen Elizabeth I; considerable additions were also made by Thomas Norcliffe in the early 17th century. Immediately on inheriting the Nunnington estate from his uncle in 1685, Richard Graham, first Viscount Preston, began to make extensive alterations to house and grounds. Within three years he had completely modernised the building both inside and out and it is at this time that a fine fireplace in Hildenley Limestone was added

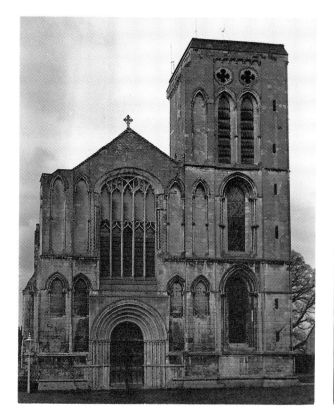

57.   The Gilbertine Priory church at Old Malton: (a) remains of the western end; (b) details of the west doorway; (c) blocking of south aisle arcading.

56. Kirkham Priory, south of Malton: (a) remains of the east end of the church; (b) heart box cut in Hildenley Limestone; (c) detail of sculptures on the north gatehouse.

59. Use of Hildenley Limestone in post-Dissolution buildings: (a) southern frontage of Howsham Hall, near Kirkham Priory; (b) details of window ashlar, Slingsby Castle, near Malton; (c) stable block at Hildenley Hall, near Malton.

to the Oak Hall. The style of this fireplace is thought to have been based on a French design included in Robert Pricke's pattern book, *The Architect's Store-House* (London 1674). This fireplace complements the excellent ?earlier stone floor constructed from hexagonal and square blocks of Hildenley Limestone.

About 1800 Sir George Strickland made extensive use of Hildenley Limestone in the construction of Hildenley Hall, the estate houses and farm buildings. Many of the buildings are now ruinous but Hildenley Home Farm, Trigger Farm, the Lodge Cottage, the extensive stables block and some other domestic buildings can still be seen (illustration 59c).

Also about 1800 C.H. Tatham used Hildenley stone for the paving and Corinthian columns in the chapel at Castle Howard (Barry *et al.* 1839, 541; Pevsner 1985, 114).

Hildenley Limestone has been used extensively in Amotherby village for the construction of 17th-to 19th-century cottages and houses. Also in several of the villages local to the Hildenley quarries, as far west as Stonegrave (illustration 47) there are a number of 18th-century vernacular buildings and walls which in part have been constructed from crudely cut Hildenley Limestone. This suggests that there was some quarrying activity during this period.

Hildenley Limestone was one of the many stone types considered by the inquiry undertaken in 1838 by Charles Barry, Henry T. De la Beche, William Smith and Charles H. Smith with reference to the selection of stone for building the new Houses of Parliament (Barry *et al.* 1839, 541). The investigators noted that if this stone were selected then a railway line would have to be constructed to the River Derwent. The stone would then be transported by shallow craft to London by river and sea, a route following that which would have been used by the Romans some 1,600 years or so before!

This limestone seems to have been used last in *c.*1933 for the construction of steps at the Royal Naval College, Greenwich, London (Mr and Mrs R. Baron; personal communication).

Conclusion

Although the limestone from the Hildenley quarries has been used sporadically over a period of at least 1,700 years, it has never gained the prominence that a stone of its properties and quality should have achieved. There is a simple reason for this: the reserves of this unique deposit of rock have always been too small for extensive and protracted exploitation.

ACKNOWLEDGEMENTS

I am most grateful to Mr and Mrs R. Baron for allowing access to the Hildenley Estate; also for the patient help given to me in this initial survey by my colleagues B. Dobson, D. Doran, R. Kilburn, J.T. Lang, D. Phillips and H.J. Smith. This study was partly financed by the University of Durham Staff Research Fund.

BIBLIOGRAPHY

Barry, C., De La Beche, H.T., Smith, W., and Smith, C.H., 1839 — Selection of Stone for Building the New Houses of Parliament, *Parliamentary Papers (HC)*, **30** (1839), 3-43

Blair, P.H., 1963 — *Roman Britain and Early England, 55 BC to AD 871*. London: Nelson, 1963

Blake, J.F., and Hudleston, W.H., 1877 — On the Corallian rocks of England, *Quart. J. Geol. Soc. London*, **33** (1877), 260-405

Bott, M.H.P., Robinson, J., and Kohnstamm, M.A., 1978 — Granites beneath Market Weighton, East Yorkshire, *J. Geol. Soc. London*, **135** (1978), 535-43

Cope, J.C.W. (ed.), 1980 — *A Correlation of Jurassic Rocks in the British Isles*, pt **2**: *Middle and Upper Jurassic*. London: Geological Society of London, 1980

Corder, M.A., 1926 — *The Roman Pottery at Crambeck, Castle Howard*. Roman Malton and District Reports, **1**. York: Yorkshire Archaeological Society, 1926

Corder, M.A., 1930 — *The Defences of the Roman Fort at Malton*. Roman Malton and District Reports, **2**. Oxford: Yorkshire Archaeological Society, 1930

Corder, M.A., and Kirk, J.L., 1932 — *A Roman villa at Langton, near Malton, E. Yorkshire*. Roman Malton and District Reports, **4**. Oxford: Yorkshire Archaeological Society, 1932

Elgee, F., and Elgee, H.W., 1933 — *The Archaeology of Yorkshire*. London: Methuen, 1933

Goodall, I.H., 1972. — Industrial Evidence from the Villa at Langton, East Yorkshire, *Yorkshire Archaeol. J.*, **44** (1972), 32-37

Hayes, R.H., and Rutter, J.G., 1964 — *Wade's Causeway*. Res. Rep. **4**, Scarborough: Scarborough Archaeological and History Society, 1964

Jenkyns, H.C., and Senior, J.R., 1977 — A Liassic palaeofault from Dorset, *Geol. Mag.*, **114** (1977), 47-52

Kent, P., 1980 — *Eastern England from the Tees to the Wash*. British Regional Geology, London: HMSO, 1980

Kitson Clark, M., 1935 — *A Gazetteer of Roman Remains in East Yorkshire*. Roman Malton and District Reports, **5**. Oxford: Yorkshire Archaeological Society, 1935

Margary, I.D., 1957 — *Roman Roads in Britain*, **2**: *North of the Fosse Way – Bristol Channel*. London: Phoenix House, 1957

Pevsner, N., 1985 — *Yorkshire: the North Riding*. The Buildings of England, Harmondsworth: Penguin, new impression 1985

RIB — Collingwood, R.G., and Wright, R.P., *The Roman Inscriptions of Britain*. Oxford: Clarendon Press, 1965

Sorby, H.C., 1851 — On the microscopic structure of the Calcareous Grit of the Yorkshire Coast, *Quart. J. Geol. Soc. London*, **7** (1851), 1-6

Stephenson, J. (trans.), 1855 — *Historical Works of Simeon of Durham*. Church Historians of England, **3**.2, London: Seeley, 1855; History of the Kings of England, repr. Felinfach: Llanerch Enterprises, 1987

Taylor, H.M., 1978 — *Anglo-Saxon Architecture*, **3**. Cambridge: University Press, 1978

Waites, B., 1959 — The monastic settlement of North-East Yorkshire, *Yorkshire Archaeol. J.*, **40** (1959), 478-95

Wenham, L.P., 1974 — *Derventio (Malton): Roman Fort and Civilian Settlement*. Huddersfield: Cameo, 1974

Wilson, V., 1933 — The Corallian of the Howardian Hills (Yorkshire), *Quart. J. Geol. Soc. London*, **89** (1933), 480-507

Wilson, V., 1949 — The Lower Corallian rocks of the Yorkshire coast and Hackness Hills, *Proc. Geol. Assoc.*, **60** (1949), 235-71

Wright, C.D., 1976   New outcrops of the Ampthill Clay north of Market Weighton, Yorkshire, and their structural implications, *Proc. Yorkshire Geol. Soc.*, **41** (1976), 127-40

Wright, J.K., 1972   The stratigraphy of the Yorkshire Corallian, *Proc. Yorkshire Geol. Soc.*, **39** (1972), 225-66

Young, G., 1817   *A History of Whitby and Streoneshale Abbey.* Whitby: Clark and Medd, 1817

Zeigler, P.A., 1975   North Sea Basin History in the Tectonic Framework of North-Western Europe, *Petroleum and the continental shelf of north-west Europe*, **I**: *Geology*, ed. A.W. Woodland, 131-49. Barking: Applied Science Publications, 1975

Chapter 11

Carved in Bright Stone: Sources of Building Stone in Derbyshire

M. F. Stanley

Newly quarried stone was probably employed during the late Anglo-Saxon building phase in many parts of the country. It is, however, generally accepted that buildings of the other main period of Anglo-Saxon endeavour were of wood, or re-used Roman brick or stone. But Derbyshire, a stone rich county, illustrates in its Anglo-Saxon, medieval and later churches, castles and domestic architecture that immediately local stone was always used and preferred.

Introduction

Derbyshire enjoys startling contrasts in scenery, reflecting its varied geology, as it straddles the divide between highland and lowland Britain. Northwards of a line from Ashbourne to Long Eaton (Pevsner 1978 suggested Ashbourne to Ilkeston but that excludes some Carboniferous outcrops) lie the Carboniferous rocks of the southern Pennines. The Dinantian Limestones (Carboniferous or Mountain Limestone) of the 'dales' form a central plateau, often referred to as the Derbyshire 'dome', almost completely surrounded by impressive edges and moors of Namurian (Millstone Grit) sandstones and shales (illustration 60). Overlying the Namurian to the east and west are the younger sandstones, shales, siltstones and coal seams of the Westphalian (Coal Measures). A small patch of Permian Lower Magnesian Limestone in turn overlies the Westphalian in the north-east of the county and forms part of a continuous outcrop from Nottingham to Durham. Southwards of the Ashbourne-Long Eaton line Triassic sandstones and marls form an undulating landscape which narrows eastwards and runs down to the gravel-floored Trent and Derwent valleys. The Trent is lined by bluffs, mainly on the south, that form the edge of a complex of Carboniferous and Permo-Triassic rocks of the Swadlincote Hill country. Dinantian Limestones are exposed at Ticknall and Calke within a surrounding patch of Namurian, overlain to the south and west by Triassic and Westphalian sandstones and shales.

Throughout the county, almost every rock type has been worked to provide building materials; all the major, and many minor, horizons (beds) of sandstone in the Namurian, Westphalian and Sherwood Sandstone Group (Bunter/Keuper Sandstones) have been employed for building, paving and walling stone; shale and clay horizons within these and the Mercia Mudstone Group (Keuper Marl) have produced bricks; stone-slates for roofing and paving were worked from the flaggy and thin-bedded upper and lower parts of sandstone horizons in the

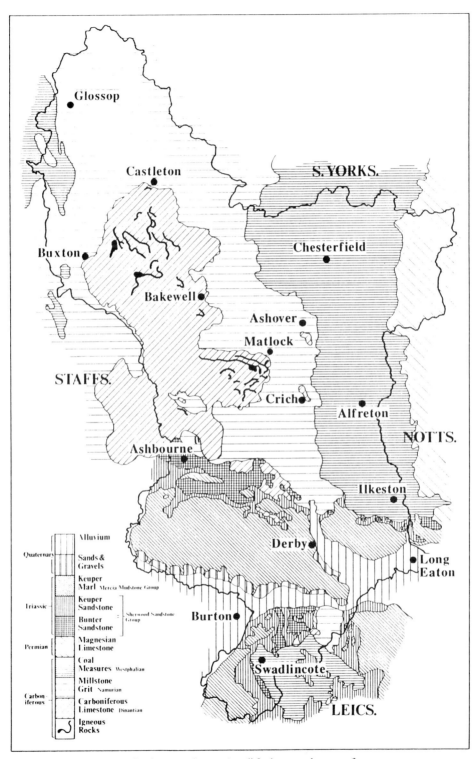

Glossop

Castleton

S. YORKS.

Buxton

Chesterfield

Bakewell

Ashover

Matlock

STAFFS.

Crich

Alfreton

NOTTS.

Ashbourne

Ilkeston

Derby

Long
Eaton

	Alluvium
Quaternary	Sands & Gravels
	Keuper Marl Mercia Mudstone Group
Triassic	Keuper Sandstone
	Bunter Sandstone Sherwood Sandstone Group
Permian	Magnesian Limestone
	Coal Measures Westphalian
Carbon- iferous	Millstone Grit Namurian
	Carboniferous Limestone Dinantian
	Igneous Rocks

Burton

Swadlincote

LEICS.

60.   Derbyshire geology: simplified general map of strata.

Namurian and Westphalian (Stanley in preparation); the limestones have given building and walling stone, lime for mortars, and cement; the Sherwood Sandstones and Quaternary deposits (river terraces etc.) the gravel and sands for concrete.

Domestic architecture

The present study of the fabric of medieval and earlier churches stemmed from preparatory work for an exhibition 'The Derbyshire Domesday' produced in 1986 to mark the 900th anniversary of the publication of Domesday Book. It also follows several years of studying country houses (Craven & Stanley 1982/84) in the county of which only the larger and well known structures have detailed building accounts. Church fabrics are far more elusive; indeed finding the date of foundation of medieval and earlier churches is fraught with problems, as many existed at the time of the Domesday survey but were not recorded, since the Commissioners 'were primarily interested in the estates of the tenant-in-chief and therefore, as a rule, only recorded those commodities which contributed to its issues' (Roffe 1986). Roffe also notes that churches with full parochial rights are noted as they contributed to the income of the manor, i.e. estate and parish, but dependent churches paid to the mother church rather than the lord of the manor and hence do not get a mention. Domesday is a record of the assets of the lord of the manor rather than the resources of communities.

It is possible, by reference to the building accounts of houses, to locate the sources of stone as both great and small houses generally obtained their stone from within a three mile radius; often a quarry or quarries would be opened specifically to supply a building. The prominent buildings on the Permian scarp, Bolsover Castle and Hardwick Halls, obtained their stone from quarries opened specifically for the building work (Craven & Stanley 1982).

The present Bolsover Castle, an extravagant adaptation of the site of a large medieval fortress mainly by John Smythson (from 1613) for Sir Charles Cavendish (son of Bess of Hardwick), used quarries in Permian Lower Magnesian Limestone, hereabouts a pinkish-cream fine-grained dolomite, from Bolsover and Bolsover Moor, and a Westphalian buff, fine-grained sandstone (below the Wales Coal) from Shuttlewood below the scarp. Bolsover Castle was the example of good weathering stone picked by the Commissioners for the rebuilding of the Houses of Parliament (Barry *et al.* 1839). The Lower Magnesian Limestone should have been quarried from Bolsover Moor but the lack of the correct block sizes promoted the use of Magnesian Limestone for the bulk of the structure from Anston Quarry just over the border in South Yorkshire (Elsden & Howe 1923). However, deposits of similar age but more sandy and hence a dolomitic sandstone, from Parliament Quarry, Mansfield Woodhouse, was used for the lower and still sound courses of the Houses of Parliament.

Robert Smythson designed Hardwick Hall for Bess of Hardwick as a large building with the revolutionary use of glass ('Hardwick Hall more glass than wall') with work commencing in 1591. This and the earlier Hardwick Old Hall, a rebuilding by Bess of her brother's house of 1582-86, are both built of a

Westphalian buff fine-grained sandstone, that below the Clowne Coal, quarried from just beneath the scarp off the drive up to the Halls. The Lower Magnesian Limestone on which the Halls sit was used only to provide lime for mortars.

Churches and monastic foundations appear also to have had an immediately local source of supply of building stone as the following examples from the 9th to the 19th century will show.

Ecclesiastical architecture
The petrographic study of selected churches and monastic foundations undertaken by the writer indicates that immediately local sources of building stone were employed, even for wholesale renovation and restoration work in the late 19th century. The source of stone is obviously influenced by the local geology and its suitability for easy working. In Derbyshire virtually all horizons provide good building stone and from the Roman occupation to the present local sources have been the norm.

Sandstone, limestone (Carboniferous or Permian) or a combination of the two are seen in churches and foundations and the use of one or a combination is entirely dependent on the local geology. Examples from the south (Repton,

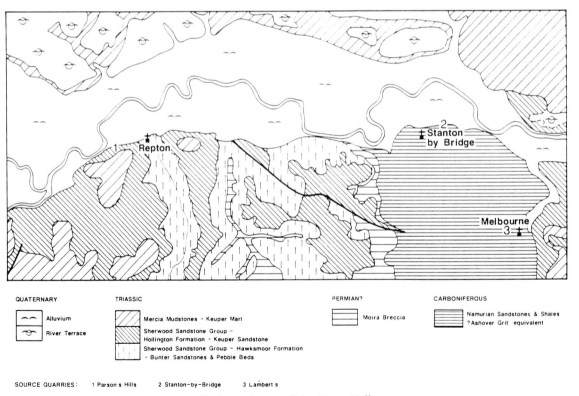

61. Geological map of the Trent Valley area.

Melbourne, Stanton-by-Bridge and Dale Abbey) and north (Steetley) of the county illustrate the use of a single rock type, while combinations, featuring a very localised dolomitised limestone, are exampled by the Thorpe–Brassington area, north of Ashbourne.

Repton

The village of Repton lies on the high ground forming the southern edge of the floodplain of the River Trent. This river cliff, with a cut-off channel the 'Old Trent Water' at its base, is composed of sandstones of the Sherwood Sandstone Group. The Hawksmoor Formation (Bunter Sandstone), a series of buff to brown, pebbly to coarse-grained sandstones with occasional pebbles, outcrops along the path to the north of the graveyard of St Wystan's church leading to the schoolyard of Repton school. It is further exposed on Tanners Lane, southwest of the school running track, and in house driveways to the east of the school cricket field. Although much weathered and poorly exposed it is discernible as being similar to the 'brown stone' used in the Saxon first phase church building of St Wystan's. Stratigraphically above the Hawksmoor Formation lies the Hollington Formation (Keuper Sandstone) which outcrops on Parson's Hill to the west and formerly on Askew Hill to the east (illustration 61).

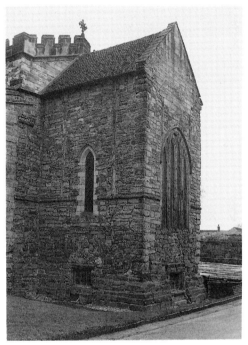

62. Repton, St Wystan's church: the chancel from the south. Note the new Hollington Formation/Keuper Sandstone (light colour) above mainly Hawksmoor Formation/Bunter Sandstone (dark colour).

In the 7th century 'it looks as if Repton had a family of ecclesiastical structures strung out along an east–west axis, like a number of other early Christian sites in England. It also seems as if a major rebuilding programme, associated with the introduction of improved masonry skills and the use of new stone, transformed the early arrangements during the 8th and 9th centuries, creating the Anglo-Saxon Church whose remains survive today' (illustration 62). Martin Biddle and Birthe Kjølbye-Biddle so described the results of the 1986 season's work on the excavations north of St Wystan's church.

My stone-by-stone identification of the standing Anglo-Saxon fabric confirms the findings of the Biddles and Dr H.M. Taylor that there appear to be two building styles at Repton. An earlier style using only brown Hawksmoor Formation (Bunter) sandstone bonded with clay and later with mortar; and a later style using finely cut green Hollington Formation (Keuper) sandstone, invariably set in mortar. The Hawksmoor undoubtedly was obtained from the immediate vicinity and to the south while the Hollington was brought the few hundred yards from open-cuts on Parson's Hill (colour plate VI). The Repton Charters (c.1227) refer to 'Rapendon Quarry near Trent' which Fraser (1947) assigns to Quarry Hill Close east of the school. Signs of stoneworking are visible but are better seen on Parson's Hill, very close to the present river channel, where several deep open cuts push south into the Hollington horizon.

Melbourne

The church of St Michael and St Mary 'is one of the most ambitious Norman parish churches of England' (Pevsner 1978, 275; see also 276-78). A brief description will have to suffice: supremely impressive within but, because unfinished and surrounded by lesser buildings, less so outside. The two-tier façade, crossing tower and six bay nave with aisles and transepts are very ambitious and exceptional in Norman parish church architecture. The building dates are not known but most of the detail looks 12th-century; the interior looks younger than 1133 when

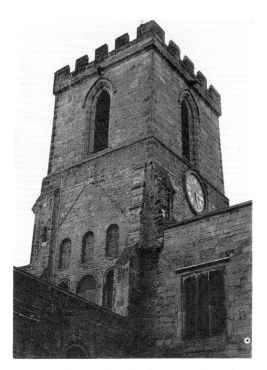

63. Melbourne church: the tower from the east, showing crossing.

64. Melbourne church: the west doorway. Note the current-bedding on the third course each side of the doorway.

the living of Melbourne went to the Bishop of Carlisle at the foundation of the see (illustration 63). The entire structure is ashlar of the local Namurian sandstone, except for late 20th-century replacement blocks which are Namurian but non-local. The sandstone is thought to be equivalent to the Ashover Grit and here in part exhibits coarse and fine grading and current-bedding illustrated by the carved detail on the south door (illustration 64). The sandstone can be seen in situ under the boundary wall of Melbourne Hall on the road to the Pool, between the hall and the church. The stone for both church and the late 16th-century part of the hall undoubtedly originate from the immediate area, in particular the present disused Lambert's quarry to the west of the church. The vanished Melbourne castle (13th century-1637) to the north of the church was also of the local Namurian.

Stanton-by-Bridge

The church of St Michael lies deep in the village at the southern end of Swarkestone Bridge (Joyce 1978), a medieval causeway of 13th-century and earlier date. The fabric of the church includes some Anglo-Saxon long and short work at the south-east angle (illustration 65) but this is unconvincing. There is the inevitable Norman south doorway with one order of colonettes and zigzagging and a Norman west window, contemporary wall and chancel arch; the remainder is 13th-century. Although probably of early 11th-century date the church does not appear in Domesday, as Stanton, together with Chellaston and Swarkestone, belonged to the mother church of Melbourne. The stonework is mainly the local Namurian sandstone, current-bedded and coarse-grained, except for a fine-grained, slightly micaceous, buff sandstone with iron staining used for the south doorway and also seen in that position in other churches, e.g. Tissington, Parwich and Hognaston. The source of the local

65. Stanton-by-Bridge, St Michael's church: south-east angle.

Namurian sandstone is the quarries at Stanton immediately east and west of the southern end of the causeway (see illustration 61). Although outcrops exist to the west and north-west of the church, these are now completely surrounded by agricultural land and any trace of quarrying has been lost.

Dale Abbey

Little remains of the house of Premonstratensian Canons, founded about 1200, except the great arch of the chancel east window (illustration 66) and many separate masonry blocks now housed in a private 'museum' on site and incorporated into houses and walls in the village. After the dissolution in 1538 much of the monastic property, including buildings, was eventually sold to Francis Pole of Radbourne, Derbyshire. He removed items for use and re-use in other local churches and it has been suggested that he and later owners used the abbey as a quarry for building stone. However Stanley (Joyce 1977) notes that the majority of the masonry was incorporated into very local buildings and walls with only tracery and other fine dressings travelling any distance. Little sign of re-use was evident except in Dale itself and buildings thought to be constructed of Dale Abbey stone proved not to be.

66. Dale Abbey: chancel east window. Note the strong current-bedding in the arch blocks, below the imposts on the right.

The main building stone is Crawshaw Sandstone, a medium- to coarse-grained sub-arkose (containing less than 25% felspar), from the base of the Westphalian (Coal Measures), and virtually indistinguishable from the main Namurian sandstones of central and north Derbyshire which are also sub-arkoses; fortunately it weathers grey and exhibits strong current-bedding. Hereabouts the Crawshaw has two main outcrops and both have furnished building stone but the main quarries were in and to the south of Stanton-by-Dale, about 2 miles (3km) from Dale. The Cartulary of Dale Abbey (Saltman 1966) mentions two quarries in two grants dated 1240; it refers to a quarry in Stanton-by-Dale granted by Ralph of Hereford 'of all his quarries in the territory of Stanton'. This would suggest that he had several which were granted to the Abbey. The second reference is a 'grant of 3 acres of arable in the territory of Kirk Hallam lying next to the place which I have given to them to make a quarry . . .' This one in Kirk Hallam could possibly be identified with the Westphalian Ashgate Sandstone, now exposed in a quarry north of Dale adjacent to the A6096, and used in Dale Abbey church and the gatehouse of the abbey.

Steetley

'Steetley Chapel is by far the richest example of Norman architecture in Derbyshire' (Pevsner 1978) and one of the most complete small-scale examples in the Norman world. Fifty-two feet long by fifteen feet wide, it was roofless for most of the 19th century, and probably earlier, and used as a chicken run. Fortunately it was carefully restored in 1880 to designs by J.L. Pearson with the result that the roof and the gable and two outer colonettes of the magnificent south porch are Victorian (illustration 67). The mid-12th-century chapel's excellence of design and building probably has its roots in its position by the Whitwell gap, one of the main routes from the Derbyshire/Nottinghamshire frontier into Yorkshire.

Except for one sill of a later window, which is a brown shelly limestone, the whole is the local Permian Lower Magnesian Limestone, here a crystalline dolomite, and an object lesson in the difficulties of sourcing and matching original stone. The Norman stonework, which makes up most of the Steetley fabric, is a fine-grained creamy dolomite which shows no sign of weathering. This is similar to the stone chosen for the rebuilding of the Houses of Parliament from Bolsover Moor (Barry *et al.* 1839) which, as already noted, was little used.

67. Steetley chapel: south porch. Note that the walling blocks of the nave do not match those of the porch, also weathering of the outer colonettes.

The Victorian replacement stone of the south porch is a coarser dolomite which is grey rather than cream and already shows signs of weathering after only 108 years. The Victorians presumably were unable to match the original and the result is obvious to see. The difference in weathering properties may be solely due to the difference in grain size of the two dolomites and may not have become apparent had it not been exposed to a polluted atmosphere for 100% of its time compared with 10% of the original stone's exposure.

Thorpe–Brassington

Bradbourne was the mother church and is noted in Domesday, but its chapelries

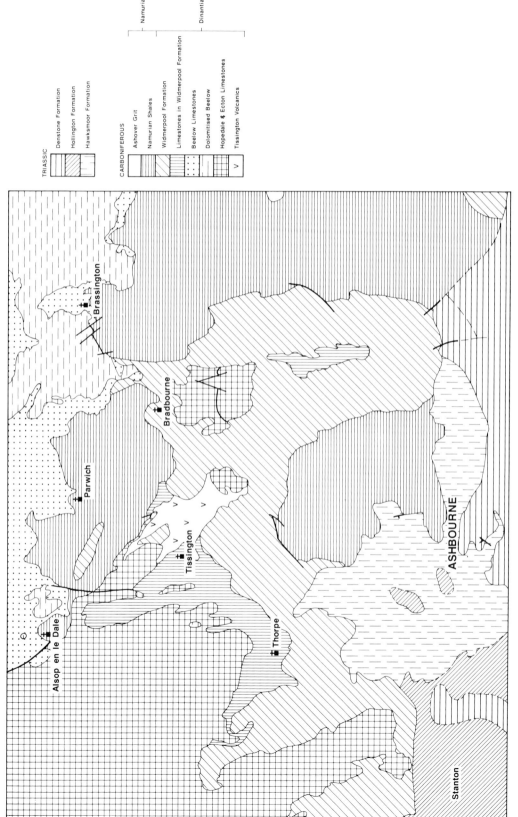

TRIASSIC
- Denstone Formation
- Hollington Formation
- Hawksmoor Formation

CARBONIFEROUS
- Ashover Grit ⎫ Namurian
- Namurian Shales ⎭
- Widmerpool Formation ⎫
- Limestones in Widmerpool Formation ⎪
- Beelow Limestones ⎬ Dinantian
- Dolomitised Beelow ⎪
- Hopedale & Ecton Limestones ⎪
- Tissington Volcanics ⎭

Brassington

Bradbourne

Parwich

Tissington

Thorpe

Alsop en le Dale

ASHBOURNE

Stanton

68. Geological map of Dinantian and later outcrop in the Brassington area.

of Ballidon, Brassington and Tissington, although having Norman features, are not recorded in Domesday. Similarly Thorpe, Alsop-en-le-Dale, Parwich and Hognaston were chapelries of Ashbourne and do not appear.

This area (illustration 68) straddles the Dinantian–Namurian junction and in part the Dinantian–Triassic junction. The juxtaposition of these produces many rock types for use as building stone. Not surprisingly the rocks have been exploited to the full and each building is a mixture of the immediately local stone, a limestone or an altered limestone, and one or more stones from slightly further afield, usually a sandstone. It is perhaps pertinent here to dispel the popular belief that sandstones and limestones do not mix well in the same building. I have yet to see in Derbyshire one building where the mixture of the two has caused difficulties with scaling of stone or other effects.

Of the eight churches noted in the area only three managed to avoid being 'Normanised' in some way by F.J. Robinson between 1854 and 1883. The Derby architect did at least employ local stone which is the one saving grace of what is now seen as vandalism.

69. Thorpe, St Leonard's church: the west tower.

Thorpe: St Leonard's has a squat, unbuttressed Norman west tower (illustration 69) with blocked west doorway, two bell openings, corbel table and nave. Crinoidal Hopedale Limestone is the main walling stone with subsidiary Widmerpool formation thin-bedded limestones and sandstones, both local. The quoins of the tower are large and are of a fine-grained sandstone with occasional pebbles, two have baryte mineralisation and all are Triassic Hollington Formation (Sherwood Sandstone Group) from the Stanton–Mayfield area some three miles to the south. The embattled parapet of the tower is Namurian Sandstone and is later, probably 14th-century.

Tissington: St Mary's was 'Normanised' by Robinson in 1854 when the north aisle was added. Fortunately the broad square-buttressed Norman west tower with south window, south doorway and tympanum was unchanged. This tower is a complete mixture, indeed an intentional alternation in part, of a brown sandstone, buff dolomite and grey limestone (illustration 70). Grey Widmerpool Formation (thin limestone with chert bands) is the main walling stone in the lower storey.

A brown sandstone, probably Triassic, forms the quoins in the upper and middle storeys and the upper half of the lower storey, and immediately above

70. Tissington, St Mary's church: the west tower, showing lighter dolomitised limestone blocks in quoins, buttresses and the south window.

and below the string course of the lower storey on the south-west and north-west corners is a dolomite. It is in fact a dolomitised Dinantian Limestone (Beelow Limestones) and is easily recognised by its buff colour and wormholed appearance (illustration 71). The dolomitised limestone is also found to form the dressings of the south window of the tower and the corbel table and was re-used by Robinson in the nave and chancel. The dolomitised limestone has a small outcrop to the west of Tissington but is more likely to have been quarried in the Brassington area.

The beautiful Norman south doorway is of a current-bedded and iron-stained fine-grained sandstone and looks Namurian. It is similar to that of the south doorway at Stanton-by-Bridge and tympana at Parwich and Hognaston (see below). The tympanum, of the same stone, has two kilted standing figures to the left and right, and a double diaper frieze between them; the field is decorated by a plain chequerboard pattern with a cross. It is recorded as Norman but is plainly earlier as kilted figures appear on undoubted Anglo-Saxon carvings in Norbury and Wirksworth churches, Brailsford churchyard, the tympana at Ault Hucknall and Hognaston and are possibly seen on the Repton Stone (Biddle & Kjølbye-Biddle 1986). The tub font is also regarded as Norman but again is earlier.

Alsop-en-le-Dale: St Michael's was heavily 'Normanised' in 1882–83 by Robinson and only the nave, south doorway and chancel arch imposts are Norman. The main walling stone is the local Beelow Limestones with little chert; the dressings are dolomitised Beelow Limestones and the plinth course and quoins are of a Namurian sandstone. The dolomitised limestone outcrops to the east of Alsop but signs of quarrying are no longer apparent. It is possible that it may have been quarried locally but more probably was brought from the Brassington area.

The south doorway (illustration 72) is particularly interesting as the pattern of

71. Brassington, boundary wall in the village: close-up of rock types. To the left is buff/red Namurian sandstone with dolomitised limestone above and to the right, sandwiching a small block of unaltered fossiliferous limestone.

the carved voussoirs, a scallop with crossed rods, is rare but can also be seen in Cartmel Priory, Cumbria.

Parwich: The medieval church was replaced by the present St Peter's by Robinson and H.I. Stevens in 1873-74, but in rock-faced local grey Dinantian limestone for the walling with Namurian sandstone dressings. Fortunately they incorporated the original north doorway and tympanum into the west doorway of the tower (illustration 73) and re-used the chancel arch and two capitals, one on each side nearest the chancel arch; the capitals are in dolomitised limestone and the chancel arch is of alternating light and dark fine-grained sandstones. The Norman double chevron arch of the doorway is a Namurian sandstone, fairly coarse in parts with heavy iron-red staining; the probable source is from the Kirk Ireton–Blackwell area. The tympanum is also a fine-grained Namurian sandstone with many crude figures and appears pre-Norman. The sandstone is now flaking and the figures are losing their form and remedial conservation work is sorely needed.

Brassington: St James's is essentially Norman and consists mainly of dolomitised Beelow Limestones. The fine west tower (illustration 74) has discrete buttressing,

72. Alsop-en-le-Dale, St Michael's church: the south doorway.

73. Parwich, St Peter's church: the west doorway with tympanum.

74. Brassington, St James's church from the south.

a clasping one at the south-west corner and a straight support near the south-east corner. The whole is in the immediately local dolomitised limestone, probably from the hillside behind which exhibits signs of working. Many of the village buildings use this stone for dressings, an uncommon sight on the limestone outcrop as most buildings of limestone have sandstone dressings. It is, however, much easier to obtain a flat surface and an arris in dolomitised limestone than it is in the unaltered Dinantian limestones.

The drums of the piers of both the south arcade and south chancel aisle are of dolomitised limestone. Robinson and Stevens used blocks of it from the north wall of the nave in their east window and north aisle building of 1879-81, incorporating them with rock-faced Namurian sandstone and Dinantian limestone.

The south porch and doorway mirror the use elsewhere of a fine- to medium-grained sandstone, which looks Namurian.

It is entirely appropriate and expected that the main area of dolomitisation of the Beelow Limestones should witness the most extensive use of it as a building stone.

75. Bradbourne, All Saints' church from the south. Note the sandstone west tower and cross shaft of c. AD 800 in the foreground.

Bradbourne: All Saints' is the mother church of Ballidon, Brassington and Tissington, and consequently had more monies expended on its fabric than its chapelries. The Norman west tower (illustration 75) is of a buff fine-grained sandstone with, unusually, a later dolomitised limestone battlement. The south doorway of the tower has one order of colonnettes, two orders of voussoirs with animals and an outer order of beakheads; all in similar stone to the tower. However the nearest sandstone is 4 miles (6.4km) south-west as the crow flies while workable dolomitised limestone is 2 miles (3.2km) away by road. Here a conscious decision must have been made to use sandstone even knowing that transport of stone would account for most of the building costs. However the Anglo-Saxons used what was available, as the north wall of the nave shows a mixture of boulders of the local Dinantian Hopedale Limestones, dolomitised limestone blocks and occasional sandstones and limestones from the Widmerpool Formation.

The cross shaft of *c.*AD 800 in the churchyard is also of a Namurian sandstone and is probably from the Bakewell workshop.

76. Hognaston, St Bartholomew's church: detail of the west tower.

Hognaston: St Bartholomew's has a fine Norman south doorway and an earlier tympanum strongly resembling Parwich, both in fine-grained brown Namurian sandstone. The west tower, 13th-century, is square and squat in three storeys (illustration 76). The upper two are of a brown Namurian sandstone, probably from Kirk Ireton, and most of the lower storey is the local Widmerpool Formation limestone and some dolomitised limestone blocks.

Apart from the 14th-century chancel arch and west tower, the remainder was rebuilt by Robinson, 1879-81, in a pebbly Triassic sandstone.

Conclusion

The series of churches typifies the use of immediately local materials in Derbyshire where the choice is usually only modified by the importance of the building or part of the building. In stone-poor counties the evidence strongly points to the extensive re-use of stone and other long-lasting materials one or more times. Derbyshire, a stone-rich county, generally has little re-use in evidence as few places are more than 5 miles (8km) from a source of good building stone and many are less distant. Prior to the end of the Second World War many quarries were in production but today only 16 produce dimensional building stone, although three have commenced new production in the past three years, a far cry from the stone-rich days of early this century when 137 quarries were producing.

ACKNOWLEDGEMENT

I am indebted to Leicestershire Museums for permission to reproduce the colour aerial photograph and in particular to Fred Hartley of their Field Archaeology Unit for taking it. I also gratefully acknowledge the graphic excellence of Janet Mellor of Derbyshire Museum Service in producing the three maps and Janine Cason of the same organisation for printing the photographs.

BIBLIOGRAPHY

Barry, C., De la Beche, H.T., Smith, W., and Smith, C.H., 1839 — Selection of stone for the New Houses of Parliament, *Parliamentary Papers (HC)*, **30** (1839), 3-43

Biddle, M., and Kjøbye-Biddle, B., 1986 — The Repton Stone, *Anglo-Saxon England*, **14** (1986), 233-72

Craven, M., and Stanley, M., 1982/84 — *The Derbyshire Country House.* 2 vols, Darley Dale: Derbyshire Museum Service, 1982 & 1984

Elsden, J.V., and Howe, J.A., 1923 — *The Stones of London.* London: Colliery Guardian, 1923

Fraser, W., 1947 — *The field names of South Derbyshire.* Ipswich: Adlard, 1947

Joyce, B., 1978 — *Swarkestone Bridge: an appraisal.* Matlock: Derbyshire County Council, 1978

Joyce, B., 1977 — Dale Abbey Conservation Area. An internal discussion document, Matlock: Derbyshire County Council, 1977

Pevsner, N., 1978 — *Derbyshire*, 2nd ed. Buildings of England, Harmondsworth: Penguin, 1978

Roffe, D., 1986 — *The Derbyshire Domesday.* Darley Dale: Derbyshire Museum Service, 1986

Saltman, A., 1966 — *A Cartulary of Dale Abbey.* Derbyshire Archaeol. Soc. Record Ser., **2**, London: HMSO, 1966

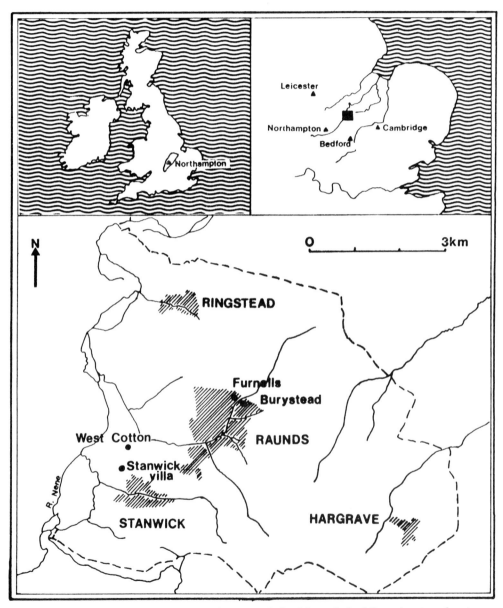

77.   General location plan. The Raunds area is defined by a dashed line, the site of major excavation by a dot.

Chapter 12

Recent Excavations on Saxon and Medieval Quarries in Raunds, Northamptonshire

Graham Cadman
with contributions by Michel Audouy

Excavations at Raunds, Northamptonshire, between 1977 and 1987 have provided valuable insights into Saxon and medieval quarrying in a Midlands rural community. The earliest excavated quarries are late Saxon and provided Cornbrash limestone for the construction of a small church. By the medieval period the underlying Blisworth Limestone was more widely quarried, being utilised as the main stone component in a mid 11th-century rebuilding of the church. Use of stone in manorial buildings commenced in the late 10th or 11th centuries and was well established by the late 12th century. By the 13th century there is evidence for stone buildings within peasant tenements. Observations on the range of excavated stone items, upon the types of quarries exploited and upon the post-medieval and modern context of the industry are included along with an initial discussion of the nature and extent of the industry within the Raunds Area Project of which the excavations are a part.

Introduction and background

Raunds is a small town on the south side of the Nene valley in Northamptonshire, some 20 miles east of the county town of Northampton (illustration 77). Since 1977 the town has been the focus for a series of rescue excavations which in 1985 were integrated into a single project, the Raunds Area Project, jointly managed by Northamptonshire County Council and English Heritage, with additional support from the Manpower Services Commission and local developers. The Project is examining the evolution of 40km² of the Nene valley's landscape, the study area being defined by the medieval parishes of Raunds, Ringstead, Hargrave and Stanwick. These stretch from the Nene floodplain and gravel terraces up onto the boulder clay plateau lying between the Nene and the Ouse valleys (Foard & Pearson 1985; Dix 1986-87a). The solid geology of the area consists of rocks of the Jurassic system. The town itself mostly overlies outcrops of Middle Jurassic rocks which include Upper and Lower Cornbrash and the underlying Blisworth Clay, Blisworth Limestone, attenuated Upper and/or Lower Estuarine Series and the Ironstone of the Northampton Sand (illustration 78).

A long established tradition of stone-working in the area is suggested by the *stan* element in the place name of the adjacent village of Stanwick, first recorded in the 10th century (Gover *et al.* 1975, 196). Quarrying continues to be an important land use at the present day with large–scale mechanised gravel extraction

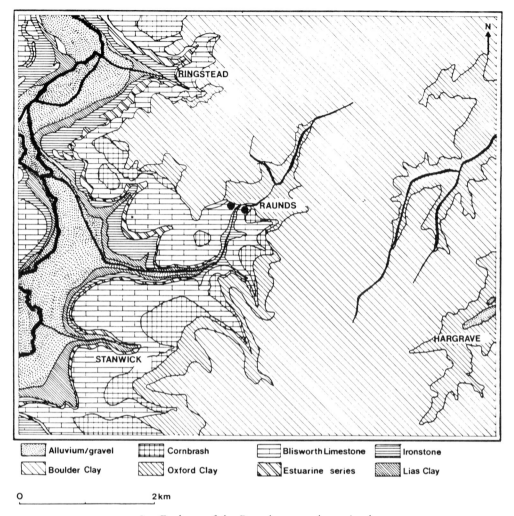

78.   Geology of the Raunds area: schematic plan.

transforming the character of the valley floor into an expanse of lagoons, whilst also prompting several of the current rescue excavations. During the post-medieval era, stone pits and quarries provided road and construction materials in Raunds. From here came the Raunds 'marble', more properly a very shelly variety of Blisworth Limestone, which attained a marble-like appearance when polished, and which was used in the 17th century for chimney pieces and window tables (Morton 1712, 107; *VCH Northamptonshire*, **2** 297). Morton (1712) listed Raunds among the 'quarries at this time of chiefest note', apparently the only one in the Blisworth Limestone. It is inferred that Raunds stone was actively worked at that time, though no information has yet come to light as to the exact location of Morton's quarry(ies), the thickness of the stone worked, or its use as a building stone other than specialised 'marble' (D.S. Sutherland, personal communication).

Important as the post-medieval industry may be, this paper is primarily concerned with those quarries of Saxon and medieval date revealed in recent excavations conducted by the present authors, with A. Boddington and S. Parry, in the town of Raunds since 1977. Dr D.S. Sutherland has provided invaluable geological advice and guidance at each site. Quarries and quarrying are here defined as those occasions when geological raw materials are extracted and removed from their place of extraction for further use. This definition justifies the inclusion in this review of extractions in addition to stone, such as sand and clay.

The sites concerned lie in the northern part of the medieval village, and subsequently of the modern town of Raunds, either side of a small tributary valley of the River Nene in areas being intensively developed for housing and light industrial use (illustration 79). To the west, the Furnells site excavated 1977-82 was the setting for an Anglo-Saxon settlement, Saxo-Norman church and a

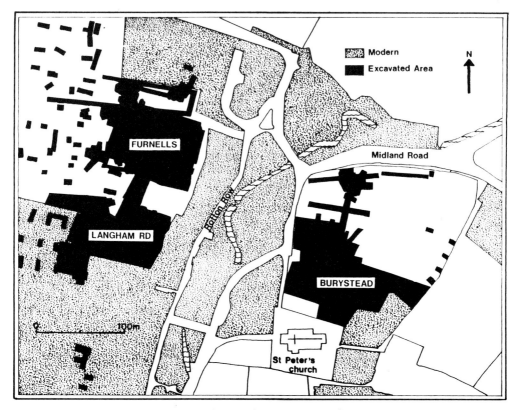

79. North Raunds: major excavations.

medieval manorial complex. Immediately to the south was the Langham Road
excavation of 1984-86, where a further portion of the extensive Saxon settlement
was recorded, along with a series of possible medieval tenements fronting onto
Rotten Row. To the east of the valley, and immediately north of the parish church
of St Peter, was the site of the post-medieval Burystead manor, excavated during
1986-87, with to its north a further series of medieval tenements fronting onto
the Midland Road (excavated 1985-87), the whole of this area also containing
evidence of Saxon occupation. The excavated settlement, church, manor and
tenements are all elements of the evolving polyfocal village which by the later
medieval period had coalesced into the single large village of Raunds.

The geology of the excavated areas was found to be extremely variable. Surface
exposures of an Upper and Lower Cornbrash pavement were present at Furnells
and Langham Road along with Blisworth Clay and a red loam (illustration 80).
Blisworth Limestone underlay the clay and although only poorly exposed was,
like the Cornbrash, subject to quarrying. Underlying the red loam on the south
side of the Furnells site were coarse and medium orange sands overlying gravels.

At Burystead on the east side of the valley similar limestone outcrops were
recorded, the Cornbrash covering most of the site with the exception of the area
to the south, occupied by a red-brown loam. Underneath lay Blisworth Clay
and Blisworth Limestone.

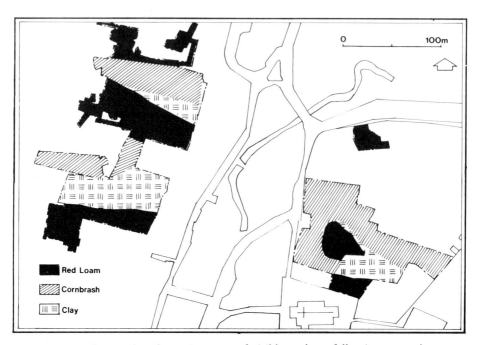

80. North Raunds: schematic extent of visible geology following excavation.

Before going on to examine the individual quarries within a basic chronological framework, four observations concerning the excavation are called for:

Excavation Objectives
The 'rescue' context precluded the total excavation of every feature encountered. The main questions posed of the quarries by the excavators concerned their extent, date of use and backfilling/abandonment, the nature of the extracted material and their relationship and function in respect to other contemporary land use. Secondary considerations tended to concern quarrying methods and retrieval of complete finds assemblages. In many cases machine-assisted sondages were sufficient to resolve many if not most of these questions.

Excavation Constraints
A general rule which applied to all quarries irrespective of their date, was that the bigger the quarry, the bigger the set of excavation problems it posed. The preponderance of large post-medieval and/or modern quarries on the east side of the valley restricted the areas available to excavation and may well have obliterated earlier quarries. Large quarries of earlier date consumed large amounts of time and labour in their excavation, whilst their depth presented a host of Health and Safety related problems. An additional factor which had to be considered was the natural reluctance of contractors to permit deep excavations beyond 1m unless followed by backfilling with costly concrete or hardcore. Modern house foundations are not guaranteed against subsidence into recently disturbed medieval quarries!

Dating
Quarries are often difficult to date precisely, particular problems being encountered in differentiating between the dates of extraction and backfilling, hence the use of date ranges within this paper, all of which are subject to revision during the ongoing post-excavation analysis.

Quantification
Much work could yet be undertaken as regards the quantification of quarried material both in terms of that extracted as well as that utilised in structures. The figures used in this paper are provisional estimates.

Chronological survey of quarries in north Raunds
The following provisional chronological summary of settlement development in north Raunds identifies where the excavated quarries fit into the sequence. For the purposes of this paper the complex internal phasing of individual sites is subsumed within the broad periods of the Early/Middle and Late Saxon and the Medieval, with a Post-Medieval postscript.

Early/Middle Saxon c.AD 550-850
Apart from some slight traces of prehistoric activity there was no indication that

any of the sites had been settled prior to the early Saxon period. During early/ middle Saxon times extensive areas of settlement existed on both the west and to a lesser extent the east sides of the valley. There was no evidence for the utilisation of stone, except sporadically as post-packing in any structures of this date. The small quantities so involved would have been easily available from surface scatters, or from the upcast of a series of partially rock cut enclosure ditches at Furnells. Clearly there was no local necessity for quarries.

Late Saxon c.850-1050 (illustration 81)
Major changes and developments characterize all the excavated areas during the late Saxon. A new settlement plan form emerges; stone is used in structural contexts for the first time, and there is evidence for the importation of highly crafted stone products.

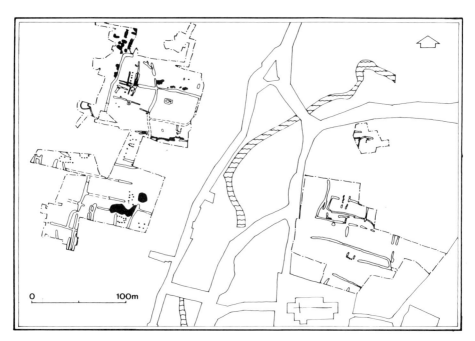

81. North Raunds: major excavated features (late Saxon), with the main quarries blacked in.

The evolving sequence is most easily summarised by site. At Furnells a timber hall and a small stone church were constructed during the late 9th century. During the following century the church was enlarged and burial initiated within a cemetery, whilst the hall was replaced by a timber-aisled structure. The stone church was rebuilt during the 11th century shortly before it and the cemetery became redundant. These buildings, presumed to be part of the manor held by Burgred in 1066 (Cadman & Foard, 1984), were enclosed by a network of ditched and banked boundaries adjacent to which lay a series of small quarries. Some lay outside the settlement's western perimeter, others were located in ditched enclosures north and south of the churchyard, the northern plot probably comprising the settlement's main access.

Cornbrash limestone was quarried in the form of small angular fragments from a series of shallow excavations, adjacent to the ditches in the latter area, those immediately north of the cemetery being but small ragged cuts into the edge of the Cornbrash pavement as exposed by the ditch edge. The largest of these had a volume of approximately 8m³, the nature of the differential backfill suggesting that stone had been removed in a series of eight or more shallow eastward moving

82. Furnells: Cornbrash Limestone quarry from the east (scale = 1m). Note the ditch to the west from which quarrying was initiated. (Photo: Northamptonshire County Council Archaeology Unit).

cuts, the debris from each being dumped back within the area previously quarried (illustration 82). Probably excavated during the early 10th century, this quarry may well have supplied stone to the Cornbrash rubble constructed church lying c.12m to its south. Rough-hewn, unsquared Cornbrash Limestone fragments not exceeding 0.2m in width were used in this building's foundation, larger flat pieces up to 0.4m across being utilised at the face of the standing wall. Stone was also extensively utilised in over 50% of the cemetery's graves, for support or protection of the interred. The stone which varied in size from small fragments to large slabs was, on occasion, derived from the excavation of the grave itself, but often it must have been collected from external quarries, including probably those just described (Boddington 1987).

Four further Cornbrash quarries lay on the outer side of the settlement's western perimeter and date to the later 10th or 11th centuries. The largest resembled a pit (5.8 x 4.0 x 0.6m). These quarries may well have been the source for the limited use of stone that is discernible within parts of the aisled hall complex at about this date. It would appear that the position of these quarries was dictated by the necessity of their being placed outside the occupied enclosures at places where the pre-existing ditches had revealed and to some extent also supplied suitable material for extraction.

Also lying exterior to the settlement's western perimeter was a single Blisworth

83. Furnells: mid 11th-century sand and gravel pits from the east (scale = 1m). These quarries were backfilled with domestic debris very shortly after having been opened. (Photo: NCC Archaeology Unit).

Limestone quarry, the greater depth of which, at 1.7m, was occasioned by the nature of the strata as well as by the apparent desire to win larger stone pieces. The finer quality of this stone, which Sutherland has identified as being akin to Raunds Stone, might suggest its use for more specialist working. Unfortunately links could not be established with much of the excavated structural material, although a lancet head window fragment and a dressed stone, found in medieval contexts were of a very similar rock type. Other pieces of locally available or imported Blisworth constructional stone were retrieved during the course of excavation although only in small quantities. There was little evidence for the use of ashlar. Most of this constructional stone was probably utilised in door or window openings or internal features of the churches, though it should be noted that the earlier church had a door and possibly windows framed in wood, as with the church at Hadstock, Essex.

Although stone quarries were prominent at late Saxon Furnells, the largest quarries were those for sand and gravel. Two concentrations of such quarries were excavated, one to the north-west and the other to the south-east. The latter comprised a linear series of 15 intercut pits, the largest measuring 3.60 x 1.9 x 1.43m and the smallest 1.26 x 0.7 x 0.46m. Most were steep-sided with flat or undulating bases. All were cut and almost immediately backfilled with occupation debris around AD 1050 (illustration 83). The group to the north-west had a date range of c.950-1050 and numbered at least 20 pits arranged in no readily apparent overall pattern. It is uncertain as to the use to which all the extracted material was put, although some may have been used in floor surfaces and the production of the limited amounts of mortar used at this date. Material from these or other nearby pits has been speculated by Boddington (forthcoming) as the source for the mortar used in the early church.

At the Langham Road site and also in the northern part of the Burystead site a series of gullies, small pits and timber structures appeared in the 10th century and were to develop into what are interpreted as a series of peasant tenements. Set amidst a series of timber buildings at Langham Road were two areas of Blisworth Limestone quarries apparently backfilled during the 11th or 12th centuries. The northernmost quarry measured 6 by 4.3m and exceeded 0.8m in depth. It was sub-rectangular in shape with steep sides. Eight metres further south lay a cluster of at least six intercut similarly shaped pits covering a total area of 25 by 9m. The deepest of these quarries reached 2.1m. Initial estimates suggest that over 180m³ of stone could have been removed.

It is an as yet unresolved question as to whether these large quarries were being utilised to supply building materials to the Furnells site or to stone buildings being erected at the Rotten Row tenement frontages late in the 11th or 12th centuries, this development following an earlier period when the tenements were occupied by timber structures which may have predominantly been set towards the rear of the tenements. It may be that a clarification of the tenurial holdings will provide a solution. Little or no quarrying activity is discernible at Late Saxon Burystead.

Medieval c.1050-1450 (illustration 84)

In the four centuries following the Conquest the manor house at Furnells was subject to two main phases of rebuilding. In the first, which occurred late in the 12th century, a stone-footed manor house was constructed atop the demolished aisled hall. Its walls comprised Blisworth and Cornbrash Limestone in the proportion 7:1, with very occasional use of Ironstone. This house was in turn demolished during the early 14th century when a new manor house with walls wholly of stone was constructed, incorporating within its fabric the remains of the abandoned church, the shell of which had itself been converted into some form of secular building upon the church's abandonment some two centuries earlier. This converted building, together with some of the aisled hall's ancillary structures which also utilised stone in their construction during the 11th and 12th centuries, represents the first large scale use of stone in non-ecclesiastical contexts

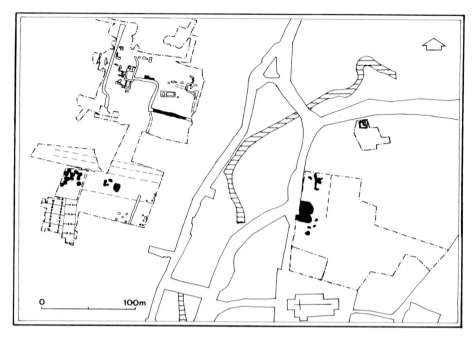

84. North Raunds: major excavated features (medieval), with main quarries blacked in.

at Furnells; though sporadic small scale use associated with the aisled hall may have been initiated as early as the late 10th century. The 14th-century manor house's walls comprised a mixture of Blisworth and Cornbrash Limestones with very small amounts of Ironstone. As with the 12th-century house there were extensive areas of flagstones, the largest of which, of Blisworth stone, measured 1.5 x 0.9 x 0.05m. In all cases the coursed walls consisted of rubble cores with rough hewn facing blocks. No use of ashlar was apparent, though there are hints, such as that provided by the lancet head window fragment referred to above and a drain cover decorated with a 'fleur de lys' design, that the 12th-century-built house did have some dressed stone features.

Only two quarries can be positively identified as contemporary with the medieval development at Furnells, although some of the previously described quarries may still have been utilised at the beginning of the period. During the 12th or 13th centuries a very shallow (0.2m. maximum depth) Cornbrash Limestone extraction with a 5.5m³ capacity, was made from the side of a large ditch, to the east of the hall. Another quarry was very much larger in extent, comprising a 40m long quarry ditch dug for Blisworth Limestone, along the line of what had been the cemetery's southern boundary during the late 11th or 12th centuries. It has been calculated that it would have supplied approximately 64m³ of rock, assuming a 25% wastage factor; not a sufficient quantity for it to have been the sole source of stone for the rebuilding of the church, which was incidentally the first building at Furnells to have been constructed predominantly of Blisworth Limestone, only 20% of its fabric being of Cornbrash Limestone (Boddington forthcoming). Additionally, or alternatively, the quarry ditch or a later recut may have helped supply stone to the late 12th-century manor house and its outbuildings which are estimated to have required a minimum of 55m³ of stone (excluding yard and floor surfaces, and estimating the use of dwarf walls). In short, the medieval quarries excavated at Furnells could only have supplied at very most 46% of the Blisworth stone required to construct the 12th-century manor house and rebuild the church. There must have been other quarries outside the immediate area covered by excavation.

The existence of further quarries may again be implied in the construction of the final manor house to occupy the site in the 14th century. This manor house and its outbuilding range may have required in excess of 200m³ of stone suggesting that even if all the stone previously used for building at Furnells had been re-used it may have been insufficient to complete the building.

Across the valley at Burystead a series of seven stone quarries was cut in the south-west part of the excavated area. All were sub-rectangular in shape and steep sided and were cut to extract Blisworth Limestone. The two largest which were intercut measured approximately 8 x 6 x 2m. The smaller ones ranged in size from 2.2 x 3.8 x 2.1m to 4.2 x 3.8 x 1.2m. It is calculated that a minimum of 100m³ of stone were removed, though it should be borne in mind that this is probably a considerable underestimate, as the quarries probably extended to the west outside the excavated area. The probable large extent of these quarries dated as having been backfilled in the 11th or early 12th centuries, suggests that they were cut either for a single building operation or as a single source supplying multiple uses. In respect of the former, it is tempting to relate them to the construction of either the nearby parish church, with its 12th-century or earlier foundation date, with the second church and/or manor house at Furnells or with the post-Conquest Burystead manor, believed to lie somewhere close by the parish church. All of these possibilities must remain speculative though it is apparent that they could not have been the sole source of stone for the parish church which would have required quantities many times greater than that available from these quarries alone. Additional sources of stone would also have been required for the 13th- and 14th-century stone tenement buildings fronting Midland Road, the Burystead quarries probably being of too early a date to have been their source.

At the Langham Road site no significant stone quarrying appears to have taken place following the abandonment of those quarries previously described in the late Saxon period, though, as at Burystead, clay removal was in progress, this occurring from a series of rounded, intercut, shallow pits.

Remnants of medieval quarries have also been identified during other excavations in Raunds. In tenements at Thorpe End, one of the medieval 'ends' of the village, some 800m south of Burystead, Steve Parry has identified a series of quarries, dated c.1350–1550, where limestone has been extracted from the steep sides of a small valley.

Post-medieval Postscript c.1450+ (illustration 85)
Following a brief period when part of the manor house was used as a temporary
smithy, the Furnells site was abandoned to pasture by the late 15th century. Stone
robbing occurred in later years, most notably in the form of a large robbing
hole where stone was removed from the collapsed medieval dovecote. Perhaps
surprisingly, though now forming a deserted plot on the fringe of the village,
the site was not further exploited for its geological resources, this presumably
being because other sites provided either easier access or sources of more favoured
materials or because tenurial holdings militated against such use. Similarly, no

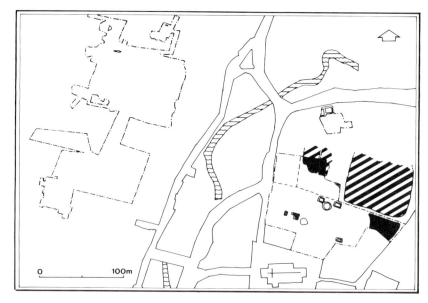

85. North Raunds: major excavated features. Post-medieval quarries are
blacked in, partially excavated quarries are cross-hatched only.

further quarrying was identified within the Langham Road tenements, though at
Burystead extensive areas of the tenements were subject to limestone quarrying,
low ridges of unquarried stone surviving to mark the boundaries between individual tenements. Elsewhere within the village there are indications of large scale
quarrying occurring throughout the post-medieval and modern periods.

Evidence for other quarried material
Apart from quarries and quarried materials already referred to, a brief mention
should be made of those stone items or artifacts for which no excavated source
was identified, and which therefore might provide information as to other local
stone sources or to a trade in stone. The evidence falls into three main categories.
Firstly, there are a small number of unworked constructional stones which have
no 'on site' source. These include Ironstone and Upper Estuarine Limestone, both
of which are known to be locally available. Secondly, there were those specialist

manufactured items, such as hones or quernstones. Investigations as to the provenances of these continues, but it is clear that the items comprise a mix of locally derived materials (some of the hones probably worked from materials found in the local Drift), and those of imported origin, such as Norwegian schist hones and Rhineland lava querns. Thirdly, and most importantly, there are the highly crafted grave slabs, coffins and other ecclesiastical stones associated with the church (illustration 86). These are of Barnack type Lincolnshire Limestone and bear witness to the well established Barnack stone industry trade (Jope 1964). It is however of interest to note the petrological similarity between Barnack stone and Blisworth Limestone of the Raunds area. Whilst some samples are readily distinguishable, others have been identified by very careful examination, and even thin section analysis (D.S. Sutherland, personal communication; see Hudson & Sutherland, above, p. 30).

86. Fragment of a late Saxon cross-shaft, 600mm in length; Barnack type stone. Note later trimming prior to re-use. (Photo: T. Middlemas, Department of Archaeology, University of Durham).

Quarrying tools and methods
(illustration 87)

Unfortunately no quarries or masons' tools (or marks), such as those described by Salzman (1967, 330-36) or by Clifton-Taylor and Ireson (1983, 64-94) have as yet been identified. Identification may be complicated, especially for the late Saxon, by uncertainty as to how far the tools used in working stone are discernible from those used in working wood. Further research would be useful. For the Middle Ages it remains to be seen whether distinctions between classes of mason, as noted by Harvey (1975, 124-25) could be identified from tools.

Four broad types of quarries and quarrying method are identifiable from the excavations in north Raunds. Each is, as would be expected, dependent upon the location and nature of the material being sought. In most cases the rock sought was located either through being exposed at the surface or through the medium

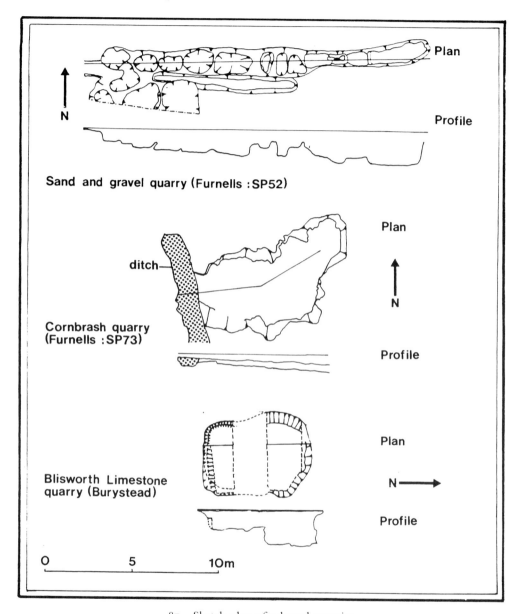

87. Sketch plan of selected quarries.

of a pre-existing cut feature, usually a ditch. Only in one instance, that of the late Saxon Langham Road quarries, was there an indication of the use of an initial evaluation or test pit having been dug. Test pits have been recognised elsewhere in Northamptonshire, most notably during the excavation of a series of post-medieval gravel pits at Ashton (B. Dix, personal communication).

In the first quarry type, Cornbrash Limestone was generally extracted from shallow surface quarries, the rock presumably being prised forth from the edges of the quarry to the depth of a conveniently located bedding plane. The resultant stone consisted of small, unfaced rubble fragments as used in the early church as well as in virtually all the later stone buildings to some degree or other.

Blisworth Limestone was worked from the second quarry type, with larger, deeper and steep-sided pit-like quarries, the deepest of which, such as those at Burystead, having a ramp or step at one side in order to facilitate access. Access ramps have also been noted by Dix (1986-87b) in Roman Ironstone quarries excavated in Kettering. Rectilinear depressions within the quarries bear witness to the extraction of larger and more angular blocks than could be taken from the Cornbrash. A single, narrow groove cut in the base of one of the Burystead quarries suggested that cutting, levering or prising was probably employed in winning the stone.

Hillside quarrying, such as identified at Thorpe End, forms the third main quarrying type identified. In this instance stone was removed across the face of the exposed strata. The final form of exploitation is only recognisable in a post-medieval context, with the appearance of large area quarrying as seen in the Midland Road tenements. Additional to these four main types, stone was also taken from ditch cuts and from the walls and floors of redundant buildings.

Those quarries used for the extraction of sand and gravel were less angular in both plan and profile than were the stone quarries, whilst pits dug for clay were generally small and shallow with rounded forms.

General discussion

The excavations in Raunds provide a valuable insight into the quarry usage of a Saxon and medieval Midlands rural community. In comparison with the contemporary builders of cathedrals and other large capital building works, the scale of stone extraction and utilisation in Raunds prior to AD 1500 may appear of little consequence and yet it was exactly such localised use in ecclesiastical, manorial and peasant contexts which must reflect the scale of quarrying involvement for the majority of the population dwelling within the Jurassic belt. One of the problems in piecing together any general observations on the quarrying in Raunds is that only those quarries identified and excavated can be drawn upon even though there are clear indications of other local sources being exploited contemporaneously.

Of the quarries excavated only those at the Furnells manor site can be directly related to the construction of stone buildings; at Langham Road and Burystead only inferred relationships to stone buildings are possible. Prior to the 9th century, at a time when all buildings were constructed of wood, evidence for stone quarrying, be it in the form of the quarries themselves or their products, is substantially lacking. The earliest quarrying, at Furnells, dates to the late 9th and 10th centuries when Cornbrash Limestone and latterly small amounts of Blisworth Limestone were extracted for use in the construction of the rubble-walled church and for use within the cemetery. Exact calculations are difficult but it is likely that most if not all the stone required would have been available from a combination of the quarries and ditches within the confines of the excavated area. There was no evidence to indicate that any re-used Roman materials had been incorporated within the church fabric as was the case for example with the, admittedly earlier, Saxon church at Brixworth.

Quarrying continued at Furnells during the medieval period but must have been supplemented by stone from quarries elsewhere as the site-extracted quantities of stone were insufficient to meet all requirements. The churches were the only buildings with mass walls of stone to occupy the site until the 12th century. The first sporadic signs of stone use in manorial buildings dates from the late 10th or

88. Furnells: 14th-century dovecote from the east (scale = 1m). This structure and the surfaces to the south typify the use of stone at medieval Furnells. Blisworth Limestone forms the major walling component, but note the single Ironstone quoin in the wall angle directly to the front of the dovecote. (Photo: NCC Archaeology Unit).

11th centuries but it was not until the end of the 12th century that such use became widespread with the building of the stone footed manor house and it was not until the 14th century and the building of the final manor house to occupy the site that all the manorial buildings were mass walled in stone (illustration 88). Apart from the early church, probably built of Cornbrash Limestone because that was the most readily available rock, all these later buildings utilised greater proportions of Blisworth Limestone. This rock was presumably favoured in construction as its tabular nature rendered it adaptable for use in coursed wall facings, as quoins and for flagged surfaces. The more fissile Cornbrash Limestone was in comparison less suitable for coursed walling though it was still usable in walls and in the stony yards that bordered the manor houses. Its poorer walling qualities may explain, at least in part, why the early Cornbrash built church was the only stone building at Furnells to have been wholly mortared. Ironstone was used only occasionally despite there being an outcrop in the valley within easy access of the sites. Its apparent lack of favour, except very occasionally as quoins, is not easily explained. It may be that post-medieval Ironstone usage in Raunds increased as settlement extended across the areas of its outcropping; this might be checked by a survey of extant buildings of that material.

The use to which the limestone from the Langham Road and Burystead sites was put is unclear. That from the former may have been used in buildings at the tenement frontage but this must remain speculation until such time as those buildings, if present, can be investigated. If they were the destination of the Langham Road stone then its use would imply an earlier date to the use of stone within tenements than was, for example, the case at the Midland Road frontage at Burystead where stone buildings are not identifiable before the 13th century at earliest. The late Saxon and early medieval stone quarries at Langham Road and Burystead are perhaps more likely to have supplied uses outside the tenements; possibly for the parish church or nearby manors including Furnells.

Throughout the medieval period the use of stone at Furnells, initially in the church and by the end of the 12th century in the manor, had clearly outstripped the supplies available from the 'on site' quarries excavated. It is suggested that whereas during the late Saxon the relatively small amounts of stone required at Furnells were available 'on site' and to a scale which did not hamper other land use, by the medieval period the increased use of stone required larger scale quarrying which would have competed with other land uses; hence the removal of most quarries to less sensitive areas, the only exceptions being when a quarry could be functionally utilised in another capacity as was the case with the quarry ditch. Presumably the quarries also lay within easy access of the intended place of building so as to minimise transport arrangements. Dependent upon the nature of tenure holdings it might be expected that additional supplies of stone for use at Furnells were being quarried either at Langham Road or Burystead; additional and later requirements such as for the stone used in the nearby tenement buildings being quarried anywhere within a radius of several hundred metres of the sites. Such extraction was perhaps most likely in those areas such as Thorpe End where the bedrock may already have been exposed. Whether quarrying extended into the areas of open field cultivation as for example happened in medieval Oundle (see Appendix) or as indeed happened with the medieval clay pits at Langham Road is an as yet unresolved question.

Though there is evidence for the use of highly crafted and dressed stone, none of the excavated quarries could be confirmed as the source of this stone nor could any craft-working waste products be identified. The absence of large quantities of worked stone is perhaps a reflection of the type of buildings present or of the efficiency of their demolishers. Most of the highly crafted worked stone such as the coffins and grave covers are of Barnack type Lincolnshire Limestone which must have been specially imported from the Barnack stone industry area for highly specific ecclesiastical uses. In contrast the Raunds quarries remained essentially a local industry serving local needs.

Towards a model for Saxon and medieval quarrying in the Raunds area

By drawing upon the excavations within the village of Raunds described above, as well as upon other evidence from within the Raunds Area Project, principally that from the deserted hamlet of West Cotton, a tentative Raunds quarrying model can be suggested.

The earliest Saxon quarrying commenced in the late 9th century and was concerned with the very localised and small scale extraction of the easily available Cornbrash Limestone for use in building a church or more strictly a manorial chapel. Quarrying for ecclesiastical use continued in later centuries and whilst the church remained proprietorial through into the 11th century, the stone was almost certainly being obtained from manorial land holdings, be these within the manorial court or from within other plots held nearby; further documentary research being necessary to confirm such tenurial linkages. Manorial use of stone commenced on a sporadic basis during the late 10th and 11th centuries and was well established by the end of the following century; stone continuing, as with the church, to be extracted on an ad hoc basis from easily accessible and in many cases adjacent manorial holdings. Better quality building stone in the form of Blisworth Limestone was now being quarried and in larger quantities than previously, the presence of local and/or imported high quality crafted stone for use in specialised ecclesiastical contexts or for constructional details in church and manor house perhaps reflecting the increasingly sophisticated aspirations of the resident lord. The manorial and ecclesiastical use of stone continued throughout the medieval period though the construction of a parish church from at least the 12th century may have demanded quantities of stone and stone working skills that drew upon a wider set of resources than those available to a single manor.

The earliest stone buildings in peasant tenements date to the 13th century though earlier usage cannot as yet be entirely discounted. Large amounts of stone would have been required for both these and the continuing manorial and ecclesiastical use and yet the excavated evidence clearly indicates that the areas previously quarried were no longer in use, implying that resources further afield were being exploited. It is suggested that this exploitation of fresh resources was accompanied by, and in part reflects, a move towards the establishment of a more commercially based quarrying industry. The examples of peasant quarrying from Oundle, quoted in the Appendix below, serve as illustration that not only was exploitation of geological resources now taking place outside the areas of the manorial court and peasant toft but that the social order of those initiating the extraction and maybe the sale of quarried materials was no longer so restricted in its base as it had been prior to the 12th or 13th centuries.

Increasing commercialisation of the industry would certainly accord with the widely acknowledged upsurge and increased specialisation in production and trade during the 13th century, as well as perhaps providing a parallel to the thesis by Dyer (1986) that argues for an increasingly commercial organisation in the supply and crafting of the timber used in constructing peasant buildings.

A more local example of late medieval commercial quarrying practice is provided by the rebuilding of Higham Ferrers castle in the 15th century. The castle, situated only a few miles from the village of Raunds, drew upon resources from several parts of the county including freestone from Weldon, stone slates from Yardley and Kirby as well as supplies of other rock from the less distant Finedon and Rushden (Kerr 1925).

That substantial quarrying continued in Raunds during the 15th or 16th centuries is attested by the excavations at Thorpe End, though the destination of that stone is unknown. By the 17th century the exploitation of Raunds stone or 'marble' is, in particular, documented by Morton (1712); is it conceivable that it was the development of this trade allied to changes in field and tenure holdings that again prompted the return of quarries to the plots adjacent to the Midland Road in Raunds?

APPENDIX
Oundle documentary references

1292 Account Roll: NRO A/4/33 (from Rockingham Castle Archive)

> 12d. from Richard Shakeloke because he made a certain quarry on his land which he holds in villenage and sold that stone withouyt licence

1453-4 Court Roll: NRO B/15/79 (from Rockingham Castle Archive)

> John Herryson (6d) is a common transgressor digging in the common and there making pits

Survey of Oundle 1565: NRO Misc. Leger 116 and 117 Howhill Field, Nether Stockwell furlong includes

> Lords Demesne – 17 lands and lees with a great mortar pit used by the lords tenants to take clay for mortar for their houses . . .

Peply Field

> A close of 17 lees and a certen pite of stone fore a quarre

ACKNOWLEDGEMENTS

Dr D.S. Sutherland provided invaluable geological expertise and advice both during the excavation and the preparation of this paper, particularly as regards the Raunds Stone. Christine Addison-Jones, Andy Boddington, Glenn Foard, Steve Parry, Terry Pearson and Tam Webster contributed much information and many useful comments and constructive criticisms during the paper's compilation. We are additionally grateful to Glenn Foard for pin-pointing the documentary sources especially those for Oundle. Christine Addison-Jones, Melanie Whewell and Teresa Eales undertook all illustrations and Carol Harrison the typing.

BIBLIOGRAPHY

Unpublished Archive

Sutherland, D.S., Geology and Stone reports in Boddington, A., and Cadman, G.E., Raunds Furnells Level III Archive, 1977-84. Northampton: Northamptonshire County Council Archaeology Unit

Published Sources

Boddington, A., 1987 — Raunds, Northamptonshire: analysis of a country churchyard, *World Archaeology*, **18**.3 (1987), 411-25

Boddington, A., forthcoming 1990 — *The Anglo-Saxon Church and Churchyard at Raunds Furnells*

Cadman, G.E., and Foard, G., 1984 — Raunds: Manorial and Village Origins, *Studies in Late Anglo-Saxon Settlement*, ed. M. Faull, 81-100. Oxford: Univ. Dept. of External Studies, 1984

Clifton-Taylor, A., and Ireson, A.S., 1983 — *English Stone Building*. London: Victor Gollancz, 1983

Dix, B. (ed.), 1986-87a — The Raunds Area Project: second interim report, *Northamptonshire Archaeol.*, **21** (1986-87), 3-29

Dix, B., 1986-87b — The Roman Settlement at Kettering, Northants; Excavations at Kipling Road, 1968 and 1971, *Northamptonshire Archaeol.*, **21** (1986-87), 95-108

Dyer, C., 1986 — English Peasant Buildings in the Later Middle Ages (1200-1500), *Medieval Archaeol.*, **30** (1986), 19-45

Foard, G., and Pearson, T., 1985 — The Raunds Area Project: first interim report, *Northamptonshire Archaeol.*, **20** (1985), 3-21

Gover, J.E.B., Mawer, A., and Stenton, F.M., 1975 — *The Place Names of Northamptonshire*. English Place-Name Soc., **10**. Cambridge: University Press, 1933, repr. 1975

Harvey, J., 1975 — *Medieval Craftsmen*. London: Batsford, 1975

Jope, E.M., 1964 — The Saxon Building-stone industry in Southern and Midland England, *Medieval Archaeol.*, **8** (1964), 91-118

Kerr, W.J.B., 1925 — *Higham Ferrers and its Ducal and Royal Castle and Park*. Northampton: Harris, 1925

Morton, J., 1712 — *The Natural History of Northamptonshire*. London: for R. Knaplock and R. Wilkin, 1712

Salzman, L.F., 1967 — *Building in England down to 1540*. Corrected ed., Oxford: Clarendon Press, 1967

VCH — *Victoria History of the County of Northampton*, **2**, ed. R.M. Serjeantson and W.R. Atkins. 1906, repr. London: Dawson, 1970

Chapter 13

Building Stone in Norfolk

A. P. Harris

Norfolk's native geology yields two building stones, flint and carstone, both extensively exploited by the medieval church builder. During the 14th and 15th centuries the aesthetic appearance of flintwork was improved by knapping and the introduction of flushwork. Other local but less suited material was used as rubble and even quoins. After the Conquest limestones from Barnack and Caen were imported to meet the need for good building stone. The use of Caen was regional and short-lived, so that by the end of the 13th century Barnack dominated the market.

Geology

The geology of Norfolk consists mainly of chalk which to the east is overlain by deposits of glacial sands and gravels. To the west, bordering the alluvium deposits of the Wash, is a thin band of clays and sand with sandstone outcropping along the north coast. The land is fairly well drained with a marked east and west watershed along a line south from Cromer passing close to Thetford on the southern border of the county, the so-called Cromer ridge. These deposits yield four materials; flint, carstone, chalk and iron-bound gravel conglomerate. Of these, only flint and carstone can be called satisfactory building materials in their own right, chalk and conglomerates having normally to be used in conjunction with other materials.

Chalk

Chalk proper has a very limited use as a building material though it is occasionally found as an inclusion in the rubble fabric. The hard chalks or clunches (extracted from the chalk marls of Cambridgeshire and from Totternhoe in Bedfordshire) were, however, widely used for internal decorative work in structures of the 13th century and later. In Norfolk clunch does not appear to have been a material employed by the 12th-century mason despite its common use in other regions, in particular those close to the source, e.g. Dunstable Priory, Bedfordshire, founded 1132 (Roberts 1974).

Flint

Flint, a very hard and durable silica, occurs in a number of forms; either banded deposits, nodules or pebbles, and can be mined from the chalk, quarried from the gravel or collected from the shore-line. With the exception of some of the major monastic or military structures, walls were built totally of this material without any external facing giving a coarse, uneven rubble appearance. Some buildings do however show an attempt to select the material to enable more close coursing and this is especially true of structures in coastal areas where uniformly sized pebbles could be selected from the beaches. Details and methods concerning the construction of flint rubble walling and their foundations are discussed in Harris (1989, 51-56) and Roberts (1974, 85-87).

Large nodules, either roughly knapped or uncut, are often found in the quoins of 12th-century churches such as at Framingham Earl (illustration 89). At Forncett St Peter, in addition to the nave quoins, many of the architectural features of the 12th-century tower (illustration 90) such as the belfry window openings and the tower arch, are entirely constructed of flint without the use of either voussoirs or ashlar. The church at Framingham Earl has several features some of which, such as the double splayed circular windows and the pilaster buttresses, are faced in rubble flint whilst others, such as the nave doorways and chancel arch, are faced in Caen stone. The Taylors indicated their belief in the assumption that the flint features pre-date those of ashlar (Taylor & Taylor 1965, 243). This can be shown not to be the case, all features being contemporary and of the early 12th century (Harris in Rogerson et al. 1987). Several later structures, for example Rackheath church (14th century), also make use of flint quoining, indicating a longer lasting tradition. In an area of abundant natural flint it is perhaps only to be expected that this style of architecture should continue. Flint-built features, as a technique, are therefore undatable and it is not true that they pre-date similar features faced in ashlar. At Haddiscoe Thorpe flint constructed arcading is located upon the round tower and is contemporary with window openings faced in Caen stone. The tower itself is an addition to an earlier 12th-century church with Caen stone dressings.

Flint construction in no way limited the decorative repertoire of the builder. Recessed blind arcading, constructed totally out of the rubble fabric without the use of any ashlar facing, is a feature of several 12th-century churches, such as Tasburgh, Haddiscoe Thorpe and Belaugh. During the 13th century and later, flint work was becoming more regular in nature with many surfaces faced with flint that had been knapped into regular sized squared blocks. In the 14th century this technique was widespread and could incorporate squared pieces of limestone in a chequerboard pattern. A similar effect was achieved by selecting flints of contrasting hue. This type of work is common upon parapets (illustration 91). Flushwork is a technique that employed very close set knapped flint as a background to limestone canopy work. It is often to be found imitating tracery upon porches and can cover entire wall surfaces, notably that between clerestory openings. In conjunction with heraldic work, it also adorns buttresess and plinth courses and was very popular during the 14th and 15th centuries. Particularly fine examples of flushwork can be found upon St Ethelbert's gate, Norwich Cathedral (c.1316), and Redenhall church (c.1460).

Carstone

The only other suitable local building material, carstone, is a fairly soft mid-brown to black ferruginous sandstone and was extensively used in that area of

89. Framingham Earl church: south-west quoin.

90. Forncett St Peter church: early 12th-century tower.

91. Haddiscoe church: chequerwork on the parapet.

north Norfolk in which it occurs (outcropping in the Hunstanton cliffs on the north-west coast). The distribution of this stone clearly shows that it was however not exported widely outside this area. Distribution westwards was probably limited by the availability of the more suitable Barnack stone which was being imported to the region via the port of King's Lynn. Carstone could be used to face entire wall surfaces, as at Shouldham Thorpe or, as on the late 11th-century church at Newton-by-Castle Acre, to dress openings and quoins and to be carved into capitals, shafts and bases. The use of carstone is not restricted to any particular chronological period, examples of its use being known in the architecture of all periods including the 19th and 20th centuries.

Iron-bound gravel conglomerate: 'ferricrete'

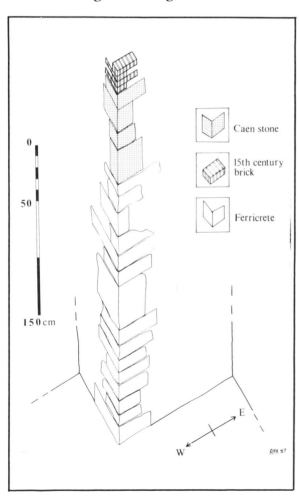

92.   Ashby church: quoin of rough-cut ferricrete.

Iron-bound gravel conglomerate is formed by iron solutions percolating into superficial gravel strata, settling around and cementing together the particles. It is a coarse material with gravel particles of up to 40mm across held within a dark brown to black ferruginous matrix. Superficial gravel deposits are widespread in Norfolk and conglomerates were no doubt extracted during flint quarrying rather than deliberately sought. When first quarried the stone can be fairly soft but soon acquires a hard skin. The material has in the past been referred to as puddingstone, gravel-stone or iron stone. In order to avoid confusion in description and recognition of these like materials, Dr Eric Robinson suggested, in discussion, that the antiquarian term ferricrete, first put forward by Lamplugh (1902, 575) should perhaps be more widely used (see also Robinson 1988).

Ferricrete's coarse texture is not suited for extensive use in building save as a constituent within the rubble fabric of a wall. As such its use is very common with a wide area of distribution which, as the stone is unlikely to have travelled far from the site of extraction, must reflect its source location. Ferricrete is employed upon the church at West Bergholt, Essex (Turner 1984). Although no extraction pit was located, a deposit of ferricrete has been sampled 200m to the east of the building (Turner 1987). Although more common within the fabric of a church, ferricrete was however also rough hewn into blocks and used occasionally as a quoin (illustration 92). At Great Ryburgh the lower courses of the west tower are made up of large numbers of rough-shaped blocks used almost as wall face. In a similar fashion ferricrete is found upon the nave of the ruined church at North Elmham dated to between 1071 and 1091. At Little Snoring well shaped blocks are used exclusively upon the voussoirs and jamb of the very imposing early to mid-12th-century tower arch. Being a widespread material, that even today is ploughed up during deep ploughing, it is only natural to expect that, as with carstone, ferricrete is to be found upon structures of all periods. In the later periods however ferricrete was seldom employed upon architectural features and was confined to use within the rubble fabric.

Both carstone and ferricrete, being of a dark hue, can sometimes be found used in conjunction with the creamy and white limestones in a fashion that recalls Romanesque two-tone paintwork. The jambs of the 12th-century crossing piers at Castle Acre priory are faced in alternating bands of Barnack stone and carstone. A similar technique, employing ferricrete, is to be found upon the jamb of the west tower arch of the ruined church at North Elmham, a structure dated by Heywood to between 1071 and 1091 (Heywood 1982). In the late 11th-century church at Guestwick alternating courses of ferricrete and Barnack can be seen upon the quoin of the tower and the jamb of the tower arch. Elsewhere upon the tower arch ferricrete is used in conjunction with flint, i.e. upon the pilaster strips flanking the arch (Rogerson in Rogerson *et al.* 1987, figs. 53-54).

Found materials and erratic

Erratic deposits were chance local finds and naturally only exploited in the architecture of the immediate surround. Many churches contain erratic material but its use within the church at Aldeby deserves closer attention. The cruciform church at Aldeby is essentially a two-phase church, the late 12th-/13th-century transeptal east arm being an addition to an unaisled single-celled structure of the early 12th century. Within the fabric of the nave can be seen substantial quantities of large flat plates of an unidentified limestone material. The material is found only within the fabric, all contemporary openings being faced in Caen stone. The stone is largely confined to a series of horizontal bands in the lower courses of the walls of the nave. It is totally absent from the fabric of the later parts of the church. Assuming that the material was only accidentally located in the course of flint extraction, then its absence in work of the later periods would imply that by now the deposit had been exhausted or, as is more likely, the flint for use in the later fabric was retrieved from new extraction pits. The absence of this material upon any other nearby church would also lead to the assumption that the extraction pit from which the material was being recovered belonged to the church at Aldeby and was used exclusively for the construction of Aldeby church. If the reverse had been true then one should have expected to find the material evident within the fabric of neighbouring churches.

All areas can produce evidence for the re-use of material, but in those areas such as Norfolk where there is an absence of freestone this re-use is more apparent. An unusual instance currently being catalogued by the Norfolk Archaeological Unit is the incorporation into the fabric of worn and broken or even complete quern or mill stones. Perhaps more significant is the use of unworked, or sometimes roughly shaped, plates of Niedermendig lava upon the quoin of the 12th-century church at Colney near Norwich. Querns made of Niedermendig lava were normally imported from the Rhineland ready made and it would seem therefore that the plates at Colney were imported as ballast upon a ship trading with the Rhineland. There is considerable archaeological evidence for trade between Norwich and the Rhineland during the 11th and 12th centuries (Hodges in Jennings 1981, 26-35).

A common feature of much of Norfolk's early rubble architecture is the re-use of Roman brick and tile material for quoins and window jambs. In contrast to the central area of Essex, especially the district around the Roman town of

93.   Howe church: detail of south-west quoin, showing re-use of long-and-short elements, flint, ferricrete and Roman tile.

Colchester, the re-use of Roman building material in Norfolk is not extensive. Nevertheless substantial amounts can be seen within the fabrics of Burgh St Peter (located just outside the walls of the Saxon shore fort) and Caister St Edmunds (situated within the walls of the abandoned Roman *civitas* of *Venta Icenorum*).

There is ample evidence for the re-use of earlier architectural features in structures of all periods. At Howe the imposts of the tower arch are monolithic. The interlace design carved into their upper surface (not visible from the nave floor) may indicate that these are in fact re-used pieces from an Anglo-Saxon cross shaft. The re-use of Anglo-Saxon material may also provide the answer to the curious rubble constructed south-west quoin (illustration 93) which in addition to flint, ferricrete and tile also uses two large Barnack ashlars that look as if they may have derived from a long and short quoin. By far the greatest opportunity to gain used stone was offered

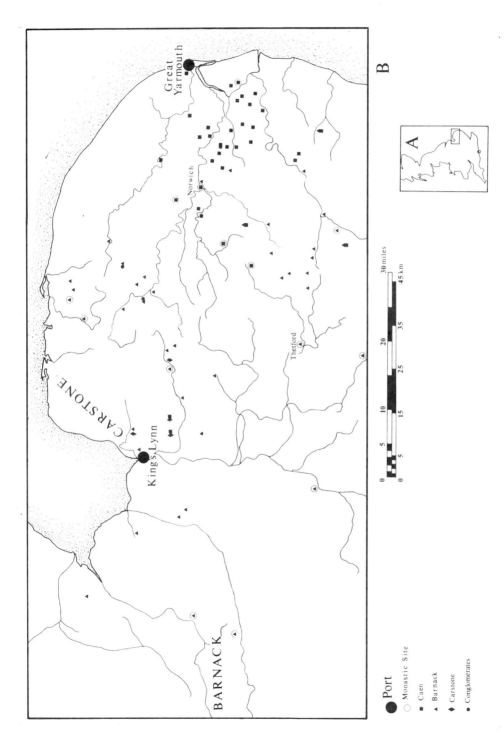

94. Provisional map of Norfolk, showing stone sources and distribution of types, in the 12th and 13th centuries.

by the dissolution of Norfolk's monastic houses. Many of the county's monasteries today remain as bare flint rubble cores, all ashlar work, whether heavily carved or not, having been systematically removed. The stone so obtained was locally distributed. At Thetford, ashlars from the Cluniac priory, many deeply sculpted, can be seen within much of the town's domestic architecture.

Imported limestones

There is no reliable evidence for the use of limestones in the pre-Conquest architecture of Norfolk. There are however several churches with long and short type quoins of Anglo-Saxon style. The better preserved examples are to be seen at East Lexham, Hempnall, Norwich St John Timberhill and Norwich St Martin-at-Palace. The long and short technique was long assumed to be characteristic of pre-Conquest architecture but it is now recognised as lasting into the post-Conquest period, employed upon the quoin of the castle chapel, Winchester, of *c.*1072. The church at Norwich St John Timberhill is also dated to between the Conquest and 1086 (Fernie 1983, 162). No diagnostic features of either the pre- or post-Conquest periods remain in association with the Norfolk examples which must therefore remain undatable. All the surviving examples of this quoin type employ megalithic Barnack ragstone ashlars. Barnack was no doubt imported into the region by river entering the western districts via the River Ouse and the port of King's Lynn, or by sea reaching eastern districts via the port of Great Yarmouth and the rivers Yare and Waveney (illustration 94).

The Norman Conquest brought with it a boom in architecture with a proliferation of castles, monasteries and smaller churches, all of which required freestones for use on the whole range of 12th-century decorative and architectural work. Many of the smaller churches however were still completed with minimum use of ashlar, i.e. for quoins and doorway dressings, but many more display much use of ashlar for quoins, doorways, windows and other decorative features. In Norfolk few reach the standard of work displayed by the mid 12th-century church at Hales (illustration 95). For this work the conquest of England by the Normans made available the limestone quarries at Caen and this stone very quickly began to be imported into Norfolk. The use of Caen was not however widespread nor

95. Hales church: mid 12th-century use of Caen stone.

dominant in Norfolk as a whole. The eastward aspect of south-eastern Norfolk, well provided with inland waterways, ensured that this area in particular is characterised by its use of Caen (illustration 94). However in the north and western districts Barnack stone seems still to have been the more dominant material. The proximity of Thetford and Bury St Edmunds to the western waterways ensured that these two large monastic sites, and smaller churches in the district, were still supplied with Barnack stone. In the north-east of the county the division between the use of the two materials is less clear cut but in general it is true to say that here too Caen stone is limited in its distribution.

The use of Caen stone in Norfolk is not only regional in its distribution but shortlived, so that by the mid 13th century Barnack stone had regained much of the market. There is little evidence for the use of Caen stone prior to the Conquest. In Norfolk the earliest datable occurrence of Caen stone would appear to be in Norwich Cathedral, begun by de Losinga in 1096. It has already been suggested that the church at St John Timberhill with its long and short quoins of Barnack has been dated to between the Conquest and 1086 and this would further seem to confirm that prior to the 1090s Caen stone was not available to the city. The reasons for the decline in use of Caen towards the end of the 12th century are no doubt related to the temporary loss of Normandy and the interruption thereafter to a constant supply of stone. Caen stone is however evident on some buildings of the 13th century, notably Norwich Cathedral, but, particularly in relation to smaller church architecture, it is true to say that in areas once rich in Caen, new work of the 13th century is devoid of the material. This development can be demonstrated at Binham Priory in north-east Norfolk; here Caen stone was never dominant but is nevertheless to be recognised in areas of the east arm. The use of Caen decreases as the nave was constructed so that by the time the west front was completed in c.1240 Barnack stone was the exclusive material.

The only other additional materials of any significance during the medieval period are a buff or pale yellow, hard, slightly oolitic limestone and a similar more shelly material. The latter can be tentatively related to material of Clipsham type whilst the former is similar to a range of materials of Ancaster type. Both of these materials are widespread on churches of the 14th century and later. The coarser material was more often used for large architectural details such as plinths and string courses, the finer grained materials being employed for decorative work.

Conclusion

Building in flint was a challenge succesfully met by all generations of church builders throughout the medieval period. The masons found flint just as versatile as limestone even though it could not be carved, and used it for quoins, window surrounds, doorways and a whole range of surface decoration techniques. Despite its rubble nature, flint was universally exploited as a walling face either coursed or uncoursed and was even knapped into smaller regular sized building blocks. So confident were the masons of this material that other materials, carstone, Barnack and Caen, only supplemented and never replaced flint architecture.

Perhaps the most telling example of the mason's confidence in his local geology was the frequent use of ferricrete as a building stone employed on architectural details as early as the 11th century. The extraordinary growth in the size of church buildings as evidenced in the so-called 'wool churches' of north–west Norfolk, and the sophistication and succesful application of techniques of surface decoration such as flushwork, attest to the competence of the Norfolk mason. Despite a lack of local raw materials he was able to construct monuments of architecture that are some of the finest in the realm.

BIBLIOGRAPHY

Fernie, E.C., 1983	*The architecture of the Anglo-Saxons*. London: Batsford, 1983
Harris, A.P., 1989	Late 11th- and 12th-century church architecture of the Lower Yare Valley, Norfolk. Unpubl. M.Phil. thesis, University of East Anglia, 1989
Heywood, S., 1982	The ruined church at North Elmham, *J. Br. Archaeol. Assoc.*, **135** (1982), 1–10
Jennings, S., 1981	*Eighteen centuries of pottery from Norwich*. East Anglian Archaeol., **13**, Norwich: Norwich Society, 1981
Lamplugh, G.W., 1902	Calcrete, *Geol. Mag.*, Decade IV, **9** (1902), 575
Roberts, E., 1974	Totternhoe stone and flint in Hertfordshire churches, *Medieval Archaeol.*, **18** (1974), 66–89
Rogerson, A., Ashley, S., Williams, P., and Harris, A., 1987	*Three Norman churches in Norfolk*. East Anglian Archaeol., **32**, Norwich: Norfolk Archaeology Unit, 1987
Robinson, E., 1988	Gravel-stone in Middlesex churches: what's in a name?, *London Archaeologist*, **5**.14 (1988), 367–71
Taylor, H.M., and J., 1965	*Anglo-Saxon Architecture*, 2 vols. Cambridge: University Press, 1965
Turner, R., 1984	Excavations at St Mary's church West Bergholt, Essex, 1978, in *Four church excavations in Essex*, Occasional Papers, **4**, Chelmsford: Essex County Council (1984), 43–63
Turner, R., 1987	The sources of indurated conglomerate from early medieval churches in North and East Essex, *Essex Archaeol. Hist.*, **18** (1987), 120

Chapter 14

Building a Fine City: The Provision of Flint, Mortar and Freestone in Medieval Norwich

B. S. Ayers

This paper assesses the problems which were encountered in the provision of stone building materials for medieval Norwich. The city lies in an area poor in good quality stone although rich in flint and chalk. A fine heritage of surviving buildings, together with increasing evidence from excavations and published primary sources, enables an appraisal to be made of the importance of the local provision of stone and the ways in which imported materials were used to augment these local supplies.

Introduction

A fine old city, truly, is that, view it from whatever side you will . . . the eye beholds a scene which cannot fail to awaken, even in the least sensitive bosom, feelings of pleasure and admiration . . . the fine old city, perhaps the most curious specimen at present extant of the genuine old English town. Yes, there it spreads from north to south, with its venerable houses, its numerous gardens, its thrice twelve churches . . . a grey old castle . . . and yonder, rising three hundred feet above the soil, from among those noble forest trees, behold that old Norman master-work, that cloud-encircled cathedral spire . . .

(Borrow, *Lavengro*)

George Borrow can be forgiven his eulogistic appraisal of Norwich; he was, after all, speaking of a place which, only a hundred years earlier, had been the second city of England, the centre of the cloth trade and, in size, outranked only by London. Furthermore, he encompasses in a few lines much of concern to this paper: venerable houses; thrice twelve churches; a grey old castle; and the cathedral church. All these structures had to be built and, although a wide range of materials from brick to timber to clay lump was used in their construction, stone of one sort or another was employed almost universally as dressings, facings, corework or lime.

Borrow's viewpoint of the city for his famous description is also appropriate. He stood to 'the east, where the ground, bold and elevated, overlooks the fair and fertile valley'. This is the edge of Mousehold Heath, an area of spectacular elevation in East Anglian terms, soaring all of 150 feet (48m) above the valley floor. Its steep slopes were ideal for quarrying and mining, both for chalk to make lime and for flint with which to build. Borrow, if he stood on St James's Hill or Kett's Heights, both viewpoints to this day, would be less than a stone's throw from some of the quarry pits that contributed material towards building his fine city.

Norwich stands in a double bend of the River Wensum, a little to the north of its confluence with the Yare. It overlies deposits of chalk and flint which are obscured by sands and gravels in the valley bottom. The river divides two substantial areas of high ground: Mousehold Heath to the north and east; and the Ber Street hill to the south and west (illustration 96). For an East Anglian town, slopes can be severe, particularly so immediately east of the river and to the south and west. It is a classic site for the development of an urban community, commanding the lowest river crossing, dominating high ground and surrounded by different types of rich agricultural hinterland.

The site is not propitious, however, with regard to building stone. There are no sources of freestone within 50 miles and few within 100 miles. Flint rubble was the only building stone to hand and this had to be won from the chalk. It has been known for some time that quarrying and mining for these two materials were practised in Norwich almost to modern times, although how far such activities were commonplace in the medieval city has yet to be quantified. It will be shown that there is a growing body of evidence to demonstrate that much quarrying dates at least from the later medieval period and that it is possible that late Saxon industrial development may have initiated the process.

Local sources of stone

Any assessment of the stone materials utilised in Norwich must start with an appraisal of the surviving buildings. Here, it immediately becomes necessary to consider the surviving churches (some 32 out of a suspected total of 60 plus) and excavated evidence, as very few domestic buildings survive from before the 16th century. Indeed, it is currently thought that, of Norwich's rich stock of some 1,500 buildings pre-dating 1830, fewer than two dozen secular structures are earlier than AD 1500 (Robert Smith, personal communication), fires in 1507 and other factors removing the rest. Norwich is thus essentially a 16th-century and later city with regard to its extant fabric.

Enough survives, however, to indicate general trends. At least one church, that of St Martin-at-Palace, contains Anglo-Saxon work and several other parish churches retain work of the Norman period. The city is indeed rich in Norman buildings: the cathedral contains substantial work from the late 11th and 12th centuries, not just in the church but also in the claustral buildings and Bishop's Palace (Whittingham 1951, 86); the Castle keep dates from the beginning of the 12th century (Drury *et al.* forthcoming); Carrow Priory, a large Benedictine nunnery, is of mid 12th-century origin; a fragment of a Lazar House or Leper Hospital survives; there exists in the Music House on King Street a fine stone house of *c.*1175 (Kent 1945) and, recently excavated and preserved at St Martin-at-Palace Plain, the remains of another house of similar date (Ayers 1987a). Thirteenth-century work is much more scarce, save for the beginning of construction on the city walls, but, by the 14th century, large merchants' houses like Strangers Hall were being constructed, while many of the city churches were rebuilt in the 15th century (Pevsner 1962, 235ff.).

All these buildings used flint, frequently in prodigious quantities, together with vast quantities of lime mortar. In buildings of quality, and the surviving buildings

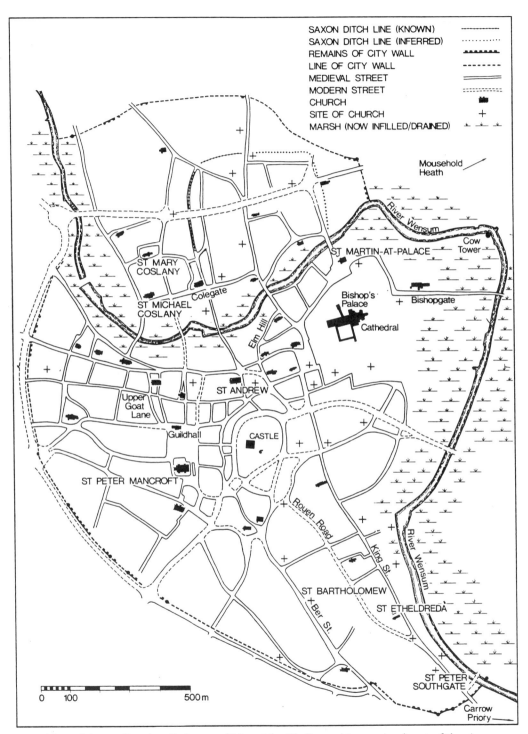

SAXON DITCH LINE (KNOWN)
SAXON DITCH LINE (INFERRED)
REMAINS OF CITY WALL
LINE OF CITY WALL
MEDIEVAL STREET
MODERN STREET
CHURCH
SITE OF CHURCH
MARSH (NOW INFILLED/DRAINED)

Mousehold Heath

River Wensum

Cow Tower

ST MARTIN-AT-PALACE

Bishop's Palace

Bishopgate

ST MARY COSLANY

Colegate

ST MICHAEL COSLANY

Cathedral

Elm Hill

ST ANDREW

Upper Goat Lane

Guildhall

CASTLE

ST PETER MANCROFT

Rouen Road

King St.

River Wensum

ST BARTHOLOMEW

Ber St.

ST ETHELDREDA

ST PETER SOUTHGATE

Carrow Priory

0   100   500 m

96.   Map of the medieval walled area of Norwich. Chalk workings existed east of the river near Rosary Road and Kett's Hill (i.e. east of Bishopgate) as well as near Rouen Road. Galleries are known in both of these locations as well as west of the walled city in the area of Earlham Road (off border, left centre).

are nearly always such, other materials such as freestone were employed, but flint was nearly always used for bulk core work. The amounts needed were enormous. To take one monument, the city wall, this structure was almost entirely built of flint and mortar, was probably at least a metre thick with an arcade frequently behind that to carry the parapet walk, stood some five metres or more in height, included 12 gates and nearly 40 towers and extended some $2\frac{1}{2}$ miles (4km), encompassing the greatest area of any medieval English city, including London. A very rough and probably highly inaccurate estimate might yield a figure of some 40,000m³ of material necessary for such a construction.

Building accounts do occasionally survive for the construction of some monuments. A very detailed account for the Cow Tower of 1398/9 (Ayers 1987b; Ayers *et al.* 1988) lists the numbers of carts of stone brought to the site, enumerating at least 170 in all (this for a brick tower; flint was used for the core). It also lists the carts of sand and lime that were brought, William Large for instance being paid 34d. for the carriage of seven carts of stone, five carts of sand and one cart of lime (Ayers 1987, 19). Payments were made to *stonmyners* for the stone as well as the carters; the cost per cart varied generally between 3d. and 4d.

The quarries for the stone were probably, for the most part, local. One *stonmyner* in the 1398-99 account was a certain John Drayton who may have mined a pit in or near the village of Drayton some five miles (8km) north-west of the city. Other sources, however, could be found much closer to hand. Some material for the building of the Cow Tower seems to have been shipped from King Street (illustration 96) and it is likely that flint extracted from the quarries cutting into the nearby Ber Street hill was amongst the stone used. The exceptionally steep slopes that survive to this day off Rouen Road reflect the abandoned quarry face while just outside the city wall close by is an abandoned and now wooded pit called the Wilderness. These quarries were, of course, producing flint *and* chalk; it is the application of the latter material as lime that engendered references in the surviving documentation for the industry.

One of the main suppliers of lime to the Cow Tower was a man called William Blakehommore (although the City Chamberlains seem also to have employed their own limeburner as Michael *Lymbrennere* was paid for seven days at 4d. a day). Blakehommore was paid £4 17s. 6d. for 67 *treyes* of *lyme* at 18d. *le Treye* (a tray measured one and three-fifths of a bushel) and is known to have had both his capital messuage and a limekiln on King Street. He sold the kiln to the city in return for an annuity in December 1399. The abuttals given locate it reasonably precisely: the hospital of Hildebronde north; the churchyard of St Peter Southgate south; the road east; and the land of Carrow and another tenement west; in other words, just north of the now ruined church of St Peter Southgate, west of King Street and a little inside the city wall (illustration 96; information from Margot Tillyard). Blakehommore's kiln was that leased by the city to Richard Sotherton in 1562; the lease included the digging of chalk within the yard (information from Elizabeth Rutledge and Geoffrey Kelly).

Other limekilns are known both north and south of this site. Carrow Priory, a large Benedictine nunnery immediately south of the city, had a limekiln (*thoralli calcis*) just outside the city wall in 1484–85 although by 1529–30 it was ruined and pulled down, no rent being paid (Redstone 1946, 49). A *kyllyard* north of St Etheldreda's is mentioned in 1553. North again, the property of John Marsham, *lymeburner*, including a *lyme kylle*, passed to Mr Thomas Gleane in 1562. North of this was a tenement owned by Richard Nixon, limeburner, which was sold in 1585. Perhaps rather tellingly a messuage south of St Etheldreda is described, also in the 16th century, as vacant and burnt down (all references courtesy of Elizabeth Rutledge and the Wensum Lodge History of King Street Group).

The limekilns and their workforce must have been utilising material drawn from the adjacent quarry face. The topographical evidence would suggest that the work extended over a long period of time as the hill has been cut back some 110 yards (100m) from King Street, creating both a cliff edge and a flat terrace. The terrace is the remains of the quarry floor, where the kilns themselves were sited. Exporting the lime had other environmental effects; an Assembly minute of 30 May 1561 records that a Mrs Bulwer had had made two staithes in Nether Conesford (i.e. King Street) for washing, but that 'certeyne parsons have used to lade lyme at the same stathes so that the people cannot wasshe there onles they should moche hurte thos clothes that they shoulde so wasshe there'. Further loading was prohibited on pain of a fine of 20s. a time (Hudson & Tingey 1910, 135). It is pleasant to have evidence of Norwich being so far in the forefront of anti-pollution measures!

The quarries off King Street were clearly an important source of stone and lime but there were others. Across the River Wensum from the Cow Tower is a large chalk pit below Kett's Heights, subsequently used as the site of a gas works (now largely gone). East of Rosary Road there is a further area where lime was extracted. Part of the resulting site became known as Lollards' Pit, being used for the burning of heretics. Both sites were probably under the lordship of the Bishop of Norwich. Remains of the early Norman St Leonard's Priory stand above Lollards' Pit and it is possible that stone and lime from this area were used in the construction of the cathedral. Much of this bank of the river was held by the prior and convent of the cathedral; a further chalk pit to the north, now known as Kett's Cave and a children's playground, may have originated as a conventual quarry.

Upon disuse the chalk pits could sometimes be utilised further. In 1581, for instance, Thomas Gleane (mentioned above as purchasing a limekiln in 1562) was granted a licence 'to build a new wall in the Lane by St Bartilmews paying yearly 12d & to be bound to receive into his Kiln ground the Drain coming out of Berstreet and also to receive into the same Ground any Compost Muck or Rubbish for 20 years so as the same be not brought in Carts' (Hudson 1889, 11; St Bartholomew located in illustration 96). This was surely not an isolated instance of using rubbish for essentially landfill purposes.

Flint and chalk were not the only raw materials quarried in the Norwich area. Sands and gravels were others and while some of these would clearly have been extracted from the river bottom, much was probably taken from Mousehold, a sandy heathland immediately east of the city of which almost 200 acres (80ha.)

still survive. It is a landscape still pockmarked by diggings and a 16th-century map clearly marks *Stonmynes* over much of the area.

It is clear from the documentary evidence that quarrying was carried on in the medieval period. What is less clear is whether mining in shafts dates from this period as well. Norwich retains a complex network of tunnels, many of which are known to be post-medieval in date but some of which could be earlier. The evidence has recently been summarised by Atkin (1983) and needs little recapitulation here. It is, however, worth reiterating that the main groups of known tunnels are localised in three areas: in the western part of the city, notably around the Earlham Road where 19th-century explorers rather quaintly named the galleries Discovery Street, Garden Lane and the like; within the Ber Street escarpment; and below the hill adjacent to Rosary Road (illustration 96). The second and third groups, of course, are near quarries; the first group does not seem to be associated with open-cast quarry working. Atkin discusses the dating evidence which is extremely tenuous in nearly all cases and concludes that most tunnels are probably 16th-century and later (recent research indicates that the earliest known recorded date for such activity is 1615: Geoffrey Kelly, personal communication) except possibly for tunnels in the Pottergate area, close to the street of *Stonegate* (now Upper Goat Lane but recorded with the earlier name in 1267, perhaps an improbable if not necessarily impossible date for a paved street).

The results of the excavation of a previously unknown late Saxon church and graveyard behind Anglia TV in 1979 are perhaps of relevance here. The work revealed numerous burials where the individuals may have suffered deficiency of Vitamin D, a causative agent of rickets which was diagnosed in bone material from the site. The combination of this deficiency with numerous upper girdle pathologies implying labouring stress suggested that some individuals may have been engaged in an arduous occupation in an environment devoid of sunlight. Mining is, of course, the obvious such occupation (Stirland 1985, 56b). The evidence is circumstantial and should not be taken too far but the possibility of pre-Conquest activity can be admitted.

The topographic effects of large-scale quarrying and mining on the city have been severe. It has already been seen that much of the physical geography immediately west of King Street was radically altered by cutting away the face of the Ber Street hill. Some pits were so deep that they have never been developed, like the Wilderness; others have become recreational areas during suburban development. The systems of tunnels continue to cause problems, especially as the locations of many galleries are unknown. Heavy rain in 1987-88 led to five major areas of subsidence in the city. Of these, one was probably associated with known late 18th- and 19th-century workings off the Dereham Road; a second was in the area of the Earlham Road system; the third was off Ber Street, an area frequently prone to such movement (examination by the City Engineer's Department revealed a partially-blocked gallery probably of post-medieval date); a fourth caused the partial collapse of a house on Kett's Hill; the fifth incident made national news when a double decker bus sank upright in a hole on Earlham Road. Such incidents are not new. On 9 December 1937 the *Eastern Evening News* reported that a Norwich butcher of Ber Street 'had an unpleasant experience yesterday when he fell into a deep cavity in his cellar caused by subsidence'. A report later in the month on 30 December 1937 stated 'that following further subsidence in Ber Street, Norwich, involving over 20 houses and a frontage of seven shops, a number of families have had to move out with all their belongings'. These problems of subsidence have another consequence: high-rise buildings are rare in Norwich; Normandie Tower was one of three planned off Rouen Road but the only one built.

It is perhaps inappropriate here to explore the various building uses to which the flint was put but it is worth mentioning that it was not employed exclusively in core-work. Many buildings were faced in flint either in cobbled courses, as in the excavated and preserved 12th-century building at St Martin-at-Palace Plain, or with squared and knapped flints as in the Guildhall of 1407 onwards or many of the churches. Flushwork was employed at some churches, most notably at St Michael Coslany, flint being carefully shaped. Celia Fiennes, on her visit to the city in 1698, noted the churches: 'they are built all of flints well headed or cut which makes them look all blackish and shineing . . .'. She also noted that 'the streetes are all well pitch'd with small stones' (Morris 1982, 136), another use for the output of the local flint industry and one replicated today only in the paving of Elm Hill (illustration 96).

Imported stone
Freestone had to be brought to Norwich. The earliest extant use of freestone is reputedly that in the east wall of the church of St Martin-at-Palace where long and short work, probably utilising Barnack material, has been dated to the 11th century. The round tower of St Mary Coslany church is often described as Saxon although its belfry openings have shafts of Caen stone and the building is now ascribed to the late 11th century (Carter 1978). The greatest surviving building or complex of buildings dating from the late 11th and early 12th centuries is the cathedral. The church remains one of the most complete major Romanesque structures in the country and its fabric employs both Caen and Barnack as well as considerable quantities of flint.

The construction of the cathedral would have involved the movement of stone on a colossal scale. While flint and lime could be procured locally, freestone, whether from Caen or Barnack, was brought a significant distance. Water transport was heavily utilised as is clear from 13th-century and later entries in the Communar Rolls of the cathedral priory. In 1288-89, for instance, stone was brought from Caen to Yarmouth, trans-shipped in Yarmouth for river transport to Norwich and then carried to the cathedral site (Fernie & Whittingham 1972, 54-55). Barnack material would probably have been shipped via Yarmouth as well in order to get into the Yare/Wensum river system. Once arrived in Norwich, the movement of stone to the site was probably facilitated by the use of a canal, cut from the Wensum to the Lower Close. This canal survived into the 18th century, although it had become a stinking ditch by the late 19th century and was infilled. Its course is occasionally seen during drainage and sewerage work.

The proportion of Caen stone to Barnack stone used in the initial construction of the cathedral would be difficult to quantify, not only because of the amount of later restoration work which has clearly removed much material but also because the use of both types of stone was not confined to the initial phase. Although Norwich Cathedral survives as a great Romanesque monument, it also contains much work of a later medieval date and both Caen and Barnack were purchased for these later building operations. The shipment of Caen stone mentioned above, for instance, was necessary for late 13th-century work on the chapter house. In 1273-74 stone was brought from both Caen and Barnack for the west walk of the cloister (Fernie & Whittingham 1972, 38) and in 1274 Base the Mason went to Caen for stone (Fernie & Whittingham 1972, 28). These continuing shipments of material over a prolonged period explain why it would appear that there may be two or three different types of Caen material in the cathedral (Keith Darby, personal communication).

Both Caen and Barnack are used throughout the church, often together and sometimes in concert for quite deliberate effect, as in the construction of the nave piers. To some extent Barnack was probably used more frequently for exterior works as it was the more durable of the two. In respect of decorated material, however, Caen was clearly preferred. A recent assessment of Romanesque worked stone, generally from the first cloister, found that all these decorative pieces were of Caen save for two items of Barnack (Borg et al. 1980, 7b). One celebrated piece of worked stone does not, however, adhere to this general rule: the carved figure of an unknown individual (variously identified as Herbert de Losinga, the first Bishop of Norwich, or St Felix, the missionary to East Anglia) set into the exterior wall above the north transept door. The material here is Barnack, used for perhaps the earliest post-Roman piece of monumental figure sculpture. The effigy was purpose-made for the recess in which it sits (information from Keith Darby).

There were of course other types of stone used in the fabric, notably flint. It is recorded in 1385-86 that 16 cartloads of flint were ready for work on the cloister (Fernie & Whittingham 1972, 40). Purbeck 'marble' was brought by sea from Corfe to Yarmouth in 1345-46 as well as freestone from Dublin. In 1346-47 Clipsham stone came from Pickworth in Rutland (Fernie & Whittingham 1972, 38).

This excursus into the later medieval building accounts at the cathedral priory has distracted attention from the Norman period during which other monuments were constructed in the city. The castle keep is second only to the cathedral as a major survival. It probably dates from the reign of Henry I, being stylistically similar to the documented keep at Falaise. Unlike Falaise, documents for the Norwich building do not survive although masons' marks parallel early work at the cathedral (Whittingham 1980, 359-60). The present structure is faced externally with Bath stone, a regrettable restoration of the 1830s. Prior to this, dressings and facings both internally and externally were of Caen stone, although they were confined to the buttresses and upper storey, not carried to plinth level as in the restoration. Eighteenth-century engravings make it clear that the ground floor level was faced in flint save for the buttresses.

Of the two Norman houses in Norwich, the Music House is of higher quality with a vault, probably of Caen stone. The excavated building at St Martin-at-Palace Plain, almost certainly a cathedral property, as late 13th-century rents were payable to the cellarer of the Benedictine priory (Ayers 1987a), is dressed at the internal and external corners with quoins of Barnack. The window openings and doorways are dressed similarly.

The construction of the principal Norman monuments was clearly the largest undertaking involving freestone in medieval Norwich but such material continued to be required. It has already been shown that there were numerous occasions in the later medieval period when it was necessary for the cathedral authorities to purchase stone for repairs or extensions. To the types itemised above can be added Quarr stone brought via Yarmouth in 1413-14 (Fernie & Whittingham 1972, 41) and a little Ketton observed within the fabric (Keith Darby, personal communication). As mentioned above, later restorations confuse matters; Weldon and Bath stone were used extensively in the 18th and 19th centuries, obscuring the scheme of earlier work.

Cathedral masons are recorded in the documentation, as in 1411-12 when the chief mason was working in the tracing house, while stone was being cut in the masons' yard (Fernie & Whittingham 1972, 41). Recent excavations (late 1987 by the Norfolk Archaeological Unit) adjacent to the north side of the cathedral church (immediately west of the north transept and north of the nave) have uncovered the probable remains of a masons' yard, characterised by spreads of limestone waste in the form of chippings and sawdust. It is not possible as yet to associate this yard with any known building phase of the cathedral but it would seem to be a deposit that is earlier rather than later in the sequence.

There are references to cathedral masons in other documentation referring to activities outside the walls of the priory. Two of them, John Antell and Robert Everard, seem to have occupied adjacent properties on St Martin-at-Palace Plain in the late 15th century. Everard, who was probably mason for the nave vaults, may have had a workshop on Bishopgate (Ayers 1987a).

Some of the cathedral masons are thought to have worked on other churches in the city and these buildings would have needed freestone, particularly for dressings as the great expense of transportation precluded the use of such stone for much else. The greater parish churches, like St Peter Mancroft, which was completely rebuilt between 1430 and 1455, did use considerable quantities of freestone such as Ancaster stone (Purcell 1967, 54) but even here it is only used for facings (40s. was left by Philip Curson in 1506 to pave the chancel in marble, another example of localised use of 'exotic' materials: Cattermole & Cotton 1983, 259). Flint remained the major building material.

The local building tradition

In conclusion, it is worth adding that it is a testimony to the importance of the local flint industry that Norwich has a rather poor timber-framed tradition for its secular buildings (and a relatively late brick tradition) but a very fine tradition of building in flint. Many 16th-century and later structures survive to illustrate the almost ubiquitous use of flint for ground-floor and gable walls (such as Bacon House on Colegate), but perhaps no finer flint building can be found than the late 14th-century Bridewell. This magnificent house, built for William Appleyard, first Mayor of Norwich, has a remarkable north wall where the flints are knapped and squared to fit extremely closely. This wall, immediately south of the churchyard of St Andrew, can only be that to which Celia Fiennes was taken in 1698: 'just by one of the Churches there is a wall made of flints that are headed very finely and cut so exactly square and even, to shutt in one to another, that the whole wall is made without cement at all they say . . . it looks well very smooth shineing and black' (Morris 1982, 137–38). Norwich was obviously proud of its indigenous stone in the 17th century and did well to show it off to visiting lady travellers.

ACKNOWLEDGEMENTS

The writer is very grateful to his colleagues for help during the preparation of this paper, especially to Keith Darby, Stephen Heywood, Elizabeth Rutledge, Robert Smith, Margot Tillyard and Geoffrey Kelly. Naturally none of them is responsible for any errors that probably litter the text. The map was drawn by Jayne Bown and Sam Brown. Alex Gibson most kindly typed the manuscript into a machine so that the writer could edit to his heart's content.

BIBLIOGRAPHY

Atkin, M.W., 1983 — The Chalk Tunnels of Norwich, *Norfolk Archaeol.*, **38**.3 (1983), 313–20

Ayers, B.S., 1987a — *Excavations at St. Martin-at-Palace Plain, Norwich, 1981* = East Anglian Archaeol. **37**, Dereham: Norfolk Archaeological Unit, 1987

Ayers, B.S., 1987b — *Digging Deeper*. Norwich: Norfolk Museums Service, 1987

Ayers, B.S., Smith, R., and Tillyard, M., 1988 — The Cow Tower, Norwich: a detailed survey and partial reinterpretation, *Medieval Archaeol.* **32** (1988), 184–207

Borg, A., *et al.*, 1980 — *Medieval Sculpture from Norwich Cathedral*, Norwich: Sainsbury Centre for the Visual Arts, 1980

Carter, A., 1978 — The Anglo-Saxon origins of Norwich: the problems and approaches, *Anglo-Saxon England*, **7** (1978), 175–204

Cattermole, P., and Cotton, S., 1983 — Medieval Parish Church Building in Norfolk, *Norfolk Archaeol.*, **38**.3 (1983), 235–79

Drury, P.J., and Ayers, B.S., forthcoming — *Norwich Castle Keep*

Fernie, E., and Whittingham, A.B., 1972 — *The Early Communar and Pitancer Rolls of Norwich Cathedral Priory with an account of the building of the cloister.* Norfolk Record Society, **41**, 1972

Hudson, W. (ed.), 1889 — *The Streets and Lanes of the City of Norwich: a memoir by John Kirkpatrick*, Norwich: Norfolk and Norwich Archaeological Society, 1889

Kent, E.A., 1945 — Isaac's Hall or the Music House, Norwich, *Norfolk Archaeol.* **28**.4 (1945), 31–38

Morris, C. (ed.), 1982 — *The Illustrated Journeys of Celia Fiennes, 1682–c.1712* London: Macdonald, 1982

Pevsner, N., 1962 — *North-East Norfolk and Norwich*. Buildings of England, Harmondsworth: Penguin, 1962

Purcell, D., 1967   *Cambridge Stone.* London: Faber & Faber, 1967

Redstone, L.J., 1946   Three Carrow Account Rolls, *Norfolk Archaeol.*, **29** (1946), 41-88

Stirland, A., 1985   The Human Bones, in Ayers, B.S., *Excavations within the North-east Bailey of Norwich Castle, 1979,* 49-58 = East Anglian Archaeol., **28**, Norfolk Archaeological Unit, 1985

Whittingham, A.B., 1951   The monastic buildings of Norwich Cathedral, *Archaeol. J.*, **106** (1951), 86-87

Whittingham, A.B., 1980   Note on Norwich Castle, *Archaeol. J.*, **137** (1980), 359-60

Chapter 15

Buildings, Building Stones and Building Accounts in South-West England

N. J. G. Pounds

The south-western peninsula has an abundance of stone, ranging from a fissile shale to granite. All has been used for rough masonry, but there is a conspicuous lack of free-cutting stone for ashlar masonry. Most early buildings made use of whatever stone was locally available, but quality stone for ashlar construction had generally to be imported. The high cost of working hard local stone had to be balanced against the high cost of bringing in good freestone. This equation is examined with reference to Exeter Cathedral and Bodmin Priory church. In general transport charges absorbed up to two-thirds of total material costs.

Sources and types of building stone

'Quarry stones', wrote Richard Carew at the end of the 16th century, 'are of sundry sorts, and serve to divers purposes. For walling there are rough and slate. For windows, dornes [doorposts] and chimneys, moor stone granite carrieth the chiefest reckoning' (Halliday 1953, 86-87). He was writing of Cornwall but, if Devon had found so competent a topographer, he could have added little more than the Permian sandstone and the Cretaceous beds along the Dorset border. John Norden, writing at about the same time, was more explicit. 'Ther is a stone', he wrote, 'called a Moar-stone, which lyeth despersed vpon the face of the mountaynes and on the confused rockes; Stones verie profitable for manie pur-poses, in buylding moste firme and lastinge; weather nor time can hardly penetrate them' (Norden 1728, 17). He went on to describe how 'the Country people cleeue them with wedges like loggs of wood, of verie great length, and of what quantities of bodye they liste; so they make of them, in steed of timber, mayne postes for their howses, Dorepostes, Chimnye and wyndow peeces . . .' There is nowhere any suggestion that the stone was quarried; reliance was placed entirely on masses of stone, bounded by their natural jointing, which occurred at the surface. The only other building material which seemed to deserve mention was slate, for which all early writers had only the highest praise: 'they are thynn, beautyfull, and lighte, and contynue verie longe without prejudice, vnles by violence' (Norden 1728, 17).

Over most of south-west England our topographers could find no workable deposits of freestone, and limestone was almost wholly absent from Cornwall, and occurred only sparingly in Devon. The south-western peninsula is largely built of rocks of Devonian and Carboniferous age, flanked on the south by the

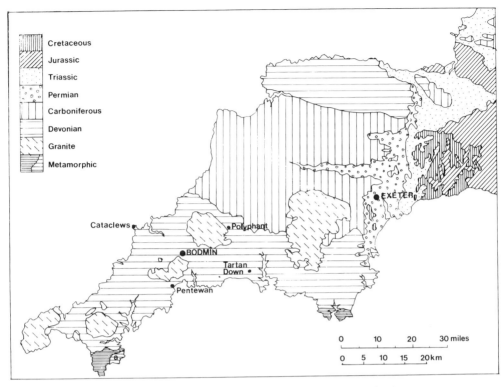

97. Simplified geological map of south-west England.

remains of a once extensive Precambrian massif (illustration 97). On the east these rocks are overlain by Permian beds, of which the most significant visually are the New Red Sandstones of south-east Devon. Lastly, the Greensand, Gault and Chalk of southern England overlap small areas of eastern Devon. The rocks are predominantly argillaceous, consisting of fissile shale, useful only in the roughest masonry, interbedded with less extensive areas of sandstone and conglomerate, and the only good freestone is from quarries in the Cretaceous beds of the extreme south-east.

The geological history of the south-west has been complicated by the intrusion of igneous rocks, some of them of great architectural importance. Broadly, they are of two types: the granites and, to use the Cornish term, the 'elvans'. During the Permian the region was intruded by granite, which lifted the crust and metamorphosed the adjacent shales to slate, forming that sequence of granite bosses which is the dominant physical feature of the region. The granites are light in colour with, as a general rule, large felspar crystals and a well formed system of joints which facilitates working. The elvans, generally speaking, followed the granites. They were intruded as veins or dykes into both the granite and the country rock. Their mineralogical composition varied, but most were fine grained and very hard. Some, however, lend themselves to working with the chisel and, in the absence of freestone, were used for monumental sculpture.

It cannot be emphasised too strongly that over all of Cornwall and most of Devon there is no limestone. Lime for mortar was always scarce, and in vernacular building was commonly dispensed with before the 19th century. The building accounts of Bodmin church show that it was bought in the ports of Padstow and Fowey. The Fabric Rolls of Exeter Cathedral do not specify the source of lime beyond stating that it was imported through the port of Topsham. At a later date this deficiency was made good by the import of limestone and Welsh coal and the burning of lime at a host of kilns on sheltered coves around the coast. In the 18th century the operation of a kiln became a profitable sideline for an enterprising landowner (Pounds 1971-73). In the medieval period the high price of lime, up to 50% above the level prevailing in lowland England, led to a general use of cob or pisé, masonry often being set in well-puddled clay.

Most medieval architecture in the south-west is ecclesiastical. There is little surviving secular building and almost no vernacular. The common practice in Cornwall and west Devon was to use granite for quoins and buttresses, and whatever rough stone was locally available for walls. Sometimes a plain, unbuttressed tower was built wholly of granite. Immense labour must have been expended on cutting blocks to size. Indeed, there was a tendency, in the absence of any more tractable material, to use granite as if it were freestone. When, in the early 16th century, Sir Henry Trecarrel rebuilt the church of St Mary Magdalene at Launceston, not only did he use granite throughout, but he also spread a low-relief carving over the whole exterior with what Pevsner termed 'barbarous profuseness' (1951, 96). An even more remarkable exhibition of carved igneous rock is to be seen in the tower of Probus church. This was contemporary with St Mary's, Launceston, and was paid for by John Tregian of nearby Golden Barton. It was built of a hard elvan, taken from a dyke in the Hensbarrow granite, a few kilometres to the north. Its most extraordinary feature, however, is the uncanny resemblance which it bears to the tower of North Petherton, in Somerset. It is, in the words of F.J. Allen, 'a most exceptional instance of the transportation of an architectural design, with very little modification, to a great distance from its place of origin' (Allen 1932, 27). More remarkable is its transfer from the medium of soft limestone to that of hard, igneous rock.

As the tower of Probus demonstrates, very effective use could be made of the elvans. They were in many instances even harder than granite, but their colouration and fineness of grain gave them a particular value. But such stone was rarely transported far from the quarries which supplied it. A particular stone usually came from a single quarry opened on the back of a dyke and incapable of being expanded. There is space to mention only a few of the elvans and the uses to which they were put.

Tartan Down stone came from a quarry in Landrake parish in south-east Cornwall. It was used in Landrake church and, most conspicuously, in the façade of St German's Priory church, less than $3\frac{3}{4}$ miles (6km) away.

Polyphant, or *Hick's Mill stone*, was, and indeed still is, obtained in Lewannick parish, close to the eastern margin of Bodmin Moor. It is grey-green in colour, works well under the chisel, and was much used for interior work. Long exposure to the weather, however, causes it to exfoliate, but it was nevertheless much used in south-east Cornwall (Reid *et al.* 1911, 128-29).

Pentewan stone is the best known and most widely used of the elvans. Its popularity derived in part from its warm colour – cream, streaked with brown – and in part from its occurrence in the sea cliffs north of Mevagissey, from which it could be shipped. It was thus distributed more widely than almost any other Cornish rock at this time. The parish church of St Mary's, Truro, largely demolished to make way for Pearson's cathedral, was built of it, and it survives in the so-called St Mary's Aisle. It was transported up the River Fowey for use in the Duke of Cornwall's Hall at Lostwithiel, and in Bodmin parish church, a piece of extravagance which will be discussed later.

Cataclews was obtained from a quarry, long since abandoned, on the eastern side of Trevose Head on the rugged north coast. It is very fine-grained and of a very dark colour. It was better suited to sculpture than almost any other intrusive rock. 'For fine tooling and for standing weather no rock in Cornwall is better than that of Cataclews' (Reid *et al.* 1910, 91). Many churches have or once had examples of Cataclews sculpture, and there would seem to have been a workshop in the vicinity of Padstow which turned out pieces that could be transported easily. The finest Cornish sculpture is in Cataclews: the 15th-century fonts at St Merryn and Padstow, both within a few kilometres of the quarry, as well as smaller fonts elsewhere in the county, and, above all, Prior Vivian's tomb in Bodmin church.

Greenstone deserves mention, but is overall of much less importance. It is an epidiorite, ranging in colour from green to near black, and occurs in almost vertical dykes. In the Tintagel area the greenstones constitute the universal building material, and their use is seen to perfection in the late medieval hall-house, known as the Old Post Office (Chesher 1968, 27-29), and in Tintagel parish church. It cuts well, and thin slabs were pierced for window openings.

Metamorphic rocks were abundant, but of little importance. *Serpentine* was used at Landewednack in the Lizard peninsula. *Slate* occurs extensively close to the granite outcrops, but little of it was of a quality to yield thin 'slates' for roofing and cladding. The coarser slate was of little value because it was too heavy for the relatively slender roof timbers. Though difficult to cut with simple tools, slate was, like granite, occasionally treated as if it were ashlar. By the end of the Middle Ages the better slates were widely used for roofing, but slate cladding came later.

By the 16th century, Delabole, close to the coast of north Cornwall, had come to be the chief source of roofing slate. The Parliamentary Survey of Crown Lands of 1649-50 listed no less than 21 slate quarries, all of them rented from the Duchy of Cornwall (Pounds 1984, 183-84). It is tempting to assume that they were the predecessors of the vast quarry, 400 feet (122m) deep, which developed in the 19th century. It is more likely, however, that they were situated in the north cliffs, where today one finds countless small, abandoned quarries. Other sources of good roofing slate lay near Liskeard and Menheniot, but their distance from waterborne transport greatly reduced their importance.

Building accounts

Few building accounts have survived from the south-west, but among them are the Fabric Rolls of Exeter Cathedral (Erskine 1981/83) and the record of income and expenditure in connection with the building of Bodmin church (Wilkinson 1875).

Between 1469 and 1472 the citizens of Bodmin undertook the rebuilding of their parish church (Maclean 1873, I, 150-58). The work was paid for by local gilds and individuals, and some was carried out by the unpaid labour of the citizens themselves. All this is noted in the record with meticulous care, but what concerns us is the expenditure on building materials. The citizens had at hand an inexhaustible supply of granite from the nearby moor, and furthermore the journey to the church was almost wholly downhill. But they had an important decision to make, whether to use the granite and the local 'killas' or shale, or to go further afield for a more attractive and tractable stone. The curious thing at Bodmin is not that they did the latter, but that they did it on a lavish scale. Of course, they used some local materials. There are very small payments – so small that they can have incorporated little by way of transport costs – for 'stonys to the grasse tabelle' (Wilkinson 1875, 11-12), by which we can only understand the rough masonry laid in the foundation trenches.

Working 'under the grase tabelle' was followed by 'scapelyng of stonys to [at] Pentewen' and 'scapelyng stonys at more for the wyndowys' and 'drawyng ston at mor and scapelyng for the peloris [pillars]' (Wilkinson 1875, 12-13). Granite was preferred, as the fabric of the church confirms, for the pillars of the arcade and the window tracery; Pentewan stone from the elvan quarry on the south coast, for the walling. The result is the delightful cream and brown ashlar masonry which covers much of the exterior of the church. The decision to use Pentewan stone must have been a hard one. Unlike the moorstone, it had to be hewn from the quarry, and to this was added the cost of transport. It was, as a general rule, carried by sea from the beach below the quarry to the River Fowey (illustration 98), and was unloaded near St Winnow. From here it was hauled the ten miles to Bodmin, 400 feet (122m) above the river. It is not easy, on the basis of the documentary record, to allocate transport costs to a particular material, but expenditure on one consignment of Pentewan stone amounted to:

Land-leave (permission to quarry)		6s.	2d.
Quarrying	£1	16s.	2d.
Transport	£4	0s.	0d.
	£6	2s.	4d.

We shall find a not dissimilar ratio of transport to total costs in the 13th- and 14th-century work on Exeter Cathedral.

In addition, 'helyng stones', or slates, were bought. Their source is not stated. It

98. Source of stone used in the rebuilding of Bodmin parish church, 1469-72, base‹ on Wilkinson 1875.

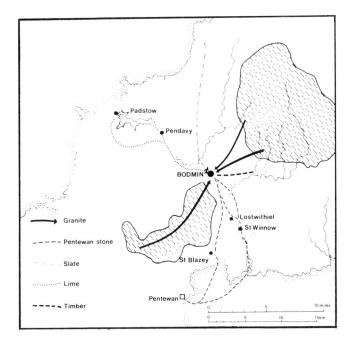

could have been the quarries near Lostwithiel, or, more likely, those near Tintagel. Timber was obtained from local woodlands, particularly those which still remain along the valley of the Upper Fowey, known today as the Glyn Valley. The supply of lime for masonry and plastering presented perhaps the biggest problem. It was obtained by sea from kilns perhaps in Somerset or Dorset – its source is nowhere specified – and imported through Lostwithiel or Padstow.

About 1270 Bishop Bronescombe began the rebuilding of Exeter Cathedral and, when the work was completed, nearly a century later, only the two transeptal towers remained of the Romanesque building (Hope & Lloyd 1973, 11-26). This work of reconstruction is chronicled in unparalleled detail in the Fabric Rolls of the cathedral for the years 1297 to 1353 (Erskine 1981/83). Exeter lies close to the eastern margin of the south-western region of Palaeozoic rocks. Its local rocks are Permian, mainly sandstones and conglomerates, intruded by dykes of trap. But only 10 miles (15km) to the east one finds the last outliers of the Cretaceous, and it was from these contrasted rocks, Permian and Cretaceous, that Exeter Cathedral was hewn.

It is difficult to assess their relative importance. In terms of volume, stone from the neighbourhood of Exeter was clearly the most important. A series of dykes yielded a trap, which was hard, red-brown in colour, and good for the rougher masonry (Usher 1902, 60, 66-70). Immense quantities were taken from quarries at Barley, to the west of the city, and carried to the cathedral by wagon.

Another local stone, used toward the end of the building period, was that from Colmanshay, in the hill to the north, and from Heavitree to the south. It was a red Permian conglomerate of the kind to be met with in many of the older buildings in Exeter. A third local source was a quarry at Silverton, some 6 miles (10km) to the north of the cathedral. Like the stone from Barley, it was a volcanic trap, and was used for much the same purpose (Usher 1902, 66-70). 'Pendants' of Silverton stone were used as filling of the vaults between the ribs. Lastly, a very small amount of Whipton stone was used from a quarry within the north-eastern suburbs of the city. It was, like Colmanshay, a Permian sandstone.

Sandstone and trap were in general unsuited for the finer work of the cathedral. For this, stone was brought in, mainly by sea, from south-east Devon, as well as from further afield in Somerset, Dorset and Normandy (illustration 99). The heaviest reliance was placed on Beer stone, a soft, cream-coloured limestone of Cretaceous age, which occurred close to the sea to the west of Beer. Closely similar was Branscombe stone from quarries between Beer and Sidmouth. Immense quantities of Beer stone were imported to Exeter, and were used in ashlar

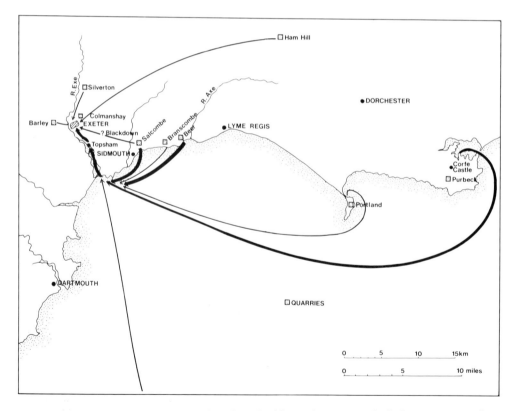

99. Sources of building stone used in the rebuilding of Exeter Cathedral, 1279-1353. The thickness of line indicates only approximately the relative importance of the types of stone used. Based on Erskine 1981/83.

masonry, as well as in the ribs and bosses of the vault. Next in importance was Salcombe stone, a calcareous sandstone from quarries in the Greensand at Dunscombe and Salcombe Regis. It was also brought largely by sea to the Exe (Woodward & Usher 1911, 83).

Only sparing use was made of other freestones: from Portland, Ham Hill in Somerset, and Caen in Normandy. Portland stone was used only in 1303-4, mainly it would seem for bases and capitals. Ham Hill or Hamdon stone from south Somerset is an oolite, found in the Upper Lias. It is, in Clifton-Taylor's words, 'one of England's most seductive stones' (1987, 88), and it contributes greatly to the beauty of many buildings in Somerset and Dorset. Only small quantities were used at Exeter, however, probably because of the high cost of overland transport. It cost, for example, 12s. to move three stones to the cathedral whereas a large load could have been brought from Beer or Salcombe for that amount. Caen stone was the only material imported from overseas. It was used particularly in the Lady Chapel, but its cost was inflated by that of transport, and in only four years is there any record of its import and use.

The only other stone in regular demand was Purbeck 'marble', described in the record as 'Corfe stone'. It was used lavishly, and expenditure on it was greater than on any other individual stone. As is well known, it was obtained from quarries to the south of Corfe Castle (Leach 1978, 1-11; Drury 1949; RCHM 1970, xl-xli). The exploitation of the thin beds was in the hands of certain families, among which the Canons of Corfe figure prominently in the rolls. It is apparent that the Canons contracted to supply finished stone, and that their price included that of transport as far as the port of Topsham. In addition to the contract price the documents record only carriage from Topsham to the construction site.

It is apparent from both building accounts which have been used that transport costs represented a very large part of total materials cost. Stone from the quarries near Exeter was brought by wagon, cart and packhorse. Ham Hill stone also came by cart, but the rest, except only a small part of that from Salcombe, came by boat to the River Exe, and was unloaded either at Topsham or at an unidentified site known as *la Sege*, which probably lay upriver from Topsham, on the east bank of the River Exe. In addition to the cost of quarrying and scappling, we have also for much of the stone brought to Exeter by sea the further costs of transport from the quarry to the waiting barge, of the voyage to the Exe, and of carriage thence to the building site. The following table presents the costs of one consignment of Salcombe stone:

148 tontight bought from Richard de Knolle at 12d. the tontight				£7	8s.	0d.
Carriage to the sea, at 3d.	£1	17s.	0d.			
Loading, at 2d.	£1	3s.	4d.			
Transport to *la Sege*, at 12d.	£7	8s.	0d.			
Unloading, at 2d.	£1	3s.	4d.			
Carriage to the Cathedral, at 9d.	£5	11s.	0d.			
	£17	2s.	8d.			
	£24	10s.	8d.			

The tontight was a measure derived from the weight of a tun of wine, and was about 2,000lb (Salzman 1952, 122). Transport thus cost more than twice as much as the purchase price of the stone itself. Few entries in the record are as clearcut as this, but it seems that, in an area as deficient in good building stone as the Exeter region, up to two-thirds of the cost of materials was made up of transport costs.

The transport of Salcombe stone presents a peculiar problem. The quarries, one might have thought, were excellently placed for the transport of their stone to Exeter by sea, if it were not for the fact that part of it was taken overland to a place which appears in the record only as *Blackdown*, and from here to Exeter. The whereabouts of *Blackdown* is quite unknown. That it lay at a considerable distance from Salcombe is suggested by the fact that transport of the stone cost 1s. 6d. per cartload. Mrs Erskine has suggested (1983, xiv) that it was in fact Black Hill, in Woodbury, a manor south-east of Topsham, then held by the cathedral chapter. This seems probable, though it is curious that neither Beer nor Branscombe stone appear ever to have been held here.

Conclusions

Certain conclusions arise from this discussion. Primary dependence was always placed on local stone, whatever its quality, but this was supplemented by stone brought from a distance, the relative importance of local and of 'imported' stone being determined by (i) the resources of the community, and (ii) the costs of purchasing and transporting stone from outside.

A second conclusion is that there was a conscious attempt to make an inferior stone look like a better material. The carving of granite or elvan, as at St Mary Magdalene, Launceston, or at Probus, is a case in point. So also is the cutting of slate to make a kind of ashlar. We cannot know what was the cost of these operations. It must have been high, and the builders, consciously or otherwise, must have been faced with the equation:

$$\left. \begin{array}{l} \text{Low cost of local stone} \\ \text{High cost of working it} \end{array} \right\} \quad \simeq \quad \left\{ \begin{array}{l} \text{High cost of imported stone} \\ \text{Low cost of working it} \end{array} \right.$$

If Sir Henry Trecarrel or John Tregian could have substituted real costs in this equation, they might have acted differently. But this 'nicely calculated less and more' was beyond their grasp, and we should not tax them both with 'vain expense'.

Lastly there is very little evidence in the south-west for the re-use of older materials, and this must be due in part to the fact that, west of Exeter, there were no Roman sites to rob and that others held little of value. The Bodmin accounts record (Wilkinson 1875, 3) the sale of a window from the demolished church to the neighbouring parish of Helland, and 'barris' – possibly iron window-bars – were sold 'yn Lestithiell (Lostwithiel) stret'. The present writer found a Celtic cross-head built into an interior wall in Wendron church tower, but it would be very difficult indeed to detect the re-use of rubble masonry or even roughly dressed granite.

ACKNOWLEDGEMENT

The author of this paper wishes to record his thanks to Dr Diana Sutherland of the University of Leicester for her great help in identifying stone used in Exeter Cathedral.

BIBLIOGRAPHY

Allen, F.J., 1932 — *The Great Church Towers of England*. Cambridge: University Press, 1932

Chesher, V.M., and F.J., 1968 — *The Cornishman's House*. Truro: D. Bradford Barton, 1968

Clifton-Taylor, A., 1987 — *The Pattern of English Building*. 4th ed., London: Faber and Faber, 1987

Drury, G.D., 1949 — The use of Purbeck Marble in medieval times, *Proc. Dorset Natur. Hist. Archaeol. Soc.*, **70** (1949), 74-98

Erskine, A.M. (ed), 1981/83 — *The Accounts of the Fabric of Exeter Cathedral 1279-1353*. Devon and Cornwall Record Society, **24** (1981) and **26** (1983)

Halliday, F.E. (ed), 1953 — Richard Carew, *Survey of Cornwall*. London: Andrew Melrose, 1953

Hope, V., and Lloyd, L.J., 1973 — *Exeter Cathedral: a short history and description*. Exeter: Dean and Chapter, 1973

Jope, E.M., 1961 — Cornish Houses, 1400-1700, *Studies in Building History*, ed. E.M. Jope, 192-222. London: Odhams Press, 1961

Leach, R., 1978 — *An investigation into the use of Purbeck Marble in Medieval England*. 2nd ed., Crediton: privately published, 1978

Maclean, J., 1873 — *The parochial and family history of the deanery of Trigg Minor*. 3 vols, London: Nichols and Sons, 1873

Norden, J., 1728 — *Speculi Britanniae pars: a topographical and historical description of Cornwall*. London: privately published, 1728; repr. Newcastle: Graham, 1966

Pevsner, N., 1951 — *Cornwall*. Buildings of England, Harmondsworth: Penguin, 1951

Pounds, N.J.G., 1971-73 — Building and operating accounts of an eighteenth century limekiln, *Devon and Cornwall Notes and Queries*, **32** (1971-73), 237-40

Pounds, N.J.G. (ed), 1982/84 — *The Parliamentary Survey of the Duchy of Cornwall*. Devon and Cornwall Record Society, **25** (1982) & **27** (1984)

RCHM 1970 — Royal Commission on Historical Monuments, *Inventory of the historical monuments in the County of Dorset*, **2**. London: HMSO, 1970

Reid, C., Barrow, G., and Dewey, H., 1910 — *The Geology of the Country around Padstow and Camelford*. Geol. Survey Gr, Br., Sheet Memoir 335-36, London: HMSO, 1910

Reid, C., Barrow, G., Sherlock, R.L., and Dewey, H., 1911 — *The Geology of the Country around Tavistock and Launceston*. Geol. Survey Gr. Br., Sheet Memoir 337, London: HMSO, 1911

Salzman, L.F., 1967 — *Building in England down to 1540: a documentary history*. Corrected impression, Oxford: Clarendon Press, 1967

Usher, W.A.E., 1902 — *The Geology of the Country around Exeter*. Geol. Survey of Gr. Br., Sheet Memoir 325, London: HMSO, 1902

Wilkinson, J.J., 1875 — Receipts and expenses in the building of Bodmin Church, 1469 to 1472, *Camden Miscellany*, **7** = *Camden Society*, ser.2, **14** (1875)

Woodward, H.B., and Usher, W.A.E., 1911 — *The Geology of the Country near Sidmouth and Lyme Regis*. Geol. Survey Gr. Br., Sheet Memoir 326 and 340, 2nd ed., London: HMSO, 1911.

Index

by Professor N. J. G. Pounds

Numbers in bold refer to pages on which illustrations of the subject appear.